Religion on the Rise
Islam in the Third Millennium

Religion on the rise

Religion on the Rise
Islam in the Third Millennium

Murad Wilfried Hofmann

Translated from German by
Andreas Ryschka

amana publications

297

First Edition
(1422AH/2001AC)
© Copyright 1422AH/2001AC
amana publications
10710 Tucker Street
Beltsville, Maryland 20705-2223 USA
Tel: (301) 595-5777 / Fax: (301) 595-5888
E-mail: amana@igprinting.com
Website: www.amana-publications.com

Library of Congress Cataloging-in-Publication Data

Hofmann, Murad Wilfried.
 [Islam im 3. Jahrtausend. English]
 Religion on the rise : Islam in the third millennium / Murad Wilfried
Hofmann.
  p. cm.
 Includes bibliographical references and indexes.
 ISBN 1-59008-003-3
  1. Islam--20th century. 2. Religious awakening–Islam. I. Title.

BP163 .H64313 2001
297'.01'12--dc21

                                                              2001046094

Printed in the United States of America by
International Graphics
10710 Tucker Street
Beltsville, Maryland 20705-2223 USA
Tel: (301) 595-5999 Fax: (301) 595-5888
Website: igprinting.com
E-mail: ig@igprinting.com

Contents

Preface

As a doctor I can only state that
humanity is caught up in a tremendous crisis.
(Friedrich Dürrenmatt, *Neue Zürcher Zeitung*, April 6, 1990)

The new millennium is upon us. Some people had barely slept off their hangover and swept up the confetti when suddenly it was January 2, 2000. We all found ourselves back at our daily, dreary treadmills. Has nothing happened? Had the Y2K computer bug been our paramount concern? Is our life-sustaining societal infrastructure not really about to collapse? Is the future still what it once was?

The turn of the millennium was indeed fraught with signs heralding crises whose amplification through the media had the potential to whip up apocalyptic frenzies and irrational doomsday anxieties. However, having faced imminent catastrophe all too long, the Western attitude towards scheduled disaster had been shifting, in recent years, from frivolous optimism to pessimistic resignation, and from there to what may be called structural indifference. Hysterical apocalyptic visions, until recently a trademark of Green culture, has given way to a new wave of cavalier equanimity. On new year's eve 1999, who was still afraid of emergency laws, nuclear war, atomic power stations, dying forests, the ozone hole, Chernobyl, global warming, dissemination of personal data, AIDS, mad cow disease or combat assignment to Chechnya? Environmentalism had begun to fade, and with it environmental paranoia. Left behind was political apathy. The social, moral, and economic state of emergency – if it did exist – had become a cozy little crisis that goes down well with beer and bubbly.

In short, the potential hot seller *Doom & Gloom* was pulled off the shelves before it ever hit the market.

The Muslims of this world reacted to the coming of the new millennium without champagne and beer yet with their usual equanimity. For one, the event took place halfway through the year 1420 of their calendar.[1] In addition, number mystics in the tradition of the Jewish Cabala fascinate very few Muslims. Above all, a new millennium cannot impress Muslims for the simple reason that it may not come to pass after all: both Muslims and Christians believe that the (final) Hour may strike at any time, without prior warning. Only God knows when.[2]

At the same time, Muslims do not look back into history without a sense of periodic-structuring. They even try to find in each Islamic century an individual who can be considered a "renewer" (*al-mujaddid*) of the faith. In the 5th Islamic century, for instance, this honorific was bestowed upon the preeminent theological philosopher Abu Hamid al-Ghazali (d.505A.H./1111); for the 8th century, it fell to Ibn Taymiyya (d.728A.H./1328), a philosophic theologian of currently resurgent popularity. For the 12th century, two men were identified as simultaneous renewers: the Indian reformer Shah Waliyullah (d.1176A.H/1763), and the spiritual forefather of Saudi Arabia, Muhammad Ibn 'Abd al Wahhab (d.1201A.H./1787). The seminal Egyptian renewer Sheik al Azhar Muhammad Abdu (d.1323A.H./1905) figured prominently for the 14th century. The Indian intellectual Ahmad-i-Sirhindi – a member of the Nakshibandi order while being critical of mystical exaggerations – in his lifetime even accepted the unofficial title of "renewer of the 2nd Islamic millennium" (*mujaddid alf thani*).[3]

This figure of recurring reformers of the faith should, however, not suggest that Muslims naively (or out of triumphalism) expected linear historical progress, although some of them are inclined to do so, based on a selective reading of the Qur'an and the *sunnah*. Knowing fully well that only God is Master of the future, the Prophet Muhammad showed himself circumspect: "I hope [sic!] that on the day of resurrection my followers will be more numerous than those of other prophets"; but he expected that at least one group of Muslims would always stay on the right path.[4] At the same time Prophet Muhammad was warning that each successive generation of Muslims might turn out less reliable than their predecessors;[5] after him, "there will be no time in the future without an even worse time following it."[6] Telltale signs for the impending end of time would be a decrease of religious knowledge, an increase of alcohol consumption, and the public display of sexuality.[7] In the course of time, the Muslims would split up into even more sects than the Jews and the Christians, into no less than 73 different groups.[8]

Obviously, except for a few isolated instances, Islam has never again been fully practiced since its charismatic beginnings under the divine guidance of a prophet. Even the Golden Period under the four Righteous Caliphs (*al-khulafa ar-rashidun*), lasting from 632 to 661, seen from close was a didactic *Utopia*, a fact that should not dim the luster of this formidable era. Indeed, Islam was never again able to put its ideals fully into reality, neither under the Umayyad dynasty in Damascus (until 750),[9] nor during the glorious cultural achievements of the Abbasids in Baghdad (until the 13th century), nor when Islamic civilization blossomed in Andalusia before 1492, even though the Spanish unwittingly still call "Allah" whenever they shout "*Olé!*" [10]

Most Muslims today assume that contemporary knowledge does not merely proceed from past knowledge, but is its cumulative result. Therefore, Muslims correctly claim today that their understanding of the Qur'an in certain respects far exceeds that of their ancestors.[11] They take the Qur'an to heart when it exhorts them as "*the best of communities created for mankind*" to "*enjoin what is right, forbid what is wrong*",[12] and when it tells them that "*Allah will never change the situation of a people until they change their inner selves.*"[13]

Even after having treated New Year's Eve 1999 as mere routine, we should not be so pollyannaish as to believe that people have completely shed their anxieties. The recent wars in Afghanistan, Rwanda, Burundi, the Caucasus and the Balkans have obviously refuted Francis Fukuyama's allegation that the "End of History" has arrived because values of Western civilization and liberal democracy had come to globalize the world.[14]

Admittedly, the economic, technological, cultural and ideological blending of the "Global Village" has already gone far. But doubts are beginning to crop up in the West whether its triumphalism after the fall of Communism was actually justified. Does the 20th Century not hold the record as the bloodiest in human history? What about its atrocious World Wars, the employment of weapons of mass destruction, extermination camps and "ethnic cleansing"? All that – of all places – took place in "civilized" Europe, known for its proud claims as a haven of Reason and Humanity, 250 years after the dawning of Enlightenment and its "Project Modernity."[15]

Are Western societies perhaps ailing and in danger of losing their moral highground, much as Bolshevism did before them?

Samuel Huntington's thesis of a likely collision between civilizations – notably the West and Islam (with its "bloody borders") – has been recognized as mainly defensive, his main purpose being to warn.[16] Since then many social scientists have loudly proclaimed the virtually timeless stability of world cultures which seem to resist any social engineering.[17] In the Occident, the existing cultural bipolarity of the world is now seen by many as naturally given, i.e., essential: here Silicon Valley – there Makkah[18] – as if the world had not made any progress whatsoever since the proclamation made by Ernest Renan, on February 23 1862, at the *Collège de France* that "Islam represents the fullest negation of Europe."

Nobody, at least halfway alert to cultural phenomena, regardless of geographic location, will deny that the future development of his world is going to be influenced, if not determined, by what will happen in the Muslim world and to Islam itself. Will it modernize, even assimilate the American Way of Life? Or is it going to reject integration? Will Islam continue to spread in the West as it did during the last third of the past century? And will this be a peaceful process?

What are the consequences for the West if a widespread moral and structural renewal of Islam fails? And what if it should succeed, thereby increasing its appeal in the West even more? Could what has always been conceptually a universal religion, in fact become a world religion, even the dominant one of the 21st century?

Could Islam, as a consequence, turn out to be the very therapy that could save the West from itself? In this case, would the West be able to perceive Islam as precisely the remedy sorely needed for surviving its crisis as a functioning civilization?

This is the background, and these are the questions that will be discussed in this book. My answers will hardly be popular because – as Sabine Audrerie once put it – "If one touches upon wounds, one relegates oneself to an unsympathetic role."[19]

This book supplies an unusually broad Bibliography featuring just about any author who has significantly contributed to the worldwide discussion on Islam over the past three decades. This is no internet-generated list; each of these books was read cover to cover, thanks in no small measure to my task as a critic for *The Muslim World Book Review* (MWBR), a British quarterly.

I am particularly indebted to two books: *The Cultural Contradictions of Capitalism*, in which Daniel Bell, former professor of Sociology at Harvard University, offered in 1976 a splendid diagnosis of the malaise and the self-destructive mechanisms undermining Western culture. The same goes for William Ophuls' *Requiem for Modern Politics*, a poignant analysis of unsurpassed elegance describing how the Western ideology of progress drives potentially fatal fault lines through society.

At the same time, I would like to point out that my observations are not just what one calls the "fruit of reading", but reflect my experiences as a Muslim activist. It was indeed most helpful that ever since my retirement from the German diplomatic service in mid-1994, I have been on extensive lecture tours throughout both the Orient and the Occident. These trips took me from Helsinki to Kuala Lumpur, from Riyadh to Los Angeles, and from Khartoum to Leipzig, with the purpose of explaining either camp to the other one, i.e., of building bridges of understanding and of allaying the pent-up feelings of anger and aggression to be found on both sides.[20]

Some of these lectures appeared in Islamic journals like *Al-Islam* (Munich), *Islamic Studies* (Islamabad), *The American Journal of Islamic Social Sciences* (Herndon, VA), *Horizons* (Indianapolis, IN), *Iqra* (San José, CA) and *Encounters* (Markfield, Leicester, UK). Some of that material was used here, but not integrally.

The size of the bibliography, as well as the inclusion of numerous foreign language titles, is not intended to impress, but to offer an impressions of: (i) the intensity and frankness of the intra-Islamic discussions on crucial issues like democracy, human rights, and the role of women; (ii) the growing visibility of Islam as a topic in vogue with current Western social sciences, and (iii) the increasing role of the English language even in intra-Islamic discourse. The fact is that, Islam lately has embraced a second semi-official language: by now more material on Islam is published in English than in Arabic. This atmospheric aspect alone should make a serendipitous perusal of the bibliography worth while.

In order to make the book less scholarly (and reading more enjoyable), bibliographic references have been used sparingly, mainly to substantiate quotations and highlight key contributions.

I have also neglected to insert, abbreviated as "(s.)" or "pbuh", the blessings Muslims commonly invoke whenever the names of prophets like Moses, Jesus or Muhammad are mentioned.[21]

Istanbul, September 1, 2000   Murad Wilfried Hofmann

Notes

1. In the year 639, the 2nd Caliph, 'Umar, stipulated that the calender begin with Prophet Muhammad's forced emigration from Makkah to al Madinah (September 10 - 22, 622). The beginning of the first year of the Islamic calender (Hijrah Year - AH) was set retrospectively to July 6, 622 (cf. G.S.P. Freeman-Grenville, *The Islamic and Christian Calenders* 622 - 2222 [AH 1-1650], Garnet: Reading (U.K.), 1995, p. 4.)

2. Qur'an 33:63; 42:18; 79:42ff. The Qur'an is quoted with Sura (before the colon) and Verse (following the colon). Absent any other reference, such numbers will henceforth identify passages in the Qur'an.

3. About his efforts to reconcile the extremes of Islamic mysticism on the one hand, and its rejection by the Hanbalite wing of Islam, see Abdul Haq Ansari, Shaykh Sirhindi's *Doctrine of Wahdat al-Shuhud* [not ontological unity, but oneness in the contemplation of Being] Islamic Studies 37, no 3, Islamabad 1998.

4. *Al-Bukhari*, vol. 6, no. 504; Muslim, no. 4215-4722.

5. *Al-Bukhari*, vol. 8, no. 686; an-Nawawi, no. 409.

6. *Al-Bukhari*, vol. 9, no. 188; an-Nawawi, no. 92.

7. *Al-Bukhari*, vol. 1, no. 80, and vol. 8, no. 800 A.

8. *Abu Dawud*, Sunan, no. 4579.

9. Modern Islamic historians disagree as to whether the government of the Umayyad dynasty was as un-Islamic as it is commonly accused of being, or whether this judgement is based on the anti-Umayyad propaganda of the Abbasids, which has survived more intact and which for transparent political reasons had made opportunistic use of Islamic themes.

10. Jayyusi offers a good insight into Andalusian culture.
11. A case in point is Surah 96:1, where in light of today's scientific understanding the Arabic expression *"al-'alaq"*, the penetration of male sperm into the female egg, is described medically correctly as "lodging, nesting", respectively "attaching itself". This term naturally escaped earlier generations.
12. Qur'an 3:110
13. Qur'an 13:11
14. See Fukuyama (1990).
15. In the 20th century an estimated 33 Million young men died in wars.
16. See Huntington (1993).
17. Turkey is the prime example. The coercive efforts on the part of the Kemalist leadership to push the country into Europe continues to be thwarted by its deep roots in Islamic history and culture. In spite of modernization and the increase in living standards, Islam is playing an even larger role today than in the 30s, Kemal's lifetime.
18. There are still scholars of cultural anthropology, the sociology of religion, Islamic and political studies, who harbor the out-dated and pessimistic view (and a taboo among postmodernists) that there are essential, predetermined differences between cultures. This leads for instance to the misconceptions that Muslim countries are congenitally unfit for democracy and thus incapable of developing civilized societies and protecting human rights. These opinions are insulting to Muslims and are typical for Bassam Tibi (1994).
19 In *Encore* no. 5, Paris, April 1997.
20. From mid 1994 to mid 1999 I gave 179 lectures on Islamic topics in ten Western and eleven Muslim countries, and visited 37 conferences focusing on Islam.
21. "s." stands for *"sallalahu alahim wa sallam"* and "pbuh" for "peace be upon him".

Preface to the 2nd Edition

This book was published shortly before the tragic events of September 11, 2001, in New York and Washington, DC. I found, however, that the analyses and predictions contained in it were not put into question, neither by the events themselves nor their aftermath.

Istanbul, August 1, 2002   Murad Wilfried Hofmann

CHAPTER ONE

Destination: West

In the absence of Gods the ghosts hold sway.
(Novalis)

*The belief that non-Western peoples should adopt
Western values, institutions, and culture is, if taken
seriously, immoral in its implications.*
(Samuel Huntington, *The West Unique, not Universal*)

Any attempt to predict the future development of the Occident and the (Islamic) Orient, or to at least describe the preconditions for a desired course, should start with a dispassionate – but by no means value-neutral – assessment of the relevant cultural factors. Then we may boldly ask: what is really going on in both domains?

In this endeavor it is useful to draw on critical minds who switched sides temporarily, without severing their roots outright. I am thinking especially of exchange students who have been looking at their home countries with different eyes since they have returned from graduating in the West or in the East. Political or economic refugees, on the other hand, are less helpful since they are likely to have lost their impartiality by becoming too close to their adopted country culturally or too dependent on it financially.

I will, therefore, proceed to interview two anonymous, but quite typical, Oriental Muslims studying in the West about life there as seen from their perspective. In the subsequent chapter, I am going to ask two anonymous European students, converts to Islam, about their impressions of the Muslim world: one who would eventually choose to live there, and another who does not see any reason for emigrating from the West.

In both sets of situations the result is puzzling indeed.

THE first student we are about to hear from is a Muslim by force of cultural habit only, but not a practicing Muslim. He had been dreaming about the West long before he ever arrived there. Even when he was child, Occidental achievements were a shining example to him, even in their Marxist perversion. No wonder, he was straining to emulate this idolized Western civilization so thoroughly that he became quite indistinguishable from his environment. I know what I am talking about, because at the tender age of nineteen, in 1950, I traveled from Germany which was then a country occupied, divided, and of fading hopes, to a seductively intact Union College in Schenectady in New York State. There, I found myself smack in the middle of the booming American post-war paradise where Coke and Milkshakes, Budweiser and Manhattans were flowing prodigiously.

America – past and present – and much of Europe have always affected young people from South America, Africa, and Asia like a drug, promising to enhance their lives dramatically and offering virtual rebirth. In the Occident, where the streets are full of golden opportunities, everything seemed possible for somebody young, healthy and hard working.

The causes for this bliss are evident: technology in the West is very advanced. After first inventing the steam engine and then harnessing electricity, the Occident is now going through its Third Industrial Revolution with the IT Revolution; always at the point where the latest infrastructure is being turned inside out by even newer innovations. Since the Internet came online, the world has never been the same.

Our "cultural" Muslim might relate his impressions of the cherished West as follows: over here everything that is driven by technology, including medicine and bureaucracy, functions so effortlessly that man has become the last remaining risk factor. The efficiency typical of the technological sector proper has been carried over into the economy, government, and education. Most citizens are law abiding – most of the time – and the administration, too, routinely obeys the law of the land: Law-and-Order government is a reassuring reality. Cases of bribery are rare. The armed forces submit to elected civilian government, and people with different religious beliefs are neither jailed nor tortured. The state promotes the general welfare of its citizens from incubator to hospice care. It follows policies for the protection of the environment. The streets are clean and the toilets do not keep running all the time. There are very few, if any, interruptions in the steady supply of power, water and heat.

(At this point, an impatient denizen of the West would love to jump in and stop what he considers to be a boring and banal portrait of his hemisphere. But for someone from the developing world there is nothing banal about those enviable achievements. The same goes for the following): state, society and the economy with its saturated markets – everything revolves around the individual. The individual enjoys utmost protection, both by police and courts, from the whims and willfulness of bureaucracy. The citizens choose their government and at times even their judges at the ballot box with a turn-out and yes-vote of less than 99.9%. The currency is stable. The brand name articles and drugs are neither forgeries nor cheap rip-offs. Quality control is not limited to technical automobile specifications and inspection. Even the unemployed do not have to beg. Labor disputes are not settled by SWAT teams.

Freedom is the supreme idea: freedom from injustice, duress, fear, want, censorship, excessive regulation, shame. Freedom of speech and association, freedom of religion, and freedom to choose whether to serve in the military or not. The major international human rights instruments are ratified without reservations. Media and academia are policed only by themselves – if that is needed. Judging from what is going on in today's workplace, and from the body-revealing female fashions, nothing seems to bar women's progress towards self-fulfillment. Sexual liberation has become a reality. Women have fully emancipated themselves. In the relationship between the sexes, every-thing goes that pleases. This includes the recognition of homosexuality as an alternative lifestyle. Gays and Lesbians do no longer need to hide but have the right to propagate their orientation.

So much for the first student's deposition. In the eyes of this Muslim student eager to assimilate, the West has realized the most perfect human civilization ever and is therefore justly destined to globalize itself as World Civilization.

THERE are of course not only lukewarm, cultural Muslims among foreign exchange students but convinced and practicing Muslims as well, and they are much more inclined to cultural criticism. In spite of the aforementioned undeniable advantages, these active Muslim students are likely to denounce the West summarily and condemn it so severely that one wonders why they do not return home right away and leave the Great Satan to its own devices.[1]

Let us now follow the deliberations of such a second anonymous Muslim student. So much can be said in advance about his negative verdict which will be as well supported and thought out as the views of his colleague who is infatuated by the West.

The critical Muslim begins – whether consciously or not – by questioning nothing less than the Western image of rationality, core of the "Project Modernity", this unique concept in the history of ideas and the pride of the 18th century:

The true course of Western history since the Enlightenment did not lead to the triumph of Reason, but triggered a series of human tragedies on a huge scale: proletarianization of entire regions, child labor, slavery and apartheid, two murderous World Wars, use of chemical and nuclear weapons, and systematic destruction of Kulaks, Jews, Roma and Sinti, homosexuals and the mentally handicapped, with the employment of industrial methods of annihilation under the Nazis. In addition, there was Bolshevist state terrorism, Fascist chauvinism, and there still is "ethnic cleansing" in Eastern Europe, Croatia, Bosnia, Serbia, and Chechnya.

This singular failure of a great idea – pure reason ruling autonomous individuals – cannot be blamed entirely on the fathers of Enlightenment, such as David Hume (1711-1776), Immanuel Kant (1727-1804), François Marie Voltaire (1694-1778), Frederick the Great (1712-1786), Gotthold Ephraim Lessing (1729-1781), or Johann Wolfgang von Goethe (1749-1832). Completely irreproachable for any of what later happened are, of course, the men who provided the initial inspiration: Michel Montaigne (1533-1592), René Descartes (1596-1650), John Locke (1632-1704) or Gottfried Wilhelm Leibniz (1646-1716), because none of them were atheists denying the existence of a God. Rather they were deists believing in the existence of a single but unconcerned, absent god (*deus absconditus*). At the same time, they rejected institutional Christianity and the concept of the Trinity. Their idea of God was not based on revelation, but arose from the observation of nature and intellectual reflection. They were not out to abolish God but the stifling dogmatism of the churches and the obscurantism of clerics, whom they considered to be uneducated, intolerant, and despotic sycophants.

Some Enlightenment philosophers even sought to enlist Islam to help shake off what they saw as the unbearable clerical yoke. Lessing took a personal risk in 1779 by following this strategy in a respectable manner: in his drama *Nathan the Wise*, he showed Muslims as role models, exclusively.[2] Voltaire, on the other hand, a bit earlier had used the same approach in a manner much less respectable and against better judgment: in his drama *Mahomet* (1742), "Prophet of Lies", he kicked the dog (Islam) and meant his master (the Church of Rome). Frederick the Great chastised his friend, if only in a roundabout way, for making Islam pay the price for this maneuver.[3]

The effects of Kant's criticisms had initially also been anti-church, not anti-religion. His *Critique of Pure Reason* (1781) did not prove the non-existence of God (nor was it intended to), but only set out to demonstrate that metaphysics going beyond epistemology becomes unavoidably speculative or, as Wittgenstein would have put it, a mere language game. To be sure, in his *Critique of Practical Reason* (1788), Kant posits God as a useful working hypothesis, necessary for the functioning of society.

And yet, in liberating people from church tutelage, the Enlightenment philosophers also marginalized religion. The French Revolution enthroned the "autonomous" (!) individual that rose to become the new idol, replacing God as the true measure of all things. In a grandiose fit of hubris, man's autonomy was celebrated as boundless and universal.

People, however, proved unable to endure the agnostic position between knowing and not-knowing represented by Kant, unable to be suspended in a theological and philosophical limbo: to live as if God existed, but without conclusive scientific proof of His existence. No wonder the average 18th century citizen was drawn to Pascal's (1623 - 1662) wager, which holds that erring in favor of faith is the smaller risk: "If you win, you win it all; if you loose, you lost nothing." All the same, the deistic 18th century inevitably transformed itself into the atheistic 19th century, spearheaded by Ludwig Feuerbach (1804-1872), Charles Darwin (1809-1882), Karl Marx (1818-1883), and Sigmund Freud (1856-1939).

The moment God was seen as a mere projection of human desires, the road was wide open to the practical deification of man, be it the deification of the collective (Marxism, Socialism, Fascism) or the deification of the individual (Individualism, Liberalism, Capitalism, Psychologism). In his book *Fröhliche Wissenschaften* (1882), written only 100 years after Kant, Friedrich Nietzsche (1844-1900) was thus able to pronounce God dead.[4] He had meant to kill the god of Christian theology but ended up introducing a century plagued by totally secular ideologies. His own experience probably told him what Muslims knew all along: that the pietistic privatization of religion is the first step towards its obliteration, especially when crude rationalism dismisses almost the entire history of ideas as symptoms of superstition. Modernity as the ideology of progress presented religion as a terminal case in need of secularization.

What mankind has been going through since then is without precedent in human history. The Occident has been the only civilization, so far, which believes in its ability to get along without the transcendental, the sacred,[5] God that is, by acting in a thoroughly materialistic fashion, even though many do not profess atheism openly.

In the Socialist camp, Atheism obviously became a *pseudo* religion, above all in Albania and Maoist China. Even ten years after the fall of the Wall, statistics prove that Communist East Germany's only sustainable success was in teaching atheism in schools. This is evident in the enduring popularity of the *Jugendweihe*, a secular imitation of Holy Communion or Confirmation ceremonies, to initiate youngsters into the adult socialist community. In eastern Germany, believers remain outsiders.[6]

In the meantime, 47% of all Germans declare themselves non-religious, 9% of them as hardcore atheists (18% in eastern Germany). At the same time, only 9% of those who call themselves believers go to church on a regular basis. This is not surprising, since today more German Protestants (32%) believe in a nondescript "higher power" than in the personal God of Christianity as taught by their church (31%). As a consequence, they are inadvertently moving away from the personal, transcendental, revealed Semitic God, and worship – equally inadvertently – the monistic-pantheistic and philosophical idea of God as pioneered by the pre-Christian thinkers of ancient Greece.

The mass exodus from the churches worldwide – with the Catholic church in Germany losing 124,000 members in 1997 alone – is a logical consequence of this development. It has less to do with the impact of Germany's negligible "church tax" on people's pocketbook, and more to do with what is going on in their minds. As of 1996, only 39 percent of Germans belonged to the Protestant, and 33% to the Catholic, church. This means that as much as a quarter of all Germans must be classified as having no religious affiliation whatsoever. In an article in its June 15, 1992 edition, the German weekly *Der Spiegel* concluded that the Federal Republic of Germany had turned into a pagan country with a Christian residue. The chairman of the German Catholic Bishops Conference, Lehmann, reportedly encapsulated this situation in his drastic observation that since the days of Saint Boniface, i.e., 1200 years ago, there have never been fewer Christians in Germany. The same could be said for France, Great Britain, and other traditional Christian countries.

Many see the cause for all this in the spread of unsophisticated pop-science. Charles Darwin is interpreted as stating that everything has come about as a result of a random chain of events which can be rewound by means of reverse engineering. From Albert Einstein we seem to learn that nothing is reliable since everything is relative, and Stephen Hawking's explanations of the Big Bang theory seem to render God superfluous for the creation of the cosmos. For most common people, finding the key to the secrets of life and mental consciousness is but a matter of time. They await a "quantum leap" (probably the funniest vulgarization of a scientific concept) in all directions. What biochemistry may fail to achieve in brain research, the computer theory of the mind will settle – quite as if brain research could ever prove that both the cognitive apparatus of our neuronal network and the living mind sustained by it are of biological origin. All this shows that 21st century man is no less science-addicted than his scientistic great-grandfather in the 19th century. Both the latter and the former – albeit with a different jargon – expect that one fine day mind (and soul) can be explained as products of material conditions. Both believe (d) that there is a "world formula" waiting to be found, which will explain without any explanatory gap all the various entities in this world as arising out of one and the same building block: our world, a world of chips.

A symptom of this condition is the widespread elimination of religious expressions from public life. When a German chancellor does not want to take the oath of office on the Bible any longer, when God is no longer mentioned in official German Christmas addresses, then we have clear evidence, not only of the alarming extent of Europe's de-Christianization,[7] but also of the crude materialism that has crept into the hearts and minds of most Westerners.

Such manifest rejection of God, less out of atheism than indifference to the Life beyond, and such manifest idolization of the individual, sooner or later, but without fail, will have devastating consequences. Otto von Habsburg believed that "Europe without Christianity is bound to collapse like a house of cards."[8] Before him, Gilbert K. Chesterton had already determined in *Heretics* (1905) that modernity thought through to its logical conclusion would necessarily lead to madness.

But not so fast. In the beginning, societies afflicted by atheism are still benefiting from a residue of traditional values, cultural habits, and a presentiment of the supernatural which is half superstition, half due to what Goethe called "forebodings" (*Ahndungen*). But even these cultural assets are slowly melting away. People are beginning to live without restraints and follow their hedonist credo by busily cramming their limited little lives with as much sensual gratification as possible, while increasingly losing sight of the common good and the family. Nowadays people can even learn hedonism at institutes for "Happiness Research", a phenomenon speaking volumes about the contemporary state of mind. That hedonism has reached the rank of an unofficial state religion can be deduced from this T-shirt imprint recently seen with the compelling message: *I want fun. N O W !*

Once this point is reached – and large parts of the Western world have indeed arrived there – the collapse of the family, as bedrock of human society, becomes imminent. Symptoms of this calamity are indeed frightening. In the USA, not more than 15 percent of all new marriages are given a statistical chance for survival. In parts of Scandinavia, more than half of all children are born out of wedlock. Millions of single mothers are about to release an entire generation of youngsters into society whose emotional development may have been hampered by the absence of a father – to a point where their mature behavior as a mate may suffer. Single motherhood may be an unavoidable fate in many cases; at any rate, more and more young women, in Germany about 30% of them, now choose to remain childless.

These days, insurance policies are available to purchase coverage for the financial consequences of unwanted parenthood. It is not just these indemnified children who suffer terribly from only being able to see their fathers on weekends – if they are lucky enough to have a father.[9] When both parents work they tend to assuage their guilty conscience by bribing their kids with the latest toys, trying to buy their love, thus raising little extortionists and a new generation hopelessly addicted to consumerism. In their formative years their kids are turned over to their peer groups, where all-too-often underage ring leaders – heavily armed budding criminals – are already running their own drug businesses.

American children since the 1960s, have been losing about 12 hours a week of former parental attention. At the same time, American grandparents have grown even more distant. Over the same time period the suicide rate of teenagers has doubled, while the crime rate among youngsters has quadrupled. If children feel rejected at home and in school and ostracized by their peers, it is only logical that violence breaks out, as in the recent American school shoot-outs. Television and video games suggest violence as the ultimate solution to problems and treat sex like merchandise. These facts would have had a smaller impact on those couch-potatoe-adolescents only if their parents had taught them to watch TV with a critical eye. But the parents are of course absent. Thus emotionally starving children gradually cross the vanishing threshold from the virtual to the real world.

An additional problem is that many children are treated as competent little grown-ups at a rather tender age. Kids who lack guidance in dysfunctional families feel that they are not loved, not wanted and superfluous. It is reported that 55.5% of American teenagers are following the lead of the adults when smoking to fight stress. About as many of them are dying in traffic accidents (30% of teenage deaths) as from suicide (12%) and murder (18%) combined. Before reaching the age of maturity, kids will have experienced 15,000 virtual killings, rapes, and brawls. No surprise then, since they tend to be "screenagers" rather than teenagers, in the worst cases spending more than 30 hours per week in front of computer games and movie screens. Thus virtual violence begets real violence. Should then people be surprised when violent outbreaks take place such as the 1999 shootout at Columbine High School in Denver, Colorado?

The only surprise about violent outbreaks like 1999 Columbine High School in Denver, Colorado is the plain fact that to some they still come as a surprise.

The deeply rooted alcoholism in Western culture is a culprit in all that. During my undergraduate years at Union College in Schenectady, N.Y., I noticed as early as 1950 that people did not drink as a means of relaxing in convivial society — but simply to get drunk. This trend for binge drinking by American students begins early in high school.

In pre-Islamic Arabia, newborn girls were sometimes killed for economic reasons, until the Qur'an outlawed this horrible practice.[10] What was a Bedouin custom is pursued nowadays in a systematic fashion. Currently, millions of unborn girls and boys are selected out by sex, with the aid of ultrasound equipment, and then aborted. In Berlin, where economic need does not play a crucial role, only every second child is given birth. Married women account for half of all abortions, and 37% of aborting women are childless. The majority of young women, after all, feel entitled to exercise a right of total control over their "belly", even if this means killing an unborn person who can arguably claim a superior right: the right to life. A particularly alarming trend are those increased terminations of pregnancies due to negative prenatal diagnoses. These individual acts of euthanasia cause otherwise perfectly viable children to be hacked to pieces at a very late stage in the pregnancy. "Extermination of worthless life" was the Nazi terminology for this aberration.

Another symptom of the "sexual wilderness"[11] spawned by the "sexual revolution" is the shift of public opinion about homosexuality. Psychiatry had been considering it a perversion far into the post-World War II years. Then, in the 1972 edition of the American diagnostic handbook on the classification of psychiatric diseases, homosexuality began to mutate into a mental "disease". In the very next edition of the same handbook, homosexuality no longer qualified for treatment; instead it had become an "orientation", just one more option, a choice of "lifestyle"; in short, a normal phenomenon which should not be subjected to therapy.

This premise enabled the suppression of strong scientific evidence suggesting that AIDS had been spreading under the immuno-depressive conditions specific to male homosexuality – in concert with other habits that damage the immune system, such as drug and alcohol abuse.[12] The fact that the AIDS epidemic originated in the homosexual milieu of San Francisco, and not somewhere among green monkeys in the African jungle, was now deemed undesirable.

This above-mentioned premise of American psychiatry has been spreading to such a degree that the institution of marriage – already under constant attack from the left – is being threatened in the process. Marriage ceases to be valued as the fundamental reproductive bedrock of society, justly privileged by the law of inheritance. Currently, marriage seems to be more popular among lesbian and gay couples than among "straight" people. Whether this can compensate for the overall decline of the institution of marriage is, however, more than questionable.

Unchecked craving for pushing orgiastic lust to ever more intensive heights has led to pornography, sadomasochism, spouse swapping, and child abuse. In each of these deviations the reckless Western abandon of inhibitions is celebrating its ultimate triumphs. Indeed, Western societies have become structurally addicted, be it to alcohol or nicotine, marijuana, cocaine, heroin, and designer drugs, or to an incessant stream of TV images and computer games, with unlimited time on the Internet. For Muslims, all this behavior represents a clear case of polytheism (*shirk*). Riding public transportation in Washington, New York City or San Francisco, one can tell which of the passengers are on drugs.

For the first time ever, we are witnessing a dance craze – "raving" to Techno music – which requires an amount of stamina impossible to command without potent stimulants like crack or ecstasy. Just as it is with drugs, increasing tolerance levels in sexuality demand ever-increasing stimulation. Taboos are lifted to reach newer and deeper recesses of intimacy. Moderated by hypocrites among star entertainers, all kinds of aberrations are happily being outed in TV shows that turn into a national sport (who confesses weirder habits?), and grabbing the ratings. It is difficult to imagine where this escalation of exhibitionism and recklessness is going to lead us. That the dignity of women is the prime casualty in all of this, not only in shamefully degrading beauty contests, is evident.

In spite of the cutting edge technology in communication systems and the resulting information overload, the Western individual feels increasingly lonely, empty and adrift. In 1970, at the flower-and-hashish festival in Tanglewood, Charles Reich's bestseller *The Greening of America* had promised America's flower children and beatniks – the "downtrodden" of the "lost (post-World War II) generation" – a "greening of America" through a spiritual and emotional renewal.[13] Instead, a chill descended on human relations in America, coupled with a heretofore unimaginable brutalization.

This disturbing, progressive isolation – primarily of old people who are getting dumped in nursing homes is not just a result of the increased mobility of "Yuppies".[14] True, these "Pyramid Climbers"[15] are constantly seeking out more lucrative jobs on their journeys from Crédit Suisse First Boston via Lehmann Brothers to Stanley Morgan,[16] and in the process loosen family ties without finding an adequate replacement in their neighborhoods. True as well is the typical modern family, shrinking down to a mini ensemble of three people – maximum.

Yet, increasing isolation is not the result of these two developments. It is mainly the consequence of a Great Emptiness which is fast becoming a structural feature of Occidental existence. Each and everyone is becoming a solitary member of a "lonely mass", segregated in traffic jams, equally alone behind the wheel and in front of the computer screen, lost in cyberspace.

For the churches, in this moral chaos everything is business as usual. The more the churches appear to be "modernizing", the more the faithful are leaving them in droves.[17] The reason for this is that the churches are gradually losing any relevance for human beings *in extremis* – above all in death and disasters – by becoming secular institutions, intent on competing with other social organizations. When a protestant minister in Upper Bavaria recently admitted from the pulpit that she did not believe in an afterlife, and when professors of theology demote Jesus to the rank of social worker, it is not surprising that even the most patient and tested Christian rank and file eventually leave their churches. As a rule, they do not turn to a better religion, but rather tend to join the rising tide of disappointed skeptics.

Living in the modern world, the basic experience thus is: failure. The "Project Modernity" was destined to fail because of a serious flaw in its design: to posit man as a rational individual who dispassionately calculates his needs; an individual who instead of "revealed" norms, only follows *apriori* rules derived from the architecture of the human mind, like Kant's Categorical Imperative.

With that, the (practicing) Muslim rested his case. It was surprising that, aside from his elaborate comments on cultural issues, he had no word to say about political or economic questions. Approached about this, he mumbled something to the effect that, upon close scrutiny, the Western citizens' vaunted liberty is not quite what it is claimed to be: where Muslims are concerned, the state was myopic and hard of hearing. And while the press was not subject to state censorship, political correctness and preemptive compliance amounted to an effective self-censorship.

THESE are the observations which moved our dedicated Muslim student to a dismissal of the West out of hand. Far from emulating a Western civilization, itself in existential crisis, he seeks to spare his homeland a similar development. He sees no point in pursuing a model of progress that has essentially failed, and in inaugurating an Age of Reason, which has brought about the irrationality of atheism and its attendant consequences.

Does this not make one sit back and wonder whether both of these students – the cultural Muslim and the practicing one – have seen and described one and the same world? Well, they both did. And both of their starkly differing judgments are correct. There are undoubtedly many things in the West deserving admiration and imitation. But then, clearly, there are also many things that are decadent and such anathemas to human nature that they can lead to the collapse of this civilization unless it changes course in midstream.

While both of our oriental students are equally correct in their opposing views of the West, they are wrong in their reactions to it. The point for them, as well as for everybody in the West, is not mindlessly to ape each and every fashion trend and manifestation of decadence, but to mount corrective efforts: to profit from the achievements of Western civilization while fighting its ills. "Selective approach" is the motto.

The same applies in the next chapter, as we join two further anonymous students. this time Western Muslims on their journey into the Muslim Orient. There, too, we find much that is deserving admiration and imitation, just as there is much that provokes disdain and tough criticism.

Notes

1. Typical of this attitude are members of the Islamic opposition movement "Hizb at-Tahrir al-Islami", founded by Shaykh Taqi ad-Din al-Nabhani in 1953, which is well represented in Jordan and the United States. It stands for non-violence and expects the solution of the world's ills by restoring the Caliphate which had formally been abolished by Mustafa Kemal in 1924, and by establishing a strict Islamic order (*Tanzim al-Islam*). Their publications are available in the U.K. through Al-Khilafah Publications, P.O Box 3669, London N8 OPW, and in the US from TINA (*Tanzim al-Islam North America*) at 13763 Kalmia Ave., Flushing, NY, 11355

2. Kuschel (1998).

3. In 1775, when Frederick was negotiating with one thousand "Mohammedan Families" over granting them "homesteads and mosques" in western Prussia, (letter to Voltaire, August 13), he was perperfectly well aware of the fact that his friend Voltaire knew about as little about Muslims as about the Emperor of China (letter January 10, 1776). As early as December 1740, Voltaire had admitted in a letter to Frederick that "Mohammed had not actually committed the kind of treason that was at the heart of this tragedy [entitled Mahomet]." At the same time, however, he justified his historical concoction and the damage it did to Islam with the following hair-raising argument: "A man who embroils his own country in war, and claims to do so in the name

of God, would he not be capable of anything?" (*Voltaire-Friedrich der Große Briefwechsel*, Zurich: Haffmans, 1992).

4. In the very first book of *Die Fröhliche Wissenschaft* Nietzsche noted that, "the greatest new event is beginning to cast it's shadow over Europe – that God is dead, that the belief in the Christian God [sic!] has lost credibility." (cf. *Nietzsche*, vol. 1, p. 489).

5. More than anybody else, Rudolf Otto has shown the consequences of losing the "sacred" .

6. Poll results from Germany's eastern and western regions differ more sharply on questions of religion than on any other issue.

7. Cf. Paul Schwarzenau, "Das nachchristliche Zeitalter. Elemente einer planetarischen Religion." In: Kirste, pp. 478. There are other Christian theologians like John Hick and Hans Küng who are also likely to believe that a Christian world is no more and won't ever exist again.

8. Otto von Habsburg, *Paneuropa*, 1991, no. 4, p. 6.

9. The French have a pithy phrase for these absentee fathers: "*pères démissionaires*" – literally "abdicating fathers".

10 6:151; 16:59; 17:31.

11. Vance Packard, *Sexual Wilderness* (New York 1968).

12. Cf. Malik Badri (1997) and Javed Jamil.

13. Reich's book was more than an analysis: a manifesto which touched a nerve among the people of his generation and their outlook on life.

14. Ambitious, upwardly mobile young business people.

15. Vance Packard coined this moniker as early as 1962 in his eponymous book on that subject.

16. Nowhere else are top managers more mobile than in Investment Banking.

17. Asad had predicted this development as early as 1934: many a thinking Christian would eventually refuse to have their intelligence insulted by church dogmas like original sin, incarnation, crucifition as deliverance, holy trinity, lately Mary's ascension. As a consequence, they will not only leave their church in droves, but religion altogether (paraphrased from p.51f.). Based on active involvement in churches and public professions of faith, statistics show surprisingly that the United States turns out to be "dechristianized" to a far lesser degree than Europe.

CHAPTER TWO

Destination: East

This must be the age when
we finally outgrow our need for religion.
(Salman Rushdie on March 6, 1999, about the Third Millennium)

Among Western students who have embraced Islam there are many who became so transformed by the process of conversion that they, like Abdul Hadi Christian Hoffmann, find themselves "striding over two chairs." Some of them were young readers of the German author Karl May (1842-1912), who set his adventure stories in the Middle East and the Americas. Having acquired a passion for everything Arabic, Islamic, and Oriental in their early years, they went on to make Islamic Studies their academic career. Now, in painstaking detail they are eagerly seeking to model their selves on the life of the Prophet as preserved in the *sunnah*,[1] even including the *hijra*,[2] an emigration into the Islamic world for reasons of faith. A few of these converts are emulating Arabic culture in dress, cosmetics, food, habits and language to such a degree that many other Muslims accuse them of exoticism, subcultural behavior, and ignorance of the timeless universality of Islam. Their approach would only confirm the prejudice that Islam is merely a religion for the Arabs, although in reality there are far fewer Arab Muslims than non-Arab Muslims now, after the separation of Pakistan from India, not to mention the 200 million Indonesian Muslims.

LET us nonetheless hear such a Muslim who has made up his mind to emigrate, so we may learn more about his personal reasons for leaving his home country for an Islamic one. What are the two dozen or so cultural factors which in his mind make a Muslim society so attractive? What moves a European to believe that, of all places, it is there – and only there – where he can recharge his moral batteries, and where he can live his life as a Muslim to the fullest? Well, let us listen:

In contrast to the very loose ties in Western nuclear family (1.8 average size), the tightly knit, extended Muslim family continues, thank God, to be the solid cornerstone of society. For Michel Houellebecq, of all social organizations, family is the only one to shield the modern individual from the brutal laws of the market. It makes no difference that the extended family is neither original to the Islamic world, nor unique to it. To be sure, nowadays even the Muslim family finds itself under the strain of modernism. Tourism, explicit movies with their unabashed glorification of adultery, and rising incomes, make solidarity dispensable and women more mobile. And yet: families in Islamic countries remain generally tightly knit to make their members feel taken care of in their emotional and physical needs, and, if anything, complain about being looked after a bit too much.

Even in oil-rich Muslim countries, the (male) family members regularly meet weekly for a so-called *majlis* (gathering) at the house of the eldest. In Bahrain, one can easily find eighty and more participants on such occasions which are not strictly limited to family members alone. As long as only one of them has an income, nobody goes hungry. The old and the frail are included in every family activity, as are the many children, day or night. Up until about ten years ago, even Turkey did not have any homes for the elderly (*huzur eviler*), and up to this very day the Moroccan king is resisting the establishment of old-age asylum, because this would be symptomatic of the unraveling of the social-safety-net provided by the family.

And indeed: in the Muslim world, whether poor or rich, the family is still the social-safety-net that it once was in the Occident, before government gradually stripped the family of its traditional functions by introducing obligatory insurance coverage for illness, unemployment, accidents, retirement, and long term care. The Muslim family continues to be the place where people live together, eat, pray, celebrate, mourn and die – and all that without squelching individuality. Odd characters do have their niche, and the family unit routinely pools support for gifted individuals, such as sponsoring them for studies abroad.

Family and hospitality go together, especially since Islamic law requires that every guest be housed and fed for up to three consecutive days. Thus, evolved a culture of hospitality which is a hard act to follow for budget-conscious Westerners subjected to the strictures of accounting.

My own experience confirms this. As ambassador to Morocco and Algeria I would often have to persuade official German visitors to resist their ingrained manner of politely admiring beautiful artifacts in their host's home: a book, a painting, a silver dagger. Those who disregarded my advice would usually find the object of their admiration in their luggage, as a farewell gift (on unconscious demand).

Whenever an acquaintance asks a traveling Muslim for a specific errand, the "order" will swiftly be turned into a "souvenir", and the traveler will always bring back more than he had on his wish list. If one music CD was requested, one will at least make it a gift of two. If you take a friend along as interpreter to the tailor where you want to order a kaftan, the next day you will receive two of them, the bill already paid.

Both family orientation and hospitality are at the source of the loving kindness and consideration typical of Muslim communities: the proverbial solidarity of the *ummah*.[3] Most Muslims have never heard that you are supposed to love your neighbor like yourself, but they read in the Qur'an that all Muslims are brothers and sisters.[4] For Europeans, it is always gratifying to witness the kind and considerate manner with which people who embraced the Muslim lifestyle treat each other in Islamic centers. Europeans feel pleasantly enfolded by sympathy and unreserved acceptance. This is one of the reasons why so many Catholic Filipinos who are guest workers in the Arabic Gulf region find themselves converting to Islam.[5]

Many Muslims who never met before embrace and address each other like friends. One may expect this more easily from an esoteric sect than from a religious community comprising over a billion people. Many Muslims suffer, of course, political persecution and oppression to such a degree that they need support.[6] But whenever Muslims ask each other for something outright, it usually is not about help, but rather to be included in the other's prayers.

Brotherhood among Muslims shows in their readiness to donate money, which achieves record-breaking proportions especially in the United States. For Muslims, giving alms (*sadaqa*) – in part as a tax on wealth targeted for social purposes (*zakat*) – is not just another onerous obligation, but one of the five "pillars (*arkan*) of Islam" and thus, an integral part of their faith.[7] A Muslim is not even allowed to embark on his pilgrimage to Makkah as long as one of his neighbors is in need, even though the *hajj* is itself one of the very pillars of Islam.

There is hardly a fund-raising dinner among American Muslims where the 80 to 120 invited guests will not donate at least $ 100,000 for the cause of Islam, sometimes even $500,000 and more. Some Muslim physicians living in the USA were still students there when they first pledged 10% of their future income to the cause of Islam, valid for life.

But this readiness for financial sacrifice alone does not account for the increase of mosque construction visible all over the Islamic world. It is also due to a unique, time-honored prophetic tradition, which holds that God will build a house in paradise for those who build a house for Him on earth.[8] This is the reason why in Turkey, all through the last decade, privately financed mosques were completed at the rate of one every six hours. The Saudi monarch, King al Fahd ibn'Abd al-Aziz, has privately financed the construction of sixty mosques all over the world – from Rome to Los Angeles.

The feeling of togetherness within the world-encompassing *ummah*, transcending all racial boundaries, is a political reality, which can be politically activated at any time. But no serious Muslim would claim that Islam had ever succeeded in fully rooting out ethnic prejudice throughout its realm. Bitter proof to the contrary does exist, not just in the Arab peninsula but also in Mauritania, which feels the strange need periodically to deny slavery in the country. At the same time, one can say with absolute confidence that no other religion has done better in pushing racism into the background than Islam – a fact of the highest significance in a time like ours, beset by chauvinism.

In particular the annual pilgrimage, *al hajj*, works like a gigantic melting pot, a colorblind festival to take note of. It was therefore not surprising that it took but a single *hajj* to convince the anti-white Malcolm X that his arch-racist "Nation of Islam" was moving down the wrong path. It was only then that as Al Hajj Malik al Shabazz, he became a true Sunni Muslim like his friends Muhammad Ali, Jamil al-Amin (Rap Brown), and W. D. Mohammed – and paid for it with his life.[9] Since then, traditionally "black", Arabic, and Indo-Pakistani mosques in the United States have increasingly become more inclusive. As it is, there is a strong egalitarian current in Islam, since the Qur'an leaves no doubt that in the final analysis piety is the only thing that counts – not power, wealth, birth, beauty or popularity.[10] In fact, the very idea of aristocracy was anathema to the pronounced sense of equality and independence among the pre-Islamic Arabic bedouins. A practical consequence of this is that, in the absence of an officially appointed prayer leader in the mosque, the congregation will spontaneously select an *imam* from amongst themselves. They will settle on the person who is worthiest or most learned in matters of faith. Age, race, or nationality are irrelevant.

That does not mean, however, that there is no such thing as hereditary aristocracy in the Muslim world. But even though *sheiks*, *emirs*, kings and their numerous princes do exist – their nobility has relatively shallow roots. A court protocol reminiscent of Byzantium survived only in the *Maghrib*. In Arabia and the Gulf region, nobody kisses hands, at most the shoulders and the bridge of the nose only. People do not bow while shaking hands, but instead proudly hold their head up high. It is impressive to see how weather-beaten Saudi bedouins, in worn-out sandals, attend their Crown Prince Abdullah's weekly open house (*majlis*), quite often giving him a piece of their mind while emphatically wagging a finger in his face.

This bedouin egalitarianism is entirely compatible with the highly developed sense of respect among Muslims. By now, many in the West consider any kind of respect as a secondary virtue, at best, if not as a detestable attitude. From early childhood on, the Muslim is taught to respect God and His Word (in the Qur'an), the moral authority commanded by the Prophet Muhammad, the principal position of father and mother, his teachers, and the elderly. Even the older brother (Turkish *abi*, from *aga bey*) and big sister (Turkish *abla*) are shown respect by their younger siblings. A situation where a youngster sues his or her parents in court or – as happened in the United States – goes so far as to file for separation from them, is unthinkable in the Islamic world. It is true that respect may be such in the Orient that in some situations, it will trump merit. After all, age does not necessarily go hand in hand with wisdom, and teachers can be foolish, too. But by embracing respect as a prime value, Muslims give their community a strong humane underpinning. One is hard pressed to find evidence of this in western countries, for instance in public transportation, where visibly pregnant women can no longer find school kids to give up their seats for them. Most likely they will be unmoved and continue to chew their gum ostentatiously.

Closely related to the attitude of respect is another exemplary feature of behavior, widespread in the Orient: the protection of privacy. This phenomenon can easily be observed in unbelievably densely settled cities like Fez. At first blush, it seems as if people could easily ogle each other from their respective roof gardens, or sneak a peek from the alley into the neighbors' windows.[11] But one realizes that everyone architecturally protects his privacy against intrusion. House entrances are built around the corner in order to shield the interior from curious gazes. On the whole, Muslim houses resemble expensive fur coats whose good sides are turned inside. In the Islamic world, even men's restrooms provide more privacy than their Western counterparts. In Makkah one will be hard pressed to find a public urinal: instead, to each his cabin, a privilege which in the West is commonly reserved for women only.

The egalitarian ideal of Islam also shows up in a place where no one would suspect it: in the oral tradition of Islam, which is an oral culture *par excellence*. The very first word of the revelation (96:1-5), which Muhammad began to receive in 610, was *Iqra*! Not only does this mean "Read!", but also "Recite!" Ever since that moment, reciting the Qur'an has become a sublime form of art, and learning it by heart is a highly acclaimed accomplishment, today mastered by hundreds of thousands of people.[12] Nevertheless, it would be misleading to follow Hans Küng who likes to equate God's becoming man in Jesus Christ, with the embodiment of His Word in the Qur'an – inlibration instead of incarnation.[13] Indeed, while Muslims do revere God's Word in recitation, they do not worship a divine physical presence in any scripture.

Artistic accomplishment in Qur'anic recitation reflects the fact that recitation of poetry – *ghazals* and (much longer) *qassidas* – is arguably the highest form of Arabic music. Declamation of poetry is therefore performed during dinners, much like a harpist's background music, only right next to the table of honor.

This is by no means intended to minimize the role of writing in Islamic sciences. How could it, given the monumental legacy of written records of Islamic scholarship, which date all the way back to the 2nd Islamic century. Already in Muhammad's lifetime, the Qur'an had been written down continuously, as a loose-leaf collection. Before long the Islamic heritage grew into the vast body of Muhammad's legacy (*hadith*),[14] multi-volume Qur'an commentaries (*tafsir*), painstaking accounts of Muhammad's life, set against prehistory (*sira*),[15] documentation of Islam's early history (*tarikh*), as well as Arabic dictionaries (*qawamis*) and grammars, both valid to this day. A glorious written tradition arose, enriched by master works of Islamic jurisprudence (*fiqh*),[16] and all the other contributions that make up the intellectual history of Islam (*adab*), so fascinating to this very day.

The above mentioned rhetorical arts, also evident during Friday prayers, were to make sure – quite in contrast to the Western church tradition – that each and every Muslim would have access to his holy texts, whether he could read or not. The Islamic revelation was never intended to be secret esoteric lore. Quite the opposite: Islam built its strength and unique resilience on oral tradition. The Soviets were bound to fail in their attempt to eradicate Islam in Central Asia, because it proves immune to the arresting of scholars and burning of libraries.

Our Orient-loving Muslim complements his deposition with a few qualities that he appreciates about life among Muslims:

Among those qualities – considered marginal in the West – are the Muslims' manifest patience and their structural sobriety. The latter prevails because drugs, including alcohol, whether available or not, do not play a significant role. According to Arab media, the Muslim region has its drug problems, too. In Dubai, the Arabic Hong Kong, everything is available – but whoever gets caught with a bottle of whiskey can expect to be deported.

In cities where people practice Islam, nobody needs to dodge drunken drivers, and no woman has to worry about drunken rapists. One is not disturbed at night by drunk and raucous voices or by rambunctious neighbors under the influence at the adjacent restaurant table. Nor will your neighbor's tobacco smoke make your eyes water, as people in the Muslim world smoke far less than in the West – even less than in today's tobaccophobic United States. Recently in Manama, an open-air coffee house under palm trees, which allowed for a measure of privacy, opened with the permission to smoke water pipes. This provoked such uproar as to flood the newspapers with letters to the editor.

Their characteristic sobriety also explains why far fewer Muslims are overweight. Being a Muslim almost always means being slim, because the *sunnah* advises people against stuffing their stomachs. In contrast to that, obesity in the United States is quite conspicuous, threatening to become a national problem. The moment one steps off the plane somewhere in the United States, one runs into overweight individuals of every age group. It would, of course, be a simplistic approach to a metabolically complex phenomenon to attribute Western corpulence to gluttony alone, and the skinny Muslim type to *Ramadan* fasting. In fact, in spite of fasting for a whole month, many Muslims do not lose weight at all. It seems certain, though, that neither junk foods nor hormone treated beef are playing a decisive role, but rather the mental makeup of overweight people, just as is the case in both chronic binge eating and anorexia. In German, one talks about *Kummerspeck* (*Kummer* standing for sorrow and *Speck* for bacon) when depressive over-eating brings about a flab. Thus we are back with religion, after all.

As a by-product of their constantly remaining sober (which implies a state of permanent readiness), in Muslim society one encounters a remarkable degree of equanimity. This could be explained by hot climate, but the same state of mind can be observed in colder regions. Some of this composure may be due to the structural tiredness of people who habitually rise at three, four, or five at dawn for their morning prayers (*fajr*). In the final analysis, however, the remarkable equanimity of Muslims can be explained best by the absence of everyday stress, and this can only be the result of a religious worldview. Of course, the Muslims' world has its own psychiatrists and patients who need them.[17] But their firm belief in divine intervention and guidance, as well as their expectation of everlasting life in the presence of God after a just Final Judgment, will indeed insulate most of them from the tragic postmodern feeling of existential, cosmic loneliness and alienation. It also helps to protect them from the depressions and anxieties of old age, which have made many a psychiatrist rich.

The Muslim's religious conviction, resulting in constant awareness of God (*taqwa*) (called God-fearing by Christians), simply renders many things dispensable which non-believers cannot seem to live without. Faith is, after all, a way of radically putting things into perspective.

All of the above makes it even more important for the Islamic world that the faithful are called to prayer five times a day, the call amplified by loudspeakers. This is to remind them in a *quasi*-official way that God is the fact of life that matters most. The call to prayer should structure a Muslim's day no matter where. But this becomes obvious only in the Islamic world, particularly when, as in Saudi Arabia, even stores close during prayer time.

In the Muslim world it is not only easy to pray on time; also shopping for meat and meat products is convenient. If as a Muslim one is intent on not buying pork products from a Western supermarket, one has to spend a lot of time deciphering the tiny print on food ingredient labels.

Finding Western butchers who sell meat of animals slaughtered according to Islamic law takes an even greater effort.[18] In Muslim stores, the beauty is that one can shop for one's meat blindly.

Oriental Muslims relate to the passing of time with particular equanimity – to the point that one might speak of a completely different, oriental sense of time. In places where "time is money", nobody has of course time. On the contrary, the Western world seems to pick up speed just as the circulation of currency keeps accelerating. The internet adds to that by enabling communication in real time, virtual – but live on screen. It seems logical that time is more plentiful among those who do not treat it as a financial commodity. Western people suffer from a bad conscience if they are late. Muslims have a more detached relationship to time and punctuality. You will be there when you get there, period. Just think of it: in a country not hung up on precision timing, although one may arrive late at the airport or railway station, one still has a good chance of catching one's flight or train. Instead of enslaving themselves to a tyrant called time, running after self-imposed deadlines, Muslims prefer to remain imprecise about appointments, not making them at 4:20 p.m. but rather for "between the afternoon and evening prayers". Everybody knows that prayer precedes everything else anyway and therefore justifies delays.

It is reported without claim to historicity that a Western tourist in southern Algeria, say in Beni Izguen, once asked a local Mozabite, waiting for the next prayer in the shadow of his oasis mosque, what time it was. The story goes that the Algerian did not respond. But after the tourist had left, he turned to the Mozabite sitting next to him and whispered in their Berber dialect: "Is he ill?"

Sobriety and composure both radiate dignity. This finds ample visual expression in the graceful strides necessitated by ankle-long Muslim gowns, such as the *galabiyya* or *thaub*,[19] and the *kaftan*. But whenever dignity is mentioned, what comes first to mind is the Muslim woman. Thanks to the dress codes of both the Qur'an and the *sunnah*,[20] she has been able to avoid following in the unfortunate footsteps of her Western sisters and eschew the competition for who will wear the smallest stitch of clothes. Nor has she been tempted to enter into direct competition with men in gender-specific areas like muscle building. This way, the Muslim women (*Muslima*) in Islamic countries have successfully managed to resist the kind of "sexploitation" other women are subjected to in fashion shows or advertisements, against which Western feminists justly protest so vehemently. Surely, the protection of women's dignity was a major goal of women's liberation movements in the West. Yet, Muslim women proved more successful at it. That explains, why in Western countries more women then men are converting to Islam, in spite of all counter-propaganda.

The Western public is in general overlooking the fact that in a Muslim home, the woman – especially as mother – holds the central role and wields considerably more influence over her sons than people commonly realize.

Muslims can only feel completely at home in an environment where God is accorded His rightful place. This undoubtedly happens more in the Muslim world than in today's Western societies. When a Muslim driver starts his engine, he invokes the "*bismillah*" ("In the Name of God."). Any speaker begins his presentation with these words, as do captains when welcoming passengers on the plane, as do parents before touching their table-ware at dinner-time. There is hardly a lecture that does not commence with a word of praise for God, a blessing for the Prophet, and a wish for peace upon the audience. [21]   The Egyptian president hosts receptions in honor of the Prophet's birthday. On the same occasion, the King of Morocco sends invitations for a religious celebration with ritual chanting. And the Saudi King's most honorific title is "Guardian of the two Holy Sites" (in Makkah and *al Madinah*). All this may be formal or formulaic and on the way to becoming fossilized ritual. Yet, it has the effect of resisting the very privatization of a faith in God which in the West is sometimes treated as something to be ashamed of, particularly by a well-educated or for that matter an intellectual person.

Finally, it is gratifying to be able to point out that Islam, in spite of its tendency towards monolithic unity, shows an equally powerful trend to pluralism. None of the caliphs ever saw himself as a pope. Nobody in Islam, Muhammad included, ever claimed to be infallible. Islamic jurists have at times tolerated up to seven schools of law (*madhahib*), competing with each other in matters of substance with often widely diverging views on important details.[22] The prevailing diversity in theology, philosophy and mysticism has always been enriching, as reflected in competing philosophical schools like the *Mu'tazila* and *Ash'ariyya*, in sects [23] and in strikingly diverse *Sufi* orders as well. [24]

In the final analysis, when he faces God, each individual Muslim is the most emancipated of all believers, without the possibility for, or necessity of, intercession by saints or via sacraments. With that in mind, Muslims are born grassroots democrats, without clerics, and the Qur'an directs them to manage all their community affairs by consultation between those who govern and the governed in a fashion resembling democracy.[25]

With this note, our prospective immigrant from the West rests his impressive case.

JUST as we did in the previous chapter, we now proceed to interview a second anonymous Western convert to Islam about his impression of the Islamic Orient. We are talking to someone like Muhammad Asad, who at the ripe old age of 85 was still thanking God that he became Muslim before knowing much about the Muslim world.[26] This way, the ideal theory of Islam could not be eclipsed by malpractice. Such a Muslim even finds himself in agreement with the renowned Egyptian Sheik Muhammad al Ghazali (d.1996), that there are few Muslims in the West, but there is a lot of Islam to be found there. This, he continued, was exactly the other way around in parts of the Muslim world. Yet, our Muslim student would not endorse the exaggeration that Islam had altogether emigrated from the Islamic world to the West, as some sardonically claim.

Curiously enough, this second Western Muslim holds decidedly negative opinions of what his brother had held in such high regard. But let us listen:

The Muslim countries all belong to the so-called developing world. Many of them have plenty enough of four things only: sun, sand, children, and time. There is no historical or climatic excuse for this deplorable underdevelopment, which is barely obscured by imported technology.

Muslim family values are highly ambivalent. They are the very roots of the rampant corruption typical of the Muslim world. There every important position in government, business, and even cultural institutions (above all in theater and literature) is filled with kins of those in power. As a result, many important functions in the Muslim world are run by unqualified or second-rate people, which puts an artificial damper on the developmental potential of these countries. To be sure, the average oriental Muslim is under moral obligations to look out for his family members. But they should do so without harming others. If one acts in the West as one does in the Muslim World one has one foot in jail already for nepotism.

The particular warmth characteristic of personal relations in the *ummah* is a fact, but not the entire truth. One can hardly pretend that the millions of Muslim guest workers on the Arabic peninsula, disparagingly called "expats" (from "expatriates"), are treated like "brothers in Islam". Otherwise they would be expected to receive permanent residency, be allowed to bring their families, and be vested in a reliable retirement plan. Should it really be so easy to expel the dirt-poor from Pakistan, Egypt, Palestine, or Morocco as "illegal aliens", without due process and under inhumane conditions? They, too, are Muslims, only seeking to scratch out a living in places privileged by God with gas and oil, as a heritage for all.

Poor countries in particular show off uncommon luxury. In Rabat, one can find local ladies who for dinner wear emerald jewelry to match green garments, or rubies with red gowns, or black sapphires that play off against white dresses. To be seen are gems of a size normally on display only in museums. Females of Western democracies that are much richer due to their higher productivity, do not stand a chance to match such luxuries of the local ladies. But that may help to explain why some countries are poor and others are rich.

It may sound cynical, but some affluent ex-bedouins seem to care less for people (even women) than for noble animals, such as sinfully expensive hunting falcons, slender, beige-colored racing camels and high-bred Arab horses that are worth millions. Not only Western Muslims but others as well, shake their heads in amazement over the extraordinary extravaganza involving these hunting falcons, even bird psychologists tending to their sensitive psyches are mused. What justification is there for the expense incurred in letting these precious hundred-thousand-dollar-birds hunt lumbering fowl, their favorite prey, 3000 miles away in the Algerian rock desert?

The much glorified brotherhood and solidarity of the *ummah* is obviously hard pressed when it comes to closing the enormous gap between the rich and the poor in the Muslim world. Many oil-rich potentates and affluent individual Muslims are doing much good, often anonymously, as recommended by the Qur'an. Let us also concede that giving money away in a constructive and controlled fashion is anything but easy; Sheik Zayd of Abu Dhabi, head of the United Arab

Emirates, maintains an entire bureaucracy solely dedicated to review aid requests, feasibility studies, evaluating cost estimates, and supervising construction projects. We also have to take into account that in some oil producing countries, public utilities like water, electricity, and local phone calls are free. At the same time, some petro-countries still tend to indulge in excessive luxuries. Somehow, this does not seem to accord with brotherhood, while it is true, of course that nobody would benefit, if millionaires scattered their money like hayseed.

It does not belittle the generosity of wealthy Muslims to say that their money would be more wisely spent, if they were less concerned with securing an abode in paradise by building yet another mosque with all the attendant maintenance costs.[27] Would they not be equally rewarded in the hereafter, if they had built instead a Muslim kindergarten or school, or funded charitable organizations like *Muslim Aid*?

Since money is the issue, it would be less than honest to ignore that Muslim states do put their capital in foreign investment in the West (and Japan) for interest, i.e., against the explicit prohibition by the Qur'an, without exception.[28] Islam permits profitable use of capital, in terms of profit-and-loss sharing between financier and finance-taker, such as when one holds shares for non-speculative purposes. This restriction is not just ethical, but of particular economic value, since it promotes the entrepreneurial spirit of risk-taking businessmen who, after all, are the foundation of the entire capitalist system. Risk-taking, however, by itself does not legitimize investment, because Islam also frowns on any sort of gambling, as in the case of derivatives.

Practicing an Islamic economy in isolation, within a world prone to destabilization by volatile hedge funds is by no means an easy feat, especially since nowadays the role of interest rates go far beyond yielding gains on savings. Interest has become an instrument of economic policy as well as of resource management. It is, nevertheless, disheartening that 1421 lunar years after the founding of the first Islamic state there is not yet one single national Muslim economy (not even in Pakistan or Malaysia) where the Islamic prohibition of interest is fully implemented.[29]

Islam has an undeniably egalitarian streak, which periodically has left its social and political mark since the earliest Islamic history, notably with the secessionist Khawarijs in the 7th century and the egalitarian Qarmatians in the 9th century.[30] But that did not prevent the emergence of aristocracies and privileged groups and families in the Muslim world, over time.

It follows that there is not a single Muslim country that could claim to be governed with significant participation of the general public, even where elections are held and representative bodies exist (which oftentimes have a mere consultative function). On the contrary: in discussing democracy, many orthodox Muslims continue to argue that this system of government is incompatible with Islam.

The abiding respect among Muslims is a fact and is rightly been characterized as positive. But there is the negative side effect that respect can pervert into unquestioned acceptance of authority, any authority. That results in a society, not only unable to promote a culture of political participation (i.e., civil society) that sees value in a peaceful exchange of ideas, but worse in an undemocratic society that is structurally hamstrung to spawn new scientific achievements. Skepticism (as a working hypothesis) is, after all, the mother of all scientific progress.

Islamic civilization did indeed begin to stagnate at a time (in the 14th/15th century) when respect for the knowledge of its elders turned into mere imitation, a process terminating in the dogma of the "closing of the door of interpretation" (*bab al ijtihad*), summed up in one terse word: *taqlid*, i.e., the blind imitation and unquestioned acceptance of authority. From this point onwards, following the example of post-Justinian jurists, Muslim scientific efforts consisted mainly in adding glosses to old glosses written on the margins of even older commentaries,

Taqlid was the wrong conclusion drawn from the correct assumptions: (i) that Islamic theology had already made available everything there is to know for man, the earthly pilgrim, to find his way to God, and (ii) that the earliest Muslims must have had a better understanding of Islam than later generations by virtue of their historical proximity to the Prophet.

The notion of *taqlid* was not decreed by any religious council, nor pronounced by a Caliph. Rather this pernicious intellectual trend seemed to prevail almost universally, all by itself. This development brought Islam perilously close to the condition of the Christian churches, which, too, had become rigid from dogmas and thought control. At any rate, *taqlid* was the cause of the very spiritual and intellectual stagnation that eventually brought about the technological, economic, and military decline of the Islamic world, and thus inaugurated its period of decadence from the 17th to the 19th century.

Most Muslims still hold Western imperialist colonialism responsible for their lingering economic underdevelopment – but it is exactly the other way around: the Islamic world was colonized, because following the principle *of taqlid* had caused it much earlier to slide into decadence.[31]

In short: the Islamic world did not decline because of colonization, it was colonized because it had declined to the point of being colonizable.

It is hard to contest that blaming other people and circumstances for one's own shortcomings and failures preserves one's self-confidence. This is a universal psychological defense mechanism enlisted by people everywhere in an attempt to cope with hideous reality. For many, however, this harmless phenomenon degenerated into a tremendous paranoia rife with conspiracy theories. From colonialism to the current socioeconomic malaise, to the political situation in Muslim countries and the "technological aggression" by Western cultural imperialists – all is quickly reduced to a monumental Western conspiracy against Islam.

The CIA, Mossad, Zionist organizations, freemasons, and even NATO surprise us in their star roles as leaders in a grand, Muslim-made conspiratorial canvas. Many seriously believe that somewhere there exists a master plan for the corruption and destruction of Islam and diligently collect whatever might fit their preconceived idea of the world. The Western failure to intervene during the first three bloody years of the Bosnian conflict, the unshakeable American commitment to Israel and the prominence of Jewish advisors in the Clinton administration have given a lot of fodder (and not the worst arguments either) to this conspiratorial paranoia.[32] In contrast to all this, would it not be much more realistic to understand that foreign policy everywhere is governed by parochial interests, and that gadgets invented, by one Bill Gates, quite naturally flood the entire world, since cutting-edge technology inevitably replaces lesser technology, just as naturally as water flows downhill?

These psychological faultlines in the Muslim mind cannot be dismissed as harmless, for they effectively hinder any helpful acknowledgement of the Muslims' own mistakes and stifle proactive initiatives. In the final analysis, Muslims are thus responsible for their own fatalist mindset.

Another Muslim belief related to the notion of *taqlid* and equally harmful, is the doctrinal ban of (theological) innovation (*bida'*), in many places still a considerable educational handicap. Because of it, in most Muslim primary schools there is more parroting or memorization going on than encouragement of critical thinking, with the consequence that the effects of illiteracy are pervasive even among those who can read. Even Muslim scientists tend to rely not on the strength of their own arguments, but on the strength in the number of authorities, which are then quoted cumulatively, rather than selectively, one by one: professor X said (qala): " . . . ". professor Y said (qala): " . . . ". [33]

The root cause of these interpretations stem from reducing the meaning of the ambivalent term bida' to mean only a "bad" innovation to the exclusion of its other meaning which can as well connote a "good" innovation. This explains why any kind of reform affecting the orthodox ways of teaching or the practice of Islam was considered out of bounds. [34] The upshot was a bida'-phobia, allowing the accusation of "innovation" to be wielded like a weapon against suspected heretics. Such a charge could have deadly consequences, as Hussain al Mansur al Halladsch and Shihab al Din Yahya al Suhrawardi "al Maqtul" (the slain) had to experience, both esoteric-ecstatic Sufis who had merely exaggerated in their theosophic speculation. [35]

The overall consequences were intellectual stagnation, seeking refuge in obscure esoterics and mysticism, as well as a decoupling from Western technological developments. This explains why the first printing of the Qur'an in 1694 was not done in a Muslim city, but in Hamburg, of all places. [36] As late as 1580, Islamic scholars in Istanbul had an observatory destroyed as "improper innovation"; it had only been erected the year before. Even the first Ottoman printing press was idled, in 1745, under pressure from the 'Ulema.

No wonder that censorship is ubiquitous in today's Muslim world. Even the text of Friday sermons is issued by governmental religious authorities. Some imams read their sermons off visibly from these instructions, with strictest compliance.

Another chronic problem for the Muslim world is the traditional overemphasis on the humanities (adab) at the expense of the hard sciences – as if God had not manifested Himself twofold: in His Book, and in His Creation. With the exception of the medical doctor, who is considered a hakim (wise man), graduates in humanities enjoy a much higher social prestige in the Islamic world than do natural scientists.

Small wonder then, that under the given circumstances, the Muslims have so far produced but two Nobel laureates in natural sciences. In the booming fields of pioneer science – brain research, genetics, cybernetics, low temperature technology, biochemistry, microphysics and astronomy, Muslims are conspicuously absent.

At the same time, the phenomenal success in medicine and computer technology of activist Muslim scientists in the United States – mostly immigrants from Egypt, India, Pakistan, Palestine and Syria – proves that the mentioned shortcomings are not due to missing talent. By now, Silicon Valley in and around Santa Clara and Palo Alto has become a Muslim valley as well, right in the middle of California. Shortcomings in science among Muslims are rather due to an educational environment that fails to nurture them from the cradle and is inimical to free research and development.

Patience is truly an Islamic virtue – God is with those who exercise patience[37] – but this is far from justifying the way in which Muslim bureaucrats, bank and transportation employees are habitually quite unapologetic about making people wait until they get around to finishing their tea or telephone chat with their girl friends. Is productivity in Muslim countries as low and inefficiency as high as it is so that believers can show patience?

Sobriety is a good thing, too. But there is not enough of it in the Muslim world. Although Muslims are forbidden to offer alcohol, only very few Muslim airlines, like Saudia, do not offer liquor on board.. How can drugs and alcohol possibly be eliminated, if Dubai accepts 92% non-Muslim residents, many of them non-Muslims entitled to alcohol under Islamic law, and that in what used to be the "House of Islam" (*dar-al Islam*)? Under these conditions it is not surprising that this place up until recently has been crawling with Russian prostitutes. Bahrain is said to tolerate posh brothels, attracting customers from the mainland via the bridge from Dhahran to Manama to indulge in sex and alcohol. Turkey, still culturally shaped by Islam, has more alcoholics than Germany – in both percentage and total numbers. But why should this faze anyone, since the Ottoman Sultans (and Caliphs!) of yore already had their share of drunkards. The Islamic world as a famously drug free haven does not exist.

Ambivalent also is the Muslims' approach to time. It may serve as a convenient excuse for un-Islamic tardiness, which is really an impolite or even arrogant act of indifference to others, as well as a waste of resources. In some cases, the casual Muslim attitude towards time is eerily reminiscent of southern European *dolce far niente* and *mañana* syndromes.

It is true that Islamic garments grace the *Muslima* with the kind of elegance the West associates with long evening gowns, and her position in the family is a very strong one, indeed. And yet, this does not mean that she is currently assuming the role in Muslim countries that both the Qur'an and the *sunnah* assigned for her. One would have to be blind to ignore the fact that women in the Muslim world have their Islamic emancipation still ahead of them. This world has remained too much of a *macho* world for its own good.

Even the diversity, which characterizes all areas of Islam, is not free from ambivalence. On the one hand, it does enrich; on the other, it leads to weakness when pluralism becomes excessive. The Muslim commonwealth of nations suffers from a chronic lack of unity, from the Arab League (founded in 1945) to the Organization of the Islamic Conference (O.I.C), which was established in 1969 and has 56 member-States to date. In Europe and the United States as well, disunity among Muslims seems to be their common denominator, and this plays straight into the hands of the enemies of Islam.

A much greater cause for concern, however, is a recent decline of the spiritual pluralism that used to be the hallmark of Islam, of the tolerance legal schools have shown towards each other, and of the refreshing polemics among Muslim philosophers.[38] Today's scene is dominated by a minority of politicized Islamic movements facing each other down with impudence, each one convinced to be on the right way, each one claiming the ultimate insight.

This growing parochialism can be explained in two ways:

Firstly, the Islamic movements in question oftentimes are caught in a life or death struggle with the regimes, Muslim by name, which are out to defend the *status quo* and therefore feel threatened by re-Islamization. People putting their life at stake for Islam and risking in the process torture and execution must be absolutely certain about the Islam they are fighting for. (It is of course possible to return to the fundamentals of one's faith without becoming a political activist or "Islamist".)

Secondly, the increased tunnel vision of Islamic movements is connected with the strange phenomenon, pointed out by Gilles Kepel, that while virtually all leaders of Islamic movements are academicians

– educators, medical doctors, engineers – very few of them have a degree in theology or philosophy.

Closely related to this phenomenon is the disconcerting fascination, particularly of young Muslims, with marginal aspects of their religion. It is hard to believe, but young minds are truly preoccupied by the following kinds of questions: is ritual ablution valid if one has painted fingernails? Are golden teeth compatible with Islam? Can cosmetics containing alcohol be used? Is it permissible to eat with knife and fork instead of using the fingers of the right hand? May wigs be used to cover a woman's hair? Is gelatin made from pork (gummibears!) forbidden? Is being left-handed acceptable in Islam? Can one give copies of the Qur'an to non Muslims? Are men and women permitted to shake hands?

All of these are real, burning questions posed by real readers of Arab-Islamic journals, conscientiously answered by religious scholars.[39] The scrupulous honesty of these young Muslims is certainly commendable. But their approach threatens to put Islam on a slippery slope towards talmudization, i.e., a legalization of Islam in the tradition of orthodox Judaism. The point is that Islam is about simplifying life, not making it harder and more complicated.[40]

This is why the Qur'an (5:101) and Prophet Muhammad advised against asking unnecessary questions, because the answers might cause distress and unnecessarily restrict the given freedom of action.[41] Indeed, the questions mentioned above betray insecurity to such a degree that a moral corset is more than welcome.

That suffices for the second Western Muslim's deposition.

AFTER listening to our Western Muslims and their observations about the Muslim world, we are left bemused as we have been after listening to our oriental Muslims and their observations about the Western world. Also this time, neither can be accused of distorting reality. Both of them observed objective but ambivalent facts, and evaluated them from different points of view. There are, after all, two sides to the Muslim world as well.

This anonymous exchange of opinions suggests that neither idealizing nor dismissing the Muslim world out of hand is the way to go. We have certainly isolated enough factors demonstrating the age-old truism that "the light shines from the Orient" (*ex oriente lux*). We get the same result when we identify the Orient with the world in terms of quality and the Occident with the world in terms of quantity. Things may not be cut and dry like that. But generalizations do contain a seed of truth.

In the West, interpersonal relations are determined (or at least codetermined) by economic laws that affect even love relationships. As Westerners we live, as Michael Houellebecq put it, not only in a market economy, but also in a market society. Whether civic society, industry, culture, sports, family or sexuality – everything is governed by the principle of maximizing profit by optimizing production through increased productivity. That which cannot be quantified or digitized (reduced to 0 and 1) has no market value in the West and hence, is classified as obscure, sentimental, irrational or merely mystical. Frills for the soul.

In that sense, the Orient in general, and Islam in particular, has truly remained a sanctuary of spirituality, living mysticism, experiencing the numinous and the holy: God. This is reflected in the appreciation of commodities without market value: Time. Silence. Peace and Serene. Contemplation. Resting in the shade. The cup of tea or coffee at the right hour. Poetry. Conversations about God. Conversation with God.

If this is so, and I am firmly convinced that it is, then the West has as much to gain from the East as the East from the West. But as the next chapter will demonstrate, both helping themselves to what the other one has to offer is a proposition fraught with obstacles.

Notes

1.   *Sunnah*, the historical record of what Prophet Muhammad said, did or tolerated, is the second most important source of Islam after the Qur'an. For Muslims, it represents the binding code of conduct in the areas of theology, morality, and jurisprudence.

2.   *Hijra* refers to the forced migration from Makkah, in the year 622, of Prophet Muhammad, followed by about 200 of his followers. After 250 miles they reached al Madinah, where they were able to live their faith for the first time without fear in a state of their own.

3.   *Umma* describes the comprehensive unity of all believers as a community of siblings.

4.   Verse 49:10 simply says: "The Believers are but a single Brotherhood."

5.   Organizations like *Discover Islam* and *At-Tabligh al-Islami* in Qatar, Bahrain and Sharjah work closely together for that purpose.

6. Since many human rights organizations do not pay enough attention,
    I would like to draw attention to the ever more precarious situation of
    the 150 million Muslims living in India. C.f. Omar Khalidi, *Indian
    Muslims since Independence*, Vikas Publishing, New Delhi,1996. I
    have seen their plight myself in 2000.
7. The five pillars of Islam are: bearing witness that there is only One God
    and Muhammad is His prophet, prayer, fasting, the pilgrimage, and
    charity in the form of *sadaqa* and *zakah*; for more on the latter, see
    Verses 2:177, 215, 219, 272.
8. The particular benefit derived from the establishment of a mosque is
    based on the following authentic records: According to a hadith
    transmitted by 'A'isha (Abu Dawud, Sunan, Nr. 455), the Prophet
    decreed that mosques be constructed wherever Muslims lived. Her
    father, Abu Bakr, the First Caliph, erected the first private mosques in
    Makkah, even before the *Hijra*. Uthman ibn Affan, the Third Caliph,
    related the popular statement by the Prophet: "Whosoever builds a
    mosque, Allah will build for him a similar place in Paradise"
    (Al-Bukhari, Nr. 1.441; Muslim Nr. 7109-7111).
9. See Barboza and Gardell. Following the death of his father and
    pilgrimage to Makkah, W. D. Mohammed, son of the founder of the
    "Nation of Islam", Elija Mohammed, became a *Sunni* Muslim
    and called upon his followers to unite with white Muslims. Jamil
    Abdullah al-Amin (Rap Brown) is the *Imam* of al-Amin Mosque, in
    Atlanta, Georgia.
10 Verse 49:13 proclaims: "The most honored of you in the sight of Allah
    is (he who is) the most righteous of you."
11. Fatima Mernissi with delicious nostalgia has described life in a house in
    Fez, as a self-contained universe. See Mernissi, *Dreams of Trespass,
    Tales of a Harem Girlhood*, Addison-Wesley: Reading, MA, 1994.
12. On a recent visit to Wad Madani, a Qur'anic school famous in all of sub-
    saharan Africa (125 miles south of Khartoum, on the Blue Nile), I was
    able to witness how today's classes are being taught exactly as they
    must have been about 400 years ago. If, on the other hand, a Christian
    learns the New Testament by heart, as the Englishman David Bathurst
    did in the Summer of 1998, it seems to make headlines (cf. Frankfurter
    Allgemeine Zeitung, June 30, 1998).

13. Hans Küng, "Islam teaches us the end of the separation of religion and politics", Die Welt, no. 55, Berlin, March 6, 1989, p. 13, bottom of 2nd column.

14. For the most authoritative collections, cf. al Bukhari, Muslim and Malik.

15. At-Tabari and Ibn Kathir are particularly famous for their Qur'an commentaries (*tafsir*) and copious Islamic historiographies (1996 and 1998). At-Tabari's multi-volume history was published in French (by Sindbad in Paris) and in English (by State University of NY, Albany); his Qur'an commentary has been in print since 1989 from Oxford University Press. Mahmoud Ayoub presents an overview of 13 Qur'an commentators throughout all periods and from all philosophical camps: *The Qur'an and Its Interpreters*, two volumes to-date, State University of New York Press: Albany, 1984 and 1992.

16. A work of monumental importance was Imam al-Shafi'i's *Risala*, a work justly considered the foundation of Islamic jurisprudence; cf. Khadduri. Another book which (not surprisingly) remains seminal today is the comparative legal textbook *al-Bidayat al-Mujtahid* by the physician, philosopher, and legendary attorney Ibn Rushd - known Averroes in Latin.

17. Cf. Badri (1979).

18. Meat (except pork) for the Muslim is halal, i.e., permitted, provided it is kosher - to use a Jewish term. This means that the animal is slaughtered after a prayer, hence in God's name, and then exsanguinated.

19. The Egyptian *galabiyya*, or the Arab *thaub*, are ankle-long, long sleeved gowns that are neck- high and primarily worn by men. Lighter colors are chosen in summertime, in Arabia only in shades of white, off-white, light green or light purple. In winter, tighter weaves with darker colors are prefered, mostly grey, blue-grey, brown, or fabrics sporting broad vertical stripes.

20. Verse 24:31; 33:53,59.

21. As a rule, a lecture is introduced with the following words: "In the name of Allah, the Compassionate, the Merciful, praise be to Allah, Lord of the Universe, and peace and prayers be upon our master Muhammad, his family and his followers. Peace be upon you, and Allah's mercy and His blessings!"

22. The four existing *sunni* schools of jurisprudence, the *Malaki*tes, *Shafi'i*tes, *Hanefi*tes and the *Hanbali*tes, have narrowed

their differences to the point that a dose of good will would be enough
to unite them. Closest to them among the Shi'ite schools is the
remarkable Zayidite Madhhab in the Yemen, founded by Zayd ibn 'Ali.

23. Among Islamic sects there are the so-called *Sevener Shia*
    (*Ismailies*), the *Twelver Shia* (Iran's state religion), the *'Ibadiyyah*
    (predominantly in Oman and the southern Algerian M'Zab region),
    and the *Zayidites* in the Yemen. The Pakistani sects *Ahmadiyya*
    and *Qadianiyya* are outside Islam, just like the *Baha'i* brotherhood.

24. Annemarie Schimmel provides a good overview of the confusing
    multitude of Islamic mystical orders, their differences in
    contemplation and gnosis. See also Parrinder.

25. This is a reference to the so-called *Shura*-principle (3:159; 42:38),
    the basis of an Islamic parliamentarism called "Shuracracy" by
    Sheik Nahnah (Algiers)

26. That is what Asad told me in 1985 in Lisbon. Asad (1988) goes even
    further when he insists that he would have never become a Muslim
    if an education in European schools had not equipped him with the
    necessary awareness.

27. A reward for building a mosque of course presupposes honest
    intentions and proper funding, but it does not imply that other
    charitable activities would not be rewarded in the same manner.

28. Verse 2: 275ff., 3: 130; 30: 39.

29. Cf. Khurshid Ahmad (1994), who discusses the problem of interest
    in exhaustive detail.

30. The Khawarij, responsible for the demise of the 4th Caliph 'Ali,
    drove the principle of allowing only the most pious to assume
    leadership to its radical conclusion. For them, a grievous sinner was
    no Muslim, and hence could not remain Caliph. The (Ismaili)
    Qarmatians rebelled against any priviledged class. They acquired
    notoriety. Cf. Hodgson, vol.1, p.215f. and 490-492.

31. Asad (1988) makes a point of this.

32. Even the fact that Monica Lewinsky is Jewish was made out to be a
    Zionist plot.

33. I call this unscientific approach the "*Qala-qala-qala* syndrome"
    ("He says-he says").

34. According to several authentic *hadiths*, the Prophet Muhammad
    admonished the faithful not to waver in their adherence to his
    sunnah. Introducing new elements into Islam would

be the worst malpractice. Any such innovation would be an error. Cf.
Al-Nawawi, Vol.1, *Hadith* 170. About the possibility of "good"
innovations, cf. Muslim, No. 6466.

35. For Hallaj, see Hallaj, *Poèmes Mystiques,* Sindbad: Paris 1985;
about Suhrawardis light mysticism, see Mehdi Amin Razavi,
Suhrawardi and the School of Illuminations, Curzon: Richmond,
Surrey (U.K.) 1997.

36. Cf. Imam, p. 73. He maintains the possibility that the Qur'an was
first printed in Venice as early as 1530, but that the Curia had it
destroyed. Since there is no extant copy, there is no evidence of that. On
the other hand, I was able to see a well preserved copy of the Hamburg
edition at the Bait al-Qur'an (Collection Dr. Kanoo) in Manama
(Bahrain).

37. Verse 2:153; 3:146, 186, 200; 8:66; 11:115.

38. In terms of the intellectual history of Islam, Abu Hamid al-Ghazali's
Tahafut al-Falasifa. (The Incoherence of the Philosophers) was a
high point in the dispute among Muslim philosophers from the 12th
century. It is a fundamental epistemological treatise, to which Ibn
Rushd replied with his *Tahafut al-Tahafut* (The Incoherence of the
Incoherence).

39. These questions are quotes from a German Muslim newsletter,
Rundbrief der Deutschen Muslim Liga (edited by Abdullah Borek
from Manama). The *sunnah* warns explicitly against this kind of
narrow-minded sophistry.

40. God does not place an undue burden on people (7:42).

41. The Qur'an says in 5:101: "Ask not questions about things which, if
made plain to you, may cause you trouble." About the *sunnah*, see
Rassoul, *Hadith* no. 5975 and 7288; also al-Bukhari, vol. 9, *Hadith*
no. 392; al-Nawawi, *Hadith* no. 9 and no. 30. According to this,
provoking a prohibition by asking is downright sinful.

CHAPTER THREE

Many long and wretched Years

*Imperialism is the necessary, logical
consequence of universalism.*
(Samuel Huntington, *The West: Unique, not Universal*)

*There are signs that over the coming century,
Islamism could grow into a major threat.*
(Peter Frisch, President of the German Federal Office
for the Protection of the Constitution, in *Der Spiegel* 36, 1997, p. 58)

We have taken stock, in a dialectical fashion, drawing a picture of both the Orient and the Occident, detailed enough to be confusing. One should think, therefore, that we are now ready to cope with the future to decide the way in which either side need to change and what can both sides learn from each other.

Alas, the road ahead is mired in an historical past that impedes any positive step either side might take. The collective memory, on both sides, is filled mostly with bitter memories that go back a thousand years. The future will be clouded by this burden of the past until the emotional rubble piled up over many centuries has been cleared by a frank dialogue, free of any taboos, conducted on their common history between Islam and the West. Only when both sides are able to see through their own campaigns that are rife with misinformation, historical spin, and psychological defense mechanisms, will they be able to engage in a beneficial partnership of give and take.

To this end, and to that end alone, let me now digress into a painful, if not disastrous history, during which, thank God, confrontations invariably also provided fruitful points of contact.

IT may well be, that polytheism in the long run, would protect and preserve world peace and stability better than monotheism. Under polytheism, every tribe and nation can keep on worshiping its own gods, while monotheism by definition is universalist and therefore expansionist – if not aggressive (at least ideologically).

Since Christianity and Islam, surrounding the same Mediterranean basin, are both global religions, i.e., "world religions", they could not but threaten to oust each other in direct competition. Speaking for the similarly universalist communist ideology, Ché Guevara succinctly made that point: "We cannot promise not to export our model, because it is a moral one, and moral examples know of no borders."[1] Hassan al-Turabi seconded this observation for Islam: "We constitute a threat in that our model is spreading as if by radiation." [2]

Within Christianity, the same idea goes back to the Greek Father Saint Cyprian (d.258) who formulated the fateful dictum that there was "no salvation outside of the church": *extra ecclesiam nulla salus.* While countless slaves, Latin American Indians, and even entire Germanic tribes had to pay their lives for this doctrine, it served as a convenient cover of conscience for those involved in Catholic inquisition. For members of the White Fathers and White Sisters, bent on Christianizing the north African Muslims, missionary work among such "heathens" was considered not only as a good deed but also an act of duty. The "good offices" of these self-appointed "shepherds" of Muslim populations came across, however, as arrogant and aggressive to those on the receiving end. (Saint Francis had been much wiser and gentler when traveling in the Muslim world during the 13th century.)

Islam, too, has organizations for *da'wa*, the invitation to become acquainted with the Islamic faith, and it, too, considers its message to be a timeless and universal one. After all, Islam is the "peace-bringing submission" (to God), and as such reflects the proper ontological attitude for mankind. A Muslim, in the original meaning of the word, is someone who submits to the One and Only God, regardless of whether he calls himself a Jew, a Christian, or a Muslim. This is why the Qur'an regards Abraham as a Muslim in the broadest sense of the word, and why it considers Islam as the historically youngest, but in terms of its theological concept as the oldest, world religion: "Abraham was neither a Jew nor a Christian; but he was true in faith and submitting to Allah [a Muslim], and he joined none in worship [with Allah]." (3:67; see also 2:140).

The first Muslims quite naturally understood early Qur'anic references to "Islam" as "submission to Allah" and not yet as the historical manifestation of the religion presently called "Islam". Whenever "Islam" remains untranslated, a concept reminiscent of *extra ecclesiam nulla salus* (no salvation outside the church), inevitably becomes associated with the religion of Islam and that immediately sets the stage for theological and military confrontations.

From the very start, however, Muslims did believe they had been charged with a global mission. This became manifest as early as 628 – even before the conquest of Makkah – when Muhammad started his famous letter writing campaign. His quick initiative was nothing less than an urgent invitation to embrace Islam that was transmitted to all the potentates of the Near and Middle East, including Heraclius I, ruler of the Byzantine empire in Constantinople; Chosroes II, Sassanid Shah of Persia in Ctesiphon; and Muqawqis, Coptic archbishop of Alexandria. (The letter received by him, written on leather, is on exhibit at the Topkapı Museum in Istanbul.)

Back then, Muhammad's challenge to present Islam as guidance came across as an outrageous provocation. (Little has changed since, as evidenced by the mostly fierce reactions in the West whenever Muslims attempt to call for prayer from a minaret.)[3] With this writing campaign began the internationalization of Islam. The earliest Muslims did not see the world divided into political or geographical regions, such as eastern or western hemispheres, but only as two domains: the "House of Islam" (*dar al-Islam*) and the unbelieving, inimical rest of the world (*dar al-harb*), where Islam has not yet been established, for the time being.

When it expanded into other lands – in North Africa, Spain, Persia, Anatolia and India – Islam ran into the very challenges to its universality that Christianity had to cope with earlier. Islam was running the risk of Arabs wishing to vest the khilafat in themselves even though the last Arab caliph, al Mu'tasim, and with him Abbasid dynasty died at the hands of Mongols in 1238. That wish became unrealistic when Sultan Selim I, after conquring Cairo wrested the office of Caliph from the Mameluks and united it, for five centuries to come. Worse, some of the non-Arab converts in the Middle East soon felt that they were not treated as full partners, in particular as far the distribution of booty and the amount of war pensions were concerned. These *mawali* (affiliates) could easily give in to neo-tribal anti-Arab feelings. This disturbing phenomenon became known as *Shu'ubiyyah*, originally a literary movement questioning the cultural superiority of Arabic."

On the other hand, there was the danger that Islam in the course of its world wide expansion would suffer the Christian fate and pick up foreign influences from Stoicism, neo-Platonism, Manichaeism, Zoroastrianism, Gnosticism, and Mazdaism. In this event, Islam would have had to pay with eclecticism for its *de facto* universalism, and that would have turned it, too, into an Oriental patchwork-religion.

Despite al-Farabi (870-950), victim of Hellenism, and Ibn 'Arabi (1165-1240), victim of spiritualistic Monism, Islam never suffered from Muslim equivalents to Saint Paul, John the Evangelist, Marcion, Saint Augustine, or the fake Dionysios Areopagita, i.e., people who drastically changed the teachings of Prophet Jesus. The credit for this relative immunity against deviations goes to a famous dispute among Islamic philosophers in 9th-10th century Baghdad. At that time, the speculative metaphysicians of the so-called *Mu'tazila* school of thought, strongly under Greek influence, were decisively defeated by the uncompromising critique of all metaphysics typical of the so-called *Ash'ariyyah* school. Flanked by popular scriptural literalism, traditionalism (*muhadithun*), and populist Islam (*ahl al-sunna*), a trend became victorious that is identical with today's orthodox Islam: intellectually fairly rigid and hostile to both philosophy and mysticism. This rejection of Hellenism – both in its extreme rationalism and intuitive gnosis – in the early Middle Ages has left its mark to this very day, for instance in the fundamentalism of the Hanabalite school, represented today by the *Wahhabi* reform movement in Saudi-Arabia.

Equally important for the defense of Islamic universality was the Qur'an's normative insistence on tolerance – *la ikraha fi-d-din* (2:256) - forbidding any compulsion whatsoever in religious matters. Important, too, was the structural religious pluralism in Islam, most impressively enshrined in *Surah al-Ma'ida (5:48)*: "*To each among you have We prescribed a law and a clear way. If Allah had so willed, He would have made of you one single community, but (His plan is) to test you in what He has given you; so compete with each other in good deeds. The return of you all is to Allah; then He will inform you about the matters in which you used to differ.*"

Thanks to this manifesto of religious pluralism, Muslims then and now tolerate other religious communities in their midst, instead of following the Christian "model", like the massacres committed by Saint Boniface in Germany and by the Catholic Reconquista in Andalusia. Indeed, missionary coercion of that kind did not convince people but forced them underground, from where their lasting convictions gradually infiltrated and corrupted the very Christian faith that had been forced down their throats.

The Qur'anic command of tolerance explains why Greece, in spite of 500 years of Ottoman rule, emerged as a Greek Orthodox nation; why *en route* to Cairo airport, one sees more Coptic churches than mosques; why the Bible is available in Moroccan bookshops and why church steeples in Damascus bear neon-lit crosses at night. It can hardly be doubted that due to this structural Muslim tolerance, Islam has been able to keep its faith pure and pristine even while penetrating for ign cultures and becoming universal. This characteristic is so remarkable that Western people, ever since the late Classical age, tend to perceive Islam as a monolithic system and to overlook its diversity and spirituality. No wonder then that Islam not only instills fear but is also viewed as a "Christian heresy".

Fear is also the fitting word for characterizing the historic relationship between the Orient and the Occident, including today's sensibilities. It all began with the breathtaking fast expansion of Islam in the 7th-8th centuries. The few available Arab warriors, rarely more than 20,000 or 30,000, with all their religious fervor and death-defying courage, would not have been able to pull off this amazing expansion had not the population on the other side – in Byzantium and Persia – surrendered in droves. Three reasons account for that: the Muslims' religious tolerance; their unheard of justice and predictable (and far less exploitative) taxation and administrative practices; and finally, the Islamic conception of God. To many heterodox Christians (chiefly Aryans and Nestorians), Islamic Christology, in particular, was by far more acceptable than the equating of Jesus and God, a dogma which had remained controversial ever since it had been pronounced by the fateful Council of Nicaea in 325.

The Christian world in Rome and Constantinople would not, and could not, face these facts. They were unable to comprehend the significance of Islam in the context of the history of religions; Islam being the first attempt at restoring Christianity, the first effort to return it to its Judeo-Christian roots. Instead, the Occident defended its claim to superiority by constructing the legend that Islam had been spread by "fire and the sword." Hadn't these barbarians even burnt down the famous library of Alexandria? [4]

Both of these accusations falsified history, but succeeded in planting an enduring fear of Islam and an enduring association of this religion with violence. These prejudices still play a major role whenever the media report on events in the Muslim world, be it in Algeria, Egypt, Palestine or Kashmir.

Thanks to Muslim Andalusians like Ibn Rushd (alias Averroës), Ibn Hazm and Ibn 'Arabi, the cultural and scientific "golden age" of the Islamic civilization blossomed, above all in Abbasid Baghdad and Umayyad Cordoba. They among others, may well have inspired and even influenced scholasticism, the troubadour singers, Gothic architecture, Western medicine, mathematics and Christian mysticism. Yet this one-way cultural globalization was unable to stave off the crusades. To be ignorant of the unique cultural achievements of Muslim civilization to this day is not yet considered in the Occident, to be a gap in basic education. However, the collective memory on both sides has been scored by violent encounters such as the periodic Turkish campaign towards Vienna which lacked cultural impact save for introducing the Viennese to coffeee. What else would have moved Max Weber to describe Islam as a "religion of war"? [5]

The Turks got beyond Vienna. Their light cavalry even scared the lower Bavarian region in Southern Germany. At that time, the Turks threatened all of Europe, and Islam was their religion. It is, therefore, both understandable as well as significant that the oldest translation of the Qur'an, into Latin, was finally printed 400 years later, thanks to the insistence of a German personality, Martin Luther.[6] Since then, Europeans quite naturally mixed Islam, the religion, with the Ottoman menace. Salomon Schweiger called his first translation of the Qur'an into German, *The Turks' Alcoran, Religion and Superstition* (1616). Johann Lange, in turn, entitled his German translation of 1688 *The Complete Turkish Book of Laws or Mahomet's Alkoran*. Even the translation which the German poet Goethe used, the one by David Friedrich Megerlin, was still called *The Turkish Bible*, as late as 1772.

These days, Turks have made it all the way to Berlin's district of Kreuzberg, now the fourth biggest Turkish city. They did not arrive there by wielding scimitars but rather by flashing work permits obtained from German Consulates. And yet, the fear of Turks persists, causing them to isolate themselves, if for no other reason, from their fellow German citizens. Reading in newspapers that the integration of Turks in Germany has failed, or that the European Council is likely to shut Turkey out from membership in the European Union, shows collective memory at work: they are dangerous (history tells us) – and Muslims to boot.

Attitudes formed during the Crusades still frame the mutual relationship. Both Claude Cahen, with his history of the Crusades, and Norman Daniel with his depressing analysis — *Islam and the West - The Making of an Image* — prove that the inventors of the Crusades had stoked hatred of Muhammad and everything Muslim with a truly professional misinformation campaign of modern sophistication. In 1143, Robertus Kettenensis and Hermanus Dalmata achieved the very first translation ever of the Qur'an, into Latin, for the abbot of Cluny, Petrus Venerabilis (d.1156). On the whole it was quite accurate. However, the translation was consciously abused to make Crusaders believe that Muslims proclaimed "there is no God besides Muhammad (literally: *non est Deus nisi Machometus*). To the Crusaders Muhammad was presented as a magician, an "idol" (person of a pagan trinity), even as a disgruntled Catholic Cardinal who had been passed over for the Papacy. To the Crusaders, Islam was not a different religion but a perversion of Christianity, whose destruction justified the worst kinds of atrocities – to wit the massacres in Jerusalem (1099) and Damiette (1219) – down to eating human flesh. The Holocaust has seared itself into the Jewish memory for centuries to come; the cruelties of the Crusades affected Muslims in much the same way.

Two hundred years of crusading failed utterly in defeating the Muslim world. The Christian invaders did not understand what they were up against, i.e., core of Islam and Muslim culture. Yes, there were exceptions such as the Italian mystic preacher, Saint Francis (founder of Franciscans) and the German Emperor, Frederick II, both were equally impressed by the erudition, piety and tolerance of Sultan al-Malik al-Kamil of Egypt when they visited him – Saint Francis while accompanying the Fifth Crusade to Damiette (1219) and Frederick II when he led the Sixth Crusade to Jerusalem (1229). They could not change the overall picture, however. Nor could Leo Africanus alias al-Hassan ibn Muhammad al-Wassan (1490-1550), another famous wanderer between two worlds and two religions.

Already, eight hundred years ealier, the Prophet of Islam was disparaged with the invectives later reemployed in Salman Rushdie's *Satanic Verses*. Already 800 years ago, Muhammad within Western jurisdictions was treated like an outlaw. And to this very day, everybody in the West is free to blaspheme and pillory him with impunity. Even for

Martin Luther, to whom we owe that first printing of a translation of the Qur'an, Islam was nothing more than God's punishment for the Papist "corruption" of the Catholic Church. Offending the feelings of 1.3 billion Muslims by degrading their Prophet has yet to be recognized as politically incorrect.

Annemarie Schimmel correctly stated: "Muhammad has generated more fear, hate, and sheer contempt in the Christian world than any other person in history. And when Dante condemns him into the deepest pits of hell, he only gives word to the feelings of countless medieval Christians..."[7] Even today, more than a generation after the Second Vatican Council, the Roman Catholic Church still refuses to recognize Muhammad as a guide to salvation, even though the Council had already recognized Islam as a particular path to salvation. This is even harder to understand if one takes into account that Michael Hart has Muhammad consistently leading his famous list of the 100 most influential people in world history.

In the "Holy Land", when exposed to Muslim faith and civilization, the Crusaders suffered a lasting cultural shock. They had begun their very dangerous and arduous journey from the Rhenish provinces with a pogrom against the Jewish population, among others, in Mayence, Speyer and Worms. That of course did not require any courage. Arriving in Palestine, they perpetrated a bloodbath of unimaginable proportions while sacking al-Quds. In 1203/4, supposedly on their way to the Holy Land, they thoroughly plundered the Christian-Orthodox capital of Constantinople, considering it a "heretical" city. (Never before or since has Istanbul suffered greater destruction than at the hands of those fellow-Christian Franconian knights!) In spite of all these "successes", the Crusaders could not help noticing the disturbing fact that the "barbarians" whom they had come to destroy enjoyed in many respects a civilization and morals far superior to theirs. This may explain the survival of the memory of "Saladin", the Kurdish hero Salah ad-Din, as folkloristic hero and legend in the West.

All in all, the Crusades do not seem to have left many deep scars in the West, although some perverted memories about fighting the "Saracens" are lingering on. For my part, I see a definite connection between such fabled memories and the strangely lurid current Western images of the Orient as reflected in Hollywood movies with an Oriental setting. In any case, no one can deny the validity of Edward Said's conclusion that the Western images of the Orient are in part a projection of hidden Western desires and sexual envy.

Initially, the lasting impact of the Crusades on the memory of the Muslim side was less obvious than in the West. The final victory had been theirs, after all. In the wake of their colonial trauma, however, it began to dawn upon the Muslim world that the Crusades, now in a secular garb, are still going on. The original Crusades had hardly ended when Ferdinand and Isabella, known as the "Most Catholic" King and Queen of Spain, innovatively embarked on a policy of ethnic cleansing in order to drive Jews and Muslims out of Andalusia, a country that had been Muslim for all of 800 years. Shortly after that the young Portuguese king Sebastião attempted to re-Christianize Morocco, eventually losing his life and his land (to Spain!) in the battle of Ksar el-Kebir near Larache, in 1578.

A couple of centuries later, the *idée fixe* (obsession) of a French *mission civilisatrice* drove Napoleon to Egypt in 1798, where he cynically cast himself as protector of Islam. Soon afterwards, in 1830, the French crossed over into Algeria, ultimately leaving behind bombastic cathedrals, consecrated as *Nôtre Dame d'Afrique*, which are still towering in and over every major port city: Tunis, 'Annaba, Algiers, Oran, Rabat, Casablanca ...

With all this in mind, it is still stunning to learn how the King of Greece commenced his efforts to re-Christianize the Aegean region in 1922 by choosing to set foot on land, outside the port of Smyrna/Izmir, at precisely the same spot where the English King Richard I ("The Lionheart") had alighted in 1190 as a knight of the Third Crusade.

The Serbian aggression against Muslim Bosnia during the last decade followed by the most recent Serbian efforts to cleanse the Kosovo province of Muslim Albanians were both religious wars, at least from the Greek and Serbian points of view: the latest in an unending series of Crusades, in this case for the purpose of ridding the Balkans of its last Muslim pockets. (By the way, both countries prohibit the building of mosques).

Indeed, from a Muslim perspective, the Crusades to this very day have never stopped, even though the Western knights have exchanged their armor for business suits. (Nor do they carry rosaries any longer.)

Not much consolation is derived from the fact that the Islamic world is not the only region to suffer the impact of contemporary Western globalization. Thus an American ambassador was recently heard sayimg to his amazed Japanese colleagues that their difficult language constituted a "non-tariff trade barrier", and as such has to be abolished according to the agreed rules of the World Trade Organization (WTO)... [8]

Even when religion is not directly targeted, the old hubris is still the same and comes through in modern efforts either to export Christianity, the *American Way of Life,* or both bundled up in one neat package. A typical proponent of that attitude was the extremely popular German mass author Karl May (1842-1912). His Muslim character "Kara Ben Nemsi" was to shape the German perception of Islam for generations to come. In his dissertation on Karl May's portrayal of Islam, for the University of Bonn, the Egyptian Shaker El-Rifai demonstrated that the author wrote at the behest of the Catholic Church. Although he knew better, he had one of his Muslim figures (in this case "Hadschi Halef Omar") claim that "women have no soul". El-Rifai found that – in contrast to Karl May's books on American Indians – noble characters in his novels played out in the Orient are exclusively Christian. "And the few noble Muslims," writes El-Rifai, "invariably end up as Christian converts." [9]

Readers in need of further proof, should immerse themselves into the most recent naive-triumphalist and determinist thinking of a Francis Fukuyama, or the segregationist strategies of a Samuel Huntington. From a Muslim perspective, either of the two expresses notions typical of cultural imperialism. Indeed, both of them are essentially guided by two major premises of the Crusades: (i) Due to its inherent superiority, the western world has matured into an authoritative model to be emulated by the entire world. (ii) Therefore the Occident has the right – not to mention the duty – to make the entire world share its blessings. A cynic rephrased this polarization as "the West – and the rest." Clearly, this kind of mentality stirs up Muslim fears of becoming marginalized or of being globalized out of existence.

None of all this, is new. It only reflects the attitudes of Orientalism in the worst sense of the word, just as it had been pursued, mostly by the British, the French, and the Dutch orientalists from the 19th and early 20th centuries. As exemplified by the notorious Lawrence "of Arabia"[10], they would serve their respective colonialist masters and treat Islam accordingly. True, even such opportunistic orientalists contributed to the knowledge about Islam, but their ingrained bias ultimately stood in the way of a true understanding of that religion and its civilization. Back then, nobody was any longer convinced of the old wisdom that the light usually comes from the East: ex oriente lux. On the contrary, people then, generally believed that with Islam they were witnessing the terminal phase of a dying religion. In 1901, an orientalist professor, Max Henning, observed in the preface to his German translation of the Qur'an that, "Islam's political role obviously has run its course." At the time, nobody could have reasonably contradicted him.

In those days, orientalists – among them a few "black sheep" from the German speaking world like Carl Becker and Gustave von Grunebaum – defined Islam primarily by how it fell short of European values. In a fashion typical for his field, Grunebaum came to the astonishing conclusion that the Muslim civilization simply did not share the "major visions" of the West, that it was not interested in self-analysis, and even less in studying other cultures.[11]

Such historical misunderstandings are prevalent today to a significant degree. This was proven yet again by a televised statement made in 1996 by Professor Peter Steinacker, president of the Protestant Church in the State of Hesse and Nassau in Germany. Believe it or not, he publicly declared that "the God of the Muslims is not identical with the God of Christianity". Just imagine what this means coming from the mouth of a non-polytheist. If there is but one God, and this God is not the God of the Muslims, then their God is not God at all, but a mere idol! German writers and thinkers like Goethe, Lessing, and the Prussian King Frederick II the Great already knew better over 200 years before.

Is it any surprise then, when a 1998 essay in the German tabloid, *Bunte* asked this rhetorical question: "Is the militancy of so many Islamists perhaps only the continuation of a historical [sic!] hostility which the western world has been drawing on itself [sic!] for some time now? Only that the menace has shifted from Moscow to Makkah?"

At the same time, the history of the relationship between the West and Islam continues to add new chapters. While Islam may have been universalist in outlook from the very start, it has become truly universal only now, thanks to the technological revolution in the areas of transportation and communication. A consequence of this development is globalization which, after all, is not a one-way street. As a result, Islam commands a large presence on the Internet, with the Prophet's *sunnah* now at a click of everybody's fingertips. The entire Qur'an can now be read on-line in every conceivable language.

It is only recently, however, beginning in the early seventies of the past century that Islam seems to have gained a permanent footing in

America and western Europe. This is a qualitative leap forward in their relationship. Even in Germany – immigrant country or not – Islam has become a permanent fixture, with or without official endorsement: The weekly *Der Spiegel* recently counted 2578 mosques and prayer rooms within the Federal Republic of Germany.[12] In both America and Europe, even in Sweden and Finland, Islam is the second largest religion, and the only one growing. On both continents it is primarily women who are converting to Islam. For the time being, it looks as if the newly arrived Muslims have been integrating, while refusing to be assimilated even though integration has been proceeding with more problems than expected. A three-generation pattern has begun to emerge which seems to be valid for England, France and Germany alike:

Upon arriving in the West, the first generation generally starts out with little Islamic conviction. But after a while they would come back to their lost faith, since it helps them feel at home in a foreign country and provides a sense of community. Returning to religion may also be a defensive reaction to discrimination experienced abroad. Another reason could be that living in an environment of civic rights, motivates many Muslims in the West to study and practice their faith without fear of governmental censorship, surveillance and oppression.

The first generation will not return to their homeland, as originally planned, because the second generation does not want to. The second-generation is sitting on the fence and is paying the piper for this experiment of emigration. They find themselves rejected and without opportunities in both their host country and their parents' homeland, especially since they cannot speak either language flawlessly. In religious terms, this is the endangered generation, because Islam seems to keep getting in the way of their struggle for acceptance, particularly in gender relations and sexual mores.

Amazingly, things turn out entirely differently for the third generation, the one significant for Islam. This generation is at home in the West, speaks both languages fluently, and should have all the opportunities in the world for integration. They are finding out, however, that this is not the case, because they are different still: because of the color of their eyes, hair, skin, and because of their names or in short because they are Muslims. The third generation reacts to this situation with defiant pride: "You think we are different? Ok, so be it, we are different!" From that point on they cultivate their otherness, form gangs, and insist on their constitutionally guaranteed rights. This young generation holds more dynamic Muslims willing to sacrifice for their faith, and do missionary work, than the older two generations. They have even begun to take charge at important Islamic centers, like the one in Aachen, Germany.

A remarkable exception to this trend can be found among many Turks. There, even the third generation still remains largely transfixed on Turkey, to a point where they live as it were on small, isolated little islands in Germany, limiting missionary work to Turkish communities only, thus limiting the effect they could have on the German scene. The same cannot be said for the Arab immigrants, especially since a large number of them are academics – as is the case in the United States, Britain, and Germany.

Over the past century, Islam's peaceful expansion through emigration has produced Islamic communities even in Korea and Brazil, Croatia, Italy, Spain, the Ukraine, Finland, Thailand, and Singapore. For a first-hand look at this impressive development I recommend a visit to the annual international conference of Egypt's Supreme Islamic Council in Cairo, where some eighty countries are represented.

THIS is the 1400-year history of Western-Islamic relations, characterized as it was by many long and wretched years of confrontation. From the beginning, the West perceived Islam as a threat. Then, for about 300 years, from the mid-18th to the mid-20th century, Islam was reduced to a mere problem. Ever since, once again, it has become upgraded to a threat. The raw emotions stirred up in the course of this mixed process, the injustices suffered and the misinformation disseminated are still with us, simmering just below the surface. The collective memory, faulty as it may be, is a politically powerful reality. William Cantwell Smith recently described this syndrome as follows: "In the special case of Islam, the West inherited from a thousand years earlier an antagonism of which few recognize the persistence (until today) or depth. Of India and China the West became aware only after it was no longer afraid of anybody; by the Islamic world .... it had at times been cowed, and over several centuries remained threatened .... Recent Western fear and bitterness expressed in anti-Communism were relatively mild, and strikingly short-lived, in comparison with centuries of medieval and anti-Islamic perceptions and emotions."[13]

The collective memory and the syndromes described play their part when Evangelical Christians, as those in Germany organized as

"Christliche Mitte" (Mainstream Christians), hand out fliers warning of a "Islamization of Germany", or when Molotov cocktails fly into Islamic centers, or when activist Muslims receive threatening phone calls.

All of this could be dismissed as short-lived narrow-mindedness if certain media did not continue to rehearse anti-Islamic prejudice, day in and day out. This is the equally sad story of the next chapter.

Notes

1. This quote taken from Richard Barnet, *Intervention & Revolution*, New York, 1972, p. 6.
2. al-Turabi (1992), p. 72.
3. Cf. *Frankfurter Rundschau*, Feb. 24, 1996, reporting on the reaction of the people of Dillenburg, Germany, to the request of the town's 2100 Muslims to be called to prayer with a 60-decibel loudspeaker. Complaints came only from those who had never heard the call.
4. Cf. Hunke (1991), pp. 85, for more on how recent research has long since refuted the persistent accusation that Caliph 'Umar had ordered the famous ancient library in Alexandria burnt down.
5. Quoted in *Salvatore*, p. 102
6. Martin Luther initiated the printing of this translation with annotations and an introduction by Melanchthon in Basle, in 1543. A copy exists at the Bait al-Qur`an in Manama (Bahrain).
7. Annemarie Schimmel, *Und Muhammad ist Sein Prophet* (Munich 1981), p. 7.
8. Cf. "Phantomschmerzen der Kunst - Kulturdialog im Zeitalter der Globalisierung" [Phantom-pain of the Arts - Cultural Dialogue in the Age of Globalization]. *Frankfurter Allgemeine Zeitung*, November 21, 1977.
9. Quoted in *NUR-Das Licht*, Nr. 19-20, Cologne, June 1979, p. 36.
10. In his book, *The Seven Pillars of Wisdom - A Triumph* (Doubleday: Garden City, N.Y., 1935), T. E. Lawrence created a legend unto himself. With all that, he was a far lesser arabist, islamologist, discoverer, and political advisor than Harry St. John Philby (1885-1960) and Leopold Weiss alias Muhammad Asad (1900-1992).
11. Quote taken from *Salvatore*, p. 121.
12. *Der Spiegel* - Special 1/1998, p. 110.
13. Smith, quoted by Parvez Manzoor, *The Muslim World Book Review*, vol. 14, no. 4, 1994, p. 6.

Targeting the Media

*This reminds me of those detractors who first
seek to disfigure the person they want to destroy
in order then to slay the monster.*
(J. W. von Goethe, *Poetry and Truth*, vol. 16, p. 1)

J ust as the collective memory is a fact of human life, so is man's fortunate ability to forget unpleasant memories – or at least to suppress them. It would seem reasonable, therefore, if Muslims relied on that mechanism, hoping that Europeans, one day would view Islam in an unbiased way with clear minds and give it a second chance.

At first glance, it does indeed look that way, thanks to today's pluralistic ethics and postmodern benevolence towards any kind of "otherness", and even the quaintly parochial. There is a religious supermarket out there, apparently with unlimited tolerance: in spite of their belief in reincarnation, anthroposophists are welcome in Christian circles. Ever since Carlos Castaneda, drug using modern shamans, emulating North American Dakotas or Central Asian medicine men, have been "in". Disciples of Hare Krishna and members of the esoteric Baghwan movement no longer provoke public reaction, nor does the conversion to Buddhism of film stars like Richard Gere. Contemporary German druids are regarded with benign indifference as they travel to Catal Höyük in Anatolia in order to revive both matriarchal societies and their goddesses, just as Celtic priestesses are currently trying to do in Wales. Without offending anybody, individuals can "out" themselves as neo-Thomists or neo-Marxists, as mystics without religion or as atheists.

Jewish customs and traditions enjoy a particularly large measure of good will, even where they do not differ one iota from those Muslim practices that are roundly decried as medieval, obscurantist, even unconstitutional. The Jewish-orthodox way of dressing comes to mind, the separation of the sexes, strict dietary rules, ritual slaughter of animals, and the uncompromising observance of detailed divine commandments. Consequently one might think that the maxim of toleration as formulated by the great Prussian King Frederick II, had finally been implemented: "Jeder soll nach seiner Façon selig werden!" (Everyone to find happiness his own way.)

Once Islam enters into view, the picture changes drastically and the threshold of tolerance drops in a heartbeat. A beard, a progressive symbol when grown by Ché Guevara, becomes a clear sign of regression when worn by Muslims. A headscarf is perceived as appropriate in paintings if it adorns an icon like Mary. But the same piece of cloth stirs up negative reactions whenever a Muslima covers her hair that way. If Muslims were to slaughter animals according to their religious obligation, they would be accused of cruelty to animals almost everywhere. When Jews do the same, it is not the same.

In a study published in 1997, the British Runnymede Trust arrived at the following conclusion: "Islamophobia is dread or hatred of Islam and of Muslims. It has existed in western countries and cultures for several centuries but in the last twenty years has become more explicit, more extreme and more dangerous. It is an ingredient of all sections of the media and is prevalent in all sections of society."[1]

Media bear, indeed, a great deal of responsibility for the fact that Islam is the most misunderstood religion, and some make sure it stays that way.

There can be no doubt that the tenacious intolerance against everything Islamic is primarily the work of certain media, who seem to excel in the perpetuation of the pernicious anti-Islamic collective memories already described.[2] Akbar Ahmed does not mince his words: "Nothing in their entire history has threatened Muslims as much as the Western media. In this media game, the Muslims cannot win."[3]

TO be sure, each people has the media it deserves. And bad journalists are to be found everywhere, together with many excellent ones. At the same time, it cannot be denied that most of those who feel a journalistic calling also tend to have a non-religious worldview. Nor can it be denied that all media are political, some more and some less, even when dealing with religion. For the United States, Peter Kreeft in 1996 detected a wide statistical gap between the religious convictions of the population at large and the members of the media – a trend which should be true for Europe as well. According to his study, 90 percent of Americans think that adultery is bad, but only 50 percent of media representatives share that opinion. While 50% of Americans go to church on a regular basis, only 9% of journalists do. And whereas 72 percent of Americans have some reservations about abortion, only 3 percent of media people think likewise.[4] It is a vicious circle: Just like everybody else in the West, journalists, too, are affected by the historically flawed view of Islam. Due to their unique position as purveyors of information, these views get reinforced and perpetuated – not only among the masses, but among media people as well.

On the whole, one gets the impression that the media present Islam more as an ideology than a religion. A typical example for that was a special edition of the German weekly *Der Spiegel (Spiegel special)* in January 1998 entitled "Enigma Islam". Its cover showed a Muslim woman with eyebrows shaped like the swords emblazoned on the Saudi national flag. The *Encyclopedia of Islam* inside neither listed "Allah" under "A", nor Muhammad under "M". Makkah was described by somebody who had never been there. So what? After all, the magazine's goal was not religion as such, but the fear of it.

The second impression of Islam, as routinely painted by the media, is that of an aggressive and expansionist "warlike religion" (Max Weber) with a tendency toward fanaticism, violence, and terrorism. Opposing voices of reason and moderation are rare. In a 1997 Spiegel interview entitled "Justification for Killing", Peter Frisch, then president of the German counter-espionage agency, warned that "Islamism" in the 21st century might grow into a global threat. After all, weren't Islamic volunteers in Afghanistan trained to kill? Frisch even expressed considerable irritation at the demands of German Muslims "to rid schoolbooks of 'anti-Islamic content'." For reasons of tolerance one could after all not accept every demand of a minority.[5]

RTL, a popular private German television channel, followed suit on September 18, 1994, with a program entitled "Terror in the Name of Allah", sounding the alarm about a fundamentalist "Islamic international". This way, the erstwhile justified fear of the now defunct Communist "red international" was adroitly redirected into paranoia of a new "green" counterpart. But even the public television in Germany shows few scruples when dealing with Islam. Take for example ARD, the largest TV network there. They reported on September 15, 1994 that Muslims in the Sudanese southern region were waging a "holy war in the name of Allah". In November 1997, a public radio station in Bavaria shocked its listeners as well with the utterly fabricated statement that carrying weapons was part of Muslim identity...

The media also continuously promote the idea of Islam as a hopelessly outdated religion which, in contrast to Christianity, had somehow missed its own Reformation and Enlightenment and was thus mired in the Middle Ages for good.[6] Characteristic for this assessment is the mental habit of defining Islam not by what it stands for but by what it is lacking in comparison to the standard-setting, supposedly obligatory Western model, especially where individualism is concerned (individual consciousness, civic attitudes, civil society, subjective rationality).[7] This attitude came to the fore in another *Spiegel* interview, in 1979, when Bassam Tibi claimed that Islam and human rights were to each other like "fire and water"; for individual human rights there was no room in Islam. According to him, even freedom of opinion was incompatible with Islam.[8]

Given such an environment, is it surprising that the German weekly *Die Zeit*, on May 26, 1995, went so far as to print an anti-Islamic satire which was not only utterly tasteless, but also downright blasphemous? In that piece by Harry Rowohlt, a buffoon "defines" Islam as follows: "Muhammad didn't have a fridge, panicked in front of women, and was dead drunk after two beers. There is all of Islam for you." Such crap could be dismissed as ludicrous if it were not so infinitely sad.

For many media, all seems to boil down to the old mantra that Islam stands for "oriental despotism", the barbaric chopping off of hands, the mummification of women in violation of their human rights; for old fashioned moralism in matters of premarital sex, marital fidelity, abortion and homosexuality. From this, most media conclude that Islam is essentially foreign, representing a paradigm that is anathema to Western values: a verdict that could not be worse.

These preconceived ideas even influenced a study conducted by the German Orient-Institute on "Islamic Organizations in Germany" which was commissioned by the German Federal Ministry of the Interior in 1997. Analyzing the study, Irmgard Pinn correctly observed that its author, Nils Feindt-Riggers, had approached the Muslims more or less like a 19th century anthropologist when studying strange and somewhat unpredictable native African savages.[9] The fact that this study confused the Saudi Minister of Religious Affairs with the Director of the Saudi Secret Service - both named "al-Turki" – would be merely an amusing anecdote if it did not reflect the negative climate of such "research". The very same attitude came to light in a letter to the editors of *Frankfurter Allgemeine Zeitung*, published on May 28, 1997. A Dr. Paul Esser there chastised the intolerance of Islamists, their primitive attitudes towards art and sciences, and their authoritarian, paternalistic and utterly undemocratic view of history, attributing all of this directly to the Qur'an. He went on to say that the latter is a text from the Stone Age, characteristic of feudalism, entertaining an "archaic-infantile" interpretation of the world. Islam, in short, constituted "a regression into barbarism."

Proofs without end.

BAD enough that these efforts to stir up hatred against Islam – what else to call it? - are torpedoing an otherwise natural regeneration of the relationship between the Occident and the Orient. One should have no illusions: Western media denigrations of Muslims and Islam are widely registered in the Muslim world, with a stifling effect on the necessary process of confidence-building there. Even more detrimental are, however, the consequences of anti-Islamic propaganda for the structural unemployment situation in western Europe. The social restlessness connected with unemployment is prone quickly to turn into open aggression if the guest workers, allegedly stealing jobs, are not just foreigners, but Muslims to boot, like the Turks in the Berlin district of Kreuzberg, the Indo-Pakistanis in Bradford, and the Maghrebians in the suburbs of Paris.

Many Muslims are absolutely convinced that the Bosnian conflict would have taken a different turn if influential Western players had not been under the influence of the abovementioned islamophobia. In an election boycotted by Bosnian Serbs, 99 percent had voted for Bosnian independence from the rest of Yugoslavia. On February 29, 1992, the member states of the European Union recognized Bosnia as independent. And yet, for three years they refused to intervene in the Serbian slaughter, and waited until August 30, 1995 when they finally launched NATO air attacks to put an end to the rape, plundering, and "ethnic cleansing".

In retrospect, the West acknowledged its moral and strategic failure, a failure caused by several quite "ordinary" reasons, among them national self-interest; a general hesitation to risk human lives; the political desire to keep Yugoslavia whole in the interest of regional stability; and fear of getting caught up in the "Balkan mess". Western human rights rhetoric calls for the universal recognition and implementation of the Western model of civilization. But nowadays, in consumer societies, the socially acceptable price for practicing idealism is money, at best. Winston Churchill's oratory of resistance against the Nazi evil in 1940, promising no more than "Blood, Sweat, and Tears", nowadays sounds rather odd.[10]

From a Muslim point of view, the Western failure was largely due to the Bosnians being Muslims. At least subconsciously this fact must have played an important role, although the West was largely in denial about the religious nature of the war. (As the syllogism goes: "It ain't so, 'cause it mustn't be".) Only Greek and Serbian media had openly stylized the massacres in Bosnia into a Crusade against the last Islamic island, the last pocket of "Turks" in Central Europe. One had been closing one's eyes also in another respect: hardly any political operator on either side cared to find out about the real nature of Bosnian Islam. Had they read "Islam between East and West" by Alija Izetbegovich, they would have encountered one of the most tolerant, open- minded, sharp and original thinkers of contemporary Islam.

This is not about ironclad proof, but about an honest response to the following hypothetical questions: is it conceivable that the West would not have taken drastic action in Bosnia as early as 1992, if the Serbs had been Muslims and had perpetrated their self-same atrocities on Catholic Bosnians? Would the massacres in Srebrenica and Zepa have been allowed to happen? Would the world have waited for 200,000 (Catholic) Bosnians to die, for three millions to be expelled, for ten thousands to be raped, for one hundred thousand buildings to be destroyed, including almost the entire architectural heritage of Islam there?[11]

Western behavior towards Bosnia in any case was eerily reminiscent of the fiasco caused by the passivity of Venice, France, and the Pope in 1443 when the Ottoman Sultan Mehmet II "Fatih", laid siege to Constantinople. Back then, too, the Western powers were dragging their feet in response to the Byzantine emperor's desperate pleas for help.

At that time as well, they counseled him to seek a "political solution", all the while consoling each other with wishful thinking – by simply denying the gravity of the situation. Worse yet, before granting any new aid whatsoever they first tried to collect outstanding debts from the sinking Byzantium. Then, all of a sudden, they reversed their earlier assessment, now judging that for military action it was "too late" anyway. (Now doesn't that sound awfully familiar?) In the back of their minds, however, in those days as well, the Western powers felt that the supplicants were damned heretics, and that religious argument turned out to be decisive.[12]

Against that double background Muslims fear that there will be many other "Bosnias", like the current bloody wars in Chechnya[13] and in Kosovo, where Muslims were targeted again. Considering the general anti-Islamic mood generated by all types of media – how could one expect things to be any different?

GIVEN the circumstances outlined above, it is not easy to keep hope alive for a miraculous transformation in the media's treatment of Islam. Fortunately, there is a silver streak on the horizon, brought about by a growing number of Western islamologists, who are exemplary in their unbiased and objective attitude towards Islam and their rich knowledge of this religion. Annemarie Schimmel is of course among them. Fortunately, by now there are a good number of qualified professors following in her footsteps: François Burgat and Bruno Etienne (both Aix-en-Provence), John Esposito (Washington), Daniel Gimaret (Paris), Angelika Hartmann (Gießen), Angelika Neuwirth, Gudrun Krämer and Armando Salvatore (Berlin), Jörgen Nielsen (Birmingham), Neil Robinson (Leeds), Reinhard Schulze (Berne), James Piscatori (Oxford Center for Islamic Studies). None of these modern islamologists would endorse old Gustave von Grunebaum`s dictum that the Muslim civilization did not share the sense of purpose ("aspirations" and "visions") ingrained in Western civilization.

Reinhard Hesse, too, went swimming against the stream with an article in *Die Woche* magazine, dated April 23, 1997, that reads like a summary of this chapter. According to Hesse, the great majority of Muslims are practicing their faith as a religion of peace and tolerance. And yet, since the Crusades, the image of Islam had never been as bad as it is today. In reality, Islam was a culture more beleaguered than belligerent. Islam, too, did not dismiss human rights and allowed not only democracy but also non-clerical governments. Hear! Hear!

Naturally, Muslims can hope for a thorough improvement of the image of their religion only if they are ready to admit without reservation that the sometimes very un-Islamic Muslim world has contributed a lot to the unflattering impression their religion has made. In an overstatement, Muhammad Asad mentioned in his 1988 interview with *Frankfurter Allgemeine Zeitung* that "Khomeini did to Islam what Hitler did to Germany." Apart from the former enigmatic ayatollah from Qum, there are a number of other personalities in the Muslim world who make people in the West regularly shake their heads, and thus have become negative household words.

In this situation, I cannot but agree with Muhammad Aman Hobohm in Bonn (75), doyen of all German-born Muslims, who repeatedly challenged Muslims to stop supporting dubious brothers all over the world unquestioningly, so to speak in the spirit of "right or wrong, my country". Such loyalty can be blind, misguided, and counter-productive. If brother Dr. Mahathir Mohamad in Malaysia unfairly treats brother, Dr. Anwar Ibrahim, there is no need for a brother in Germany or the United States to defend his behavior, gloss it over, or to issue denials.

Furthermore, it is not enough for the Muslims to idly twiddle their thumbs while waiting for a psychological sea change. They have to do their part to bring it about. And they are doing it, for instance, with scholarships for Muslim students of journalism, arranged by organizations like CAIR (Council on American-Islamic Relations) in the U.S. The media follow rules that can be mastered when it comes to writing acceptable letters to newspaper editors, coming up with snappy bumper stickers or video clips, attracting visitors to a website, or producing prepackaged radio- and television programs.[14]

Two of the media laws are, however, that "bad news is good news" and "good news is no news". Islam, too, has media chances only in connection with the public's quest for the sensational, intimate, and unusual. For television this implies that bad programming displaces good programming, much as bad coins replaced good mint in the Middle Ages. Thus, any attempt to establish a Muslim TV channel for a non-Muslim, Western public, would be utterly pointless. One cannot rake in ratings with a lot of prayer, Friday sermons and reports from the pilgrimage, without nudity, violence and sensations.

More promising are coordinated activities like the annual "Day of the

Open Mosque", organized by the Central Council of Muslims in Germany on October 3, a public holiday. This activity is more likely to reduce prejudice and fear, and to educate better, than any Islamic television channel could. The thing to do now is not to be present with television, radio, and newspapers,[15] but to be represented in them. To make this work, more Muslims will have to learn how to get articles published in the mainstream press: articles so concise, objective, well researched and well written as to be virtually ready-to-print. Why not profit from the fact that journalists, like everybody else, would rather work less than more?

Notes

1. Runnymede Trust, p. 2
2. As former director for information of NATO (1983-1987), I believe to have gained some insights as to what the media business is capable of.
3. Akbar Ahmed (1992), p. 223.
4. Kreeft, p. 62, 67.
5. Frisch, *Der Spiegel* no. 36, September 1997, pp. 58-60.
6. Salvatore, p. 73; Woods (with 28 anti-Islamic carricatures from American media).
7. Kreeft, p. 67, Said (1978, 1981, 1993).
8. Tibi, *Der Spiegel,* no. 3, January, 1994, pp. 170-172.
9. Irmgard Pinn, "Islamische Organisationen in Deutschland" (Review). In: *Newsletter,* no. 2, Gesellschaft der Muslimischen Sozial- und Geisteswissenschaftler: Cologne 1997, p. 11.
10 Professor Klaus Hornung called attention to this point in a letter to the editors of *Frankfurter Allgemeine Zeitung,* Nov. 19, 1999. Whether the German airforce could have continued its mission if it had suffered so much as one casualty, remains an open question.
11. In his richly illustrated book *Islamic Architecture in Bosnia and Hercegovina* (IRCICA: Istanbul, 1994), Amir Pasic, winner of the Agha Khan Prize for Architecture and associate at the Istanbul Research Institute for Islamic Culture and History, documented how Serbs and Croats had joined forces during the Bosnian war to destroy or severely damage 349 out of 591 Islamic architectural monuments dating from 1463 to 1878.
12. Cf. Steven Runciman, *Die Eroberung von Konstantinopel* 1453, 4th ed. (C.H. Beck: Munich, 1990).

13. Cf. Muhammad Iqbal Khan, *The Muslims of Chechnya*, (The Islamic Foundation: Markfield, Leicestershire, UK, 1995).

14. For more information on Islam on the Internet, see Blunt, and also Imran Ali Maskatiya, "The Internet", in: IQRA, vol 17, no. 2, San José, March 1997, p. 32.

15. *The Freitagsblatt (Friday Paper)* of the Islamic community in Hesse, Germany (IRH) has, however, been published succesfully in Frankfurt since 1998. It is a monthly but comes close to serving the functions of a regular Islamic newspaper. The same is true of the monthly *Islamische Zeitung* published from Potsdam. Exceptions make the rules.

CHAPTER FIVE

Blond, blue-eyed
and human Rights

*Why should we accept declarations of human rights
drafted by the same powers that colonized and
pillaged our countries?*
(Shirin Sinnar[1])

Where there is smoke, there is fire, the saying goes. This folk wisdom forces Muslims to prove a negative: they have to disprove three major accusations leveled at them by the West, i.e., that (1) Islam has prevented them from respecting human rights, (2) especially the basic rights of women, and that (3) Muslims have yet to show that they are capable of democracy. In essence, these are questions of morality, not theology, but sooner or later they become the focus of every Islamic-Christian dialogue.

This is quite obvious as far as the West is concerned. However, a productive discussion of these three topics is a prerequisite – *conditio sine qua non* – for any normalization of relationship with Islam. What happens in these three fields is of even greater importance for the Muslim side since the global future of Islam itself may hinge on it. On the other hand, as Neil Hicks sees it, it is also quite evident that certain forces in the West have a vested interest in perpetuating the myth of Islam's incompatibility with human rights and democracy.[2] It is never easy to prove a negative; however, this chapter sets out to demonstrate that Muslims are indeed not incapable of protecting human rights, for human rights are distinctively an integral Islamic issue.

WHEN discussing human rights, Muslims often discover to their surprise and dismay that their Western interlocutors believe to have both invented and patented the subject. People in the Occident really expect that human rights are respected only in the West, as a matter of principle, and generally disrespected, again as a matter of principle, all over the Muslim world.

The first conviction is quite understandable, because it was indeed the Occident – notably England – where a specific human rights codex emerged that was designed to protect the individual citizen from state abuse, essentially as defensive freedom *from* something. Back then, in the 17th and 18th centuries, it had not yet occurred to anybody to demand from the monarchs the very civic entitlements which have become so important today, the active freedom *to do* something.

Important landmarks in the Western history of human rights were the British Magna Charta Libertatum (1215), the Act of Habeas Corpus (1679), the Bill of Rights (1689), the American Declaration of Independence of 1776 (making reference to God), and the French Declaration of the Rights of Man and the Citizen of 1789 (less explicit about God). The famous, but not binding, Universal Declaration of Human Rights, adopted by the United Nations in 1948, was exclusively based on these Western precedents. It was not much different with the two (binding) International Pacts on Civic, Political, Social, Economic, and Cultural Rights of December 19, 1966 and also with the human rights instruments of the European Council.

And yet these developments became possible not due to Christianity, but in spite of it. Up until Pope John XXIII in the past century, the concept of human rights was condemned as secularist, laicistic, and naturalist. Only with his Encyclical *Pacem in Terris* of April 11, 1963, were human rights finally admitted into the Vatican.

This history does not imply that Islam did not possess any legal concepts comparable to human rights, notably based on the Qur'an. The Western pride of invention and ownership of human rights, is an assertion which simply ignores the fact that, throughout history, the states have always and everywhere disregarded the rights of ordinary people, also in the Christian Occident. Even today, the state of human rights is deplorable worldwide, also in – but not limited to – Muslim countries; Amnesty International maintains depressing files.

Fairness requires non-Muslims to admit that violations of human rights in nominally Islamic states, such as torture, police brutality, election fraud, censorship, and infringements on religious freedom are neither motivated by Islam nor legitimized by it. The fact that jails in the Muslim world are primarily populated by Muslim activists of strong religious convictions proves the contrary. One should accept once and for all that a country like Turkey, with a Muslim population, is not necessarily an Islamic state, just as a country like Spain, populated by Christians, must not necessarily be called a Christian state.

Western human rights experts cannot be spared answering the following question repeatedly asked in this book: have there ever been worse violations of human rights, in quantity as well as quality, than during the two World Wars, with the use of chemical and nuclear weapons, during the Stalinist terror regime and the Holocaust; under apartheid in South Africa and ethnic cleansing in Bosnia and Kosovo? Muslims committed none of these atrocities. The noted Kenyan social anthropologist, professor Ali Mazrui at Binghamton University in the State of New York says: "If Islam in the twentieth century has not always been the most fertile ground for democracy, it has also been less fertile ground for the greatest evils of this century: Nazism, fascism, communism, and genocide .... Muslims are often criticized for not producing the best, but they are not congratulated for having standards of human behavior that avert the worst. There are no Muslim equivalents of Nazi concentration camps, American racial lynching, apartheid under the Dutch Reformed Church, Japanese racism before the Second World War, or genocide under Stalin and Pol Pot."[3]

Even so, Western interlocutors still claim the moral high ground, demanding the worldwide implementation of a Euro-American value system of individual human rights under penalty of canceling their developmental aid. Given the two widely differing yardsticks with which Western people judge themselves and others, they should not be surprised when young Muslims cynically observe that human rights probably are "blond and blue-eyed."

Human rights, whether blond and blue-eyed or not, can be wielded like a club. Therefore, Parvez Manzoor was correct when stating, in 1994, that "Human Rights talk is power talk."[4] This is the reason why there are still voices heard – although they are fading out – who talk about Islam or human rights, as if they were opposites. They consider human rights a "holy cow of modernity ... which should not be blindly worshipped, but subjected to critical scrutiny ... especially since the *Shari'ah* offers solutions to every issue, independent of time and place."[5]

But no use complaining, Muslims have to take a stand. Most Muslims states belong to the group of Third World countries euphemistically called "developing countries", even those basking in a warm petrodollar rain. These Third World countries, inclusive of Muslim ones, traditionally defended their human rights record by pointing towards the interdependence of civil rights on the one hand, and social, economic and cultural rights on the other hand. They convincingly argued that elections amount to little more than the confirmation of tribal chiefs as long as voters remain illiterate. It may not fit into the political pigeonhole of Third World ideologues but, according to Panajotis Kondylis, it is self-evident that "human rights, which promise each individual autonomy and dignity equally, can only thrive in societies where a highly differentiated division of labor atomizes the collective, and where mass production and consumption are running in high gear."[6] It is equally undeniable that democracy needs a civil society which, in turn, is only possible when structural poverty is overcome.

By using such arguments, Third World countries have managed to slip in a catalog of their own particular human rights, such as the right to education, work and livelihood, into some of the more recent human rights treaties.

The same countries think they can ward off the human rights by questioning their universal validity. (This is their second line of defense.) In effect, they characterized the existing human rights statutes as Euro- and ethnocentric, and therefore as alien to other cultures, such as those of Asia or Sub-Saharan Africa. Behind the theory of universality they even detected Francis Fukuyama's flawed assumption that history had come to an end by endorsing the Western model of civilization, once and for all.[7]

This view of human rights may be correct as far as inflamatory and stylish legal innovations are concerned, such as the "right to be afraid" (of all things nuclear), the "right to intoxication" (by means of legalized drugs), or the "right to homosexual marriage." The assumption of a cultural limitation of human rights is, however, not correct in respect to the classical core rights, such the right to life, and freedom from torture, freedom of opinion, conscience, expression and religion, and the personal liberties (freedom of movement, assembly, association, etc.).

Muslims damage their own cause whenever they get carried away towards questioning any of these core human rights. In particular, they should not exploit for their own purposes Samuel Huntington's pessimistic assessment that worldwide unanimity on human rights exists in but one point: the total reprehensibility of torture.[8]

A far better strategy would be to deal with the human rights phenomenon in the framework of Islamic jurisprudence, i.e., on the basis of the Qur'an and the *sunnah*. Of course, the term "human rights" was not developed by Judaism, Christianity, or Islam. Indeed, if this modern term were found in any holy scripture, it would be a glaring anachronism betraying forgery. The absence of the term "human rights" in religious discourse is due as well to the following. the very idea that a created being could be possessor of rights evidently goes against the grain of people – Jews, Christians, and Muslims alike – for whom God, the Creator, is the sole source of rights. Divine rights for individuals: yes. Rights of the individual: no. It was, after all, only logical that the formulation of the concept of "human rights" had to await a historical period, i.e., the 18th century Enlightenment, during which man was proclaimed to be the autonomous measure of all things. For people with transcendental links this was, and continues to be, a downright blasphemous piece of irreligious fiction.

Muslim jurists have been particularly handicapped: given that the entire *Shari'ah* is divine law, attempts to give particular norms, such as human rights, higher rank or greater importance cannot be justified. Muslim jurisprudence, to this day, has therefore resisted a prioritization of norms. Muslims consistently refuse to establish a normative hierarchy by distinguishing, according to human fancy, between divine rights of a higher and lower order. Non-religious legal systems like Roman Law, Civil and Common Law, French and German law, deal with such a normative hierarchy, starting at the top with (a) international law, and cascading down via (b) constitutional law, (c) statutory law, to (d) decrees (d) government regulations, and (e) administrative directives. Muslim jurists cannot, and do not, follow suit. They continue to accord equal rank to all the norms set by the *Shari'ah*, from the rules for ritual ablution to the prohibition of earning interest. Thus there is no conceptual room for a particular set of superior "human rights".

Although the term "human rights" is thus both absent and

theologically flawed, a positive Islamic approach to the human rights phenomenon would yet have been possible. The fact that this opportunity was missed opened Islam up to the nasty suspicion that it was hostile to human rights and failing to take the protection of individuals from despotism seriously enough. In fact, just a little ingenuity would have gone a long way towards showing that Islam, from the very beginning 1400 years ago, has not only known but substantially protected the core human rights, and that Islam has anchored these rights more solidly in its divine prime sources, the Qur'an and the *sunnah,* than the Occident could with any number of man-made treaties.

The evidence is right there: take the statutory prohibition of murder in *Surah an-Nisa (4: 92)* and Allah's equating the murderer of a single person with someone killing the entire human race in *Surah al-Ma'ida* (5: 32). While not specifically spelling it out, both passages indirectly – as a legal reflex – permit one to discover in the Qur'an a God-given right to life, enjoyed by all human beings. Take *Surah ash-Shura* (42: 38) with Allah's command for Muslims to settle their affairs through mutual consultation. This obligation, phrased as a duty, can be taken indirectly as implying the right to political participation. The fact that the first three caliphs were elected into office without being blood-relatives of Muhammad is sufficient evidence to prove that an Islamic state could be a republic and need not be a monarchy. Along these lines it can be shown that the protection of individuals against abuse is an original Islamic concern. Should it not then, also be possible to reinterpret the offensive terminology of human rights as being consistent with the Qur'anic rights of man?

It should be evident that rights laid down by God are more securely rooted than rights merely granted by treaties and hence subject to negotiations and social change. In the West – whether in the former Soviet Union or in the United States – the beautiful catalogues and bills of human rights oftentimes were hardly worth their paper in actual practice. Do not ask the Klu-Klux-Klan, ask African-Americans and North American Indians.

It cannot be denied that mankind never succeeded in finding a universally acceptable system of "natural rights", either from observing nature or by sheer force of reasoning.[9] This may be one of the reasons why former German chancellor Helmut Schmidt (Hamburg) and former professor of Catholic theology Hans Küng (Tübingen) are working towards a United Nations declaration on human obligations. Obviously, human rights are insufficiently secured without correspondding duties and need further buttressing by more and more paper! When will people realize that human rights cannot stand the test of time unless solidly founded on divine revelation?

In the wake of the above mentioned, somewhat self-righteous Occidental human rights offensive, the Organization of the Islamic Conference (OIC), the most important Muslim intergovernmental organization, finally got its act together. On August 5, 1990, as regional sub-organization of the United Nations, it issued the "Cairo Declaration of Human Rights in Islam", a document not legally binding, but of political significance only.[10] Of even lesser legal weight had been the preceeding "Declaration of Human Rights" issued on September 19, 1981, by an "Islamic Council of Europe", a rather obscure outfit of dubious legitimacy.

Important Islamic personalities and scholars have also entered the human rights debate, among them individuals as influential as Muhammad Hamidullah, Abul 'Ala Mawdudi and Prince Hassan of Jordan. During a round table conference for the purpose of "Promoting the Universality of Human Rights", which he had convened in 'Amman from December 10 - 13, 1994, Prince Hassan said, "Regarding human rights, we absolutely need a global consensus (....). The Universal Declaration on Human Rights circumscribes the minimum standards of human life. I believe that my faith, Islam, pursues the same goal. Each of the 30 articles of the Declaration corresponds to a passage in Qur'an, *Hadith*, and *sunnah* of the Prophet." The first conclusion drawn at the conference was: "Human rights dwell in all human beings."[11]

THE foregoing observations will make it easier to delineate those few differences which appear to distinguish the catalog of Islamic human rights from the Western ones. At issue are (a) apostasy, (b) slavery, (c) law of asylum, (d) the status of women, and (e) corporal punishment. If current efforts (*ijtihad*) towards a better understanding of the relevant Islamic sources, wholeheartedly supported by me, are successful, the positions of both sides will become far closer than they now appear to be. Required was, and is, a contemporary exegesis of Islamic sources by major scholars like Muhammad Asad (1900-1992), Rashid al-Ghannoushi, Hassan and Mather Hathout, Alija Izetbegovich, Jeffrey Lang, Fathi Osman, Yusuf al-Qaradawi, Fazlur Rahman (1919-1988),

Mohamed Talbi and Hassan al-Turabi.

Concerning apostasy, any conflict with international law disappears once the Muslim side recognizes that neither the Qur'an nor the *sunnah* specify any punishment in this world (*fi-d-dunya*) for merely breaking with Islam.[12] The Qur'an describes no less than 13 cases of apostasy; invariably severe consequences are announced, but only for the afterlife. Earlier, the universally valid maxim "no compulsion in matters of religion!" (*la ikraha fi-d-din; 2:256*) had been interpreted as applying only to the relationship between Muslims and non-Muslims. In this day and age, however, all Muslims should admit that this fundamental rule of religious tolerance must form the relationship among Muslims as well. Should they not be at least as tolerant among each other as they are bound to be toward outsiders? Those who deny the universal application of the Qur'an verse 2: 256, among them many an overzealous Muslim, forget that "no compulsion in matters of religion!" also restates that, given the crucial importance of intention (*niya*), coercion in matters of personal conviction means attempting the impossible. Muslim states can enforce proper behavior except when its validity requires personal assent. Pummeling the faithful into praying and fasting should become a thing of the past.

Originally, apostate ex-Muslims were only prosecuted, and rightly so, if in addition they also committed high treason (*ar-ridda*), i.e., if they actively fought against the Muslim community in the sense of *Surah al-Ma'ida (5): 33*. High treason includes hurting the cause of Islam by withholding legitimate taxes, espionage, sabotage, counter-propaganda, and any other way of "causing mischief on earth".

It remains true, however, that apostates under an Islamic community are discriminated against in matters of inheritance, because according to the *sunnah,* Muslims and non-Muslims cannot inherit from each other.[13] Here, being a member of the Islamic community is equated to modern citizenship, and international civil law, as a matter of principle, sees nothing wrong in tying inheritance to citizenship.

The problem of slavery can be defused in similar fashion. The Qur'anic provisions in that regard (which only served to humanize the existing practice of slavery) can, of course, not be deleted. In fact, they still help to protect people who, if not *de jure*, are *de facto* enslaved and disenfranchised. Slavery is, after all, still suspected to be a fact of life in remote areas of Mauritania. On the whole, the Qur'anic provisions for slavery suggest, however, that Allah intended the (gradual) abolition of slavery as a legal institution. Thus slaves had to be given the opportunity to buy their freedom; releasing a slave was declared a good deed, and frequently prescribed as an act of penitence.[14] It follows that a Muslim state without any reservation can endorse international prohibitions of slavery.

Islam's pronounced protection of ethnic groups, religious minorities and the status of women will be discussed in more detail in the chapters "Similar or Identical?", "Colorblind", and "What are they here for?". Relevant for the present discussion is the fact that religious minorities in the Muslim world would feel today like second-class citizens if they did not enjoy full citizenship but simply remained, as in the past, "under protection" (*dhimmi*).

According to Fathi Osman and others, there is no legal obstacle to granting non-Muslims full citizenship, if they so wish, as long as Muslim countries organize themselves as nation-states, and not as religious foundations.[15] One innovation follows from the other. An important aspect of the Shari´ah`s minority statute is that it assures a specific standard of protection without capping allowable rights. The *dhimmi* status is the minimum, not the maximum, to be granted to non-Muslim subjects.

The Muslim Brothers in Egypt, too, no longer dispute full civil rights for the large Coptic minority.[16] As full citizens, as a matter of course, non-Muslims lose their special privileges and are thus subject to both general taxation and the military draft.

The next logical step is to question whether or not it is compatible with international law if a Muslim state excludes a non-Muslim from becoming head of state. Although logically compelling, this question is without practical relevance. It is, after all, unlikely that a non-Muslim could get elected state president in a truly Muslim country. But if this were to happen, the country in question could no longer be considered 'Muslim' anyway, so that the election would have to be honored on that ground.

The corporal punishments foreseen by the *Shari‘ah's* penal provisions (*hudud*) are deemed cruel and demeaning by Western human rights standards, hence a violation of international law. On trial here, in particular, are the stoning or flogging of adulterers[17] and amputations for theft.[18]

Westernized Muslims panic easily apologetically whenever this subject comes up. Rather they should call attention to the fact that even the self-appointed paragon of Western morality, the United States of America, clings to the death penalty, executing hundreds of people (mainly black) year after year, by hanging, lethal injection or the electric chair. Execution is arguably the most gruesome of all corporal punishments – and demeaning to boot. As long as this is so, it appears hypocritical to complain about Islam, especially since the Muslim judicial practice differs widely from what is theoretically permitted under Islamic law. This also pertains to capital punishment, which Qur'anic law permits, but does not necessarily demand, as the most severe punishment for murder, robbery, and high treason.[19]

It should also be pointed out that the deterrent effect of penal law is recognized in the West, as well, even though the prospect of punishment seems not to make an impression on every single type of criminal. Nowadays however, in the West, particularly in Europe, penal codes are no longer implemented in such a way that they would deter. Even convicted murderers are hardly doing more than a handful of years, "languishing" in prisons of bed-and-breakfast quality. Even a major spy can expect weekend passes for good behavior. Early release has gone from being an act of mercy to being an entitlement. "Violence against property", graciously sparing people, is being trivialized.

In contrast to all that, the deterrent effect of the Islamic penal code definitely provides higher public safety, mainly for women, and also reflects a higher regard for personal property. These positive effects endure for a while, even in places where Qur'anic law is no longer applied. Thus in Istanbul, a city of 15 million people, the streets are still largely safe, even at night.

I am not alone in holding that there is no Islamic justification for "stoning" In fact, a provision for stoning married adulterers cannot be found in the Qur'an, but only in the Bible, in the Fifth Book of Moses (*Deuteronomy* 22: 20-22). This Biblical norm is not binding for Muslims any more, since it is superseded by *Surah an-Nur* (24: 2) – a typical *lex posterior generalis*.

It was always questionable in terms of *Hadith* scholarship whether such a far-reaching penalty "stoning" could be admissible in contradiction to *Surah an-Nur* (24: 2), since the *sunnah*, according to Taha Jabir al-'Alwani's convincing arguments, cannot alter the Qur'an. The purpose of the *sunnah* – as legitimized by the Qur'an – is to explain and supplement the teachings of the Qur'an, not to supersede or cancel them. The *sunnah* cannot derogate the Qur'an.[20]

In case of adultery, this conclusion is even more valid, because the stoning of the guilty party had been justified in the past by what amounts to weak traditional records.[21] It is not even clear whether the stoning incident mentioned in *Hadith* literature and the Prophet's reported acquiescence took place before or after the revelation of the Qur'anic verse dealing with adultery.[22] If the incident had taken place before the respective revelation, the *sunnah* in question would have been overruled by the Qur'an as a procedural matter.

In view of the fact that the Qur'an does not prescribe stoning for any crime whatsoever, it is curious but legally irrelevant that the Second Caliph 'Umar spoke of a "verse of stoning". That stoning for adultery is not envisaged by the Qur'an should at least be accepted on the basis of Verse 4: 25. This verse reduces the penalty for adultery by "one half" whenever slaves are the culprits.[23]

At any rate, the standards of evidence in the Islamic law of criminal procedure are so exacting that hardly anybody can be convicted of adultery who is not out to provoke his or her conviction. Normally, except in cases of pregnancy, adultery can only be proven through voluntary confession. (Ex-President Clinton would have fared far better under the Islamic rules of evidence for adultery[24] than under the American system.)

In order to understand the Qur'anic punishment for theft and its deterrent effect in *Surah al-Ma'ida* (5: 38), one first has to grasp its socio-economic function. It is important to know how much the social security of women, especially their old-age insurance, in regions under Islamic law depends on their ability to safeguard their life-time savings of cash and bridal gifts of gold, silver and diamonds, they had received and not having any of that stolen. Except for modern credit card societies functioning with little cash on hand, theft has to be considered as a severe attack against the social foundations of the entire community.

In a humanitarian spirit, Islamic jurisprudence has, nevertheless, bent over backwards in order to limit the prosecution of this criminal offense to exceptional cases. In this endeavor it has succeeded so well that presently one can spend years in the Muslim world without ever encountering someone who has lost a hand for theft. This has less to do with a shortage of thieves than with the liberal legal definition of what constitutes the type of theft mentioned in the Qur'an. Accordingly, theft presupposes the stealing of well-guarded assets of more than petty value that are not public property. In times of economic crisis the prosecution of thieves had already been suspended under the Second Caliph 'Umar. A society cannot punish thieves produced by its own neglect! In addition, the Islamic statute of limitations for theft is extremely short, running out within a few weeks. Consequently, conviction for theft is rare in the Muslim world, and execution of the harsh Qur'anic punishments for theft is even rarer.

Whenever critics of Islam find attractive regulations in the Qur'an – such as the command of tolerance in *Surah al-Baqara (2: 256)* and *Surah al-Ma'ida* (5: 48) - they tend to dismiss these and other impressive norms by arguing that they do not square with Muslim reality. However, wherever they find a Qur'anic provision distasteful to them – like the punishment for theft – they exclusively focus on these norms without regard to everyday practice. Holding the normative treatment of theft against Islam without simultaneously considering its humane implementation in real life is a stark case of double standards.

This overview (and the discussion of the status of women in the subsequent chapter "Similar or Identical?") leads to the conclusion that Islamic law does not fully accord with the 1966 Human Rights Pacts of the United Nations. In view of that, some Muslim countries ratified them with the proviso that the *Shari'ah* remains unaffected. But surely, as we have seen, the areas of conflict are so limited in scope that people of good will can acknowledge Islamic law as a complementary system of human rights.

As far as the areas of conflict are concerned, I have tried to demonstrate that while all differences cannot be resolved, at least they can be narrowed down thanks (i) to a reinterpretation (*ijtihad*) of some source materials, fully in conformity with the principles (*maqasid*) of the Qur'an and the *sunnah*, and thanks (ii) to strict adherence to Islamic criminal procedure. But this approach has its limits because ultimately, as divine law, the *Shari'ah* is not subject to human yardsticks. That is how it is, regardless of whether manipulation of that law would appear to serve public interest (*maslaha*) or improve the image of Islam in the West.

What good would Islam do the West (and Muslims, too) if it were no longer different?

Notes

1. Sinnar, "Reflections on the 50th Anniversary of the Universal Declaration of Human Rights", in: *Commentary*, no. 19, Petaling Jaya, Selangor, Malaysia, December 1998, p. 1-5.
2. Hicks, p. 1
3. Mazrui, "Islam and the End of History", in *The American Journal of Islamic and Social Sciences,* vol. 10, no. 4, Herndon, VA, 1993, p. 534; Mazrui, "Islamic and Western Values", in: *Iqra*, San José, CA, January 1998, p. 13-18.
4. Manzoor, *The Muslim World Book Review*, vol 15, no. 1, Markfield, LE (UK), 1994, p. 9.
5. "Islam oder Menschenrechte", in *Explizit*, Vienna, December 1998, p. 12-15.
6. *Frankfurter Allgemeine Zeitung*, December 28, 1995.
7. Manzoor, p. 8.
8. *Berliner Zeitung,* Magazin, June 28/29, 1997.
9. With the possible exception of the principle that contracts are binding, pacta sunt servanda, cf. Friedrich Berber, *Lehrbuch des Völkerrechts*, vol. 1, (Munich: C.H. Beck, 1960), p. 165.
10. Printed in "Zeitschrift der Weißen Väter" (Gazette of the White Fathers), CIBEDO, Frankfurt 1991, pp. 178.
11. See periodical *Ma'ab*, vol. 6, no. 18, 'Amman 1995, p. 6.
12. Osman (The Children, 1996), p. 30; Lang (1995), pp. 195-199; al-Turabi (1992), p. 41.
13. al-Bukharı, no. 6764.
14. Cf. 2:177; 4: 36; 5: 89; 9: 60; 58: 3.
15. Supported by Osman (The Children, 1996), p. 20, 43; and (Human Rights, 1996), p. 19.
16. Cf. "Bürgerrechte auch für Kopten" (Civil Rights also for Copts), *Frankfurter Allgemeine Zeitung,* April 19, 1997.
17. 24: 2 prescribes 100 lashes.
18. Verse 5: 38.
19. Sahrour, p. 7.
20. al-'Alwani, Preface to Ahmad 'Ali al-Imam, *Variant Readings of the Qur'an,* p. XIV.
21. Abu Dawud, Sunan, *Hadith* No. 4405; al-Bukhari, no. 8805 and 8810; Muslim no. 4191-4225; al-Nawawi, no. 220.

22. *al-Bukhari*, vol. 8, no. 804 and 830, and vol. 9, no. 281.
23. 4:25; Osman (1997), p. 914, rejects the stoning for adultery for this and other reasons.
24. Verse 24:61.

CHAPTER SIX

Democracy or *Shuracracy*

He who says that democracy is disbelief, neither
understands Islam, nor democracy.
(Cheih Yuuuf al Qarndaui in the London newspaper
Ash-Sharq al-Awsat, February 5, 1990)

We do not view democracy as an alternative to
. *Islam, or as better than Islam. We view*
democracy as an Islamic principle that was taught
and practiced by Prophet Muhammad and his companions.
(Radwan Masoudi in the first issue of the Washingtonian
periodical *Muslim Democrat,* May 1999)

What was discussed on human rights, in the previous chapter is equally relevant for debating democracy with the Muslims, within and outside the Muslim world. The outcome of this heated debate will be critically important for the entire future of Islam, and certainly for its chances in the West. Unless the Islamic world rediscovers and whole-heartedly accepts and fulfills its democratic potential, it will also fail to become a model for the Occident in any other field. Nor will it realize its economic possibilities, thereby in turn solidifying its political power deficit. I am saying this without subscribing to Muhammad Said Ashmawi's sardonic statement, "God wanted Islam to become a religion, but people turned it into politics."[1] For Muslims, religion and politics is not a contradiction. They do not want to sacralize politics, but to Islamize it by grounding it on Islamic values.

FOR a discussion of democracy, it is helpful that Islam is not a Manichean or Gnostic religion that preaches otherwordliness, a rejection of this world and flight into the other (*al-akhira*). Except for some mystic schools,[2] Muslims actively participate in public life in a balanced way, equally concerned with both worlds, the present and the future. Islam is, therefore, an eminently political religion. For Muslims, God is both transcendent and immanent. Therefore, after their ritual prayers, they like to recite: "*Our Lord! Give us good in this world and good in the hereafter*" (2: 01). The Qur'an even exhorts them: "*Do not forget your portion in this world*" (28: 77). Consequently, every Muslim is expected to shoulder responsibility for his particular sphere of influence.[3] A popular *hadith* states that whenever a Muslim witnesses evil, he is to remedy it "by his hand" or, if this is not possible, "by his tongue" or, if even this proves impossible, at least "in his heart."[4] Therefore, without any doubt, Muslims must implement Islam by materializing it in their community's polity and economy. No real Muslim can rest by merely professing his faith.[5]

In the past, almost all orientalists believed that this political calling of Islam was in clear contrast to the Occident. Some Muslims and most Occidental people still believe so. True, by integrating religion and politics – considering religion as Faith and State (*din wa daula*) – Muslims break with the Eurocentric and secularist understanding of separation of religion and state which has become the standard definition in the West. In a speech at the *Oxford Center for Islamic Studies* on October 27, 1993, Prince Charles emphasized the reductionist nature of these definitions by pointing out that we are falling victim to our arrogance if we expect to measure "modernity" in other countries by how closely they come to resemble us. He went on to point to the unifying worldview at the heart of Islam, a vision the West had lost over time.

It is equally true that at least the earliest Christians viewed politics differently than Islam does. Jesus did not come from an influential family, nor did he grow up in the capital of the Jewish kingdom. Muhammad, on the other hand, was born into a distinguished family of hereditary office holders in Makkah, the religious and commercial heart of Arabia. These differences intensified because Jesus expected the Last Judgment to be imminent. With him, the first Christians saw themselves also as the last ones. In an atmosphere rife with such eschatological premonition, any thought of establishing a Christian state would have been pointless, not to mention that Jesus did not see himself as founder of a new religion, but as a reformer of Judaism in the tradition of the Qumran community.

Muhammad, however, considered both eventualities: the possibility of the Hour coming soon and the possibility of a continuation of history for a considerable period of time. He was almost irresistibly driven into nation building when his earliest companions, fiercely persecuted in heathen Makkah, did not settle permanently in their Ethiopian asylum but were offered refuge in the hometown of their Arab sympathizers, Yathrib (today's *al-Madinah*). There, as a simple matter of survival, they were able – if not forced – to establish their own confederation in 622.[6]

Given these rather different circumstances it is quite understandable that the New Testament knows only few rules of a legal nature, such as those governing divorce, while the Qur'an and *sunnah* contain hundreds of regulations for everyday life, that include rules of state and economy. The Islamic *Ummah* entered into history as a 'nation', whose citizenship did not derive from language, skin color, or descent, but from a solidarity of faith and law.[7]

In spite of this, there was no difference between Christianity and Islam with regard to their impact on society and world affairs. Following its conquest of the imperial throne of the Eastern Roman Empire through the conversion of Emperor Constantine in the fourth century, Christianity, too, became a state religion (and still is in the Eastern European, Orthodox Christian region). What came of this fateful development is common knowledge, but a few concepts from that history speak volumes: sacred kingship; Holy Roman Empire; the doctrine of the divine rights of kings; the doctrine of the Two Swords (one held by the emperor, the other by the pope); Investiture Controversy (who is to crown whom?); penance at Canossa (after the German emperor Henry IV had been excommunicated by the pope); Vatican State; the Concordat (treaty between the Vatican and other states); the Crusades; the Inquisition; the Witch Trials; the reconquest of Muslim Spain under the "Most Catholic Kings" Ferdinand and Isabella...

If any proof of Christian involvement with secular affairs was needed, there it is. The Renaissance, the Reformation and the Enlightenment in Europe can only be explained as a backlash to the ubiquitous, overbearing dominance of the Church in the political realm.

One may let history be history, but only if history is all there is. An analysis of Western secularism demonstrates, however, that Occidental states and societies, despite all protestations to the contrary, continue to show the formative influence of Christianity, both as religion and civilization. Jeffrey Lang therefore flatly rejects as a misnomer any reference to a supposedly "secular" West.[8]

In the Federal Republic of Germany, for instance, Church and State are supposedly separate. However, the state enforces religious holidays, legally recognizes religious organizations as public institutions, and collects payroll taxes for Protestant churches, the Catholic Church, and the Jewish community (but not for or from Muslims). In public schools civil servants teach religion. In court and the German military, oaths are sworn to God, and the preamble of the German constitution even refers to Him. The German armed forces employ chaplains, school walls are adorned with crucifixes, and the penal code contains articles dealing with "crimes relating to religion and ideology". Article166 of the German penal code, the so-called blasphemy statute, is designed to safeguard religious sensitivities. Both the Chancellor and the Federal President traditionally address the German people on Christmas Day. (The situation in other European countries, except France, is not entirely dissimilar.)

The Germans are right not to dismiss all this as medieval obscurantism. Why, then, denounce Islam as a defender of theocracy? All Muslims strive for is a state construed along those lines, where religion and politics, religion and society, are in harmony.

No arabized Germanistan, no theocracy ruled by an autocratic cleric. There are radical liberals, left-wing socialists, as well as militant atheists from all over the political spectrum who cringe at any ongoing entanglement of Church and State. They are not satisfied with the present marginalization of God and the de-Christianization of Europe. Rather, they take 'laicistic' nations like Mexico and France as models to be followed. Such people are, however, mistaken in two respects: for one, they forget that religion can appear in surprisingly different guises, such as pseudo-religious Kemalism, for instance, or as militant French laicism. Symptomatic of an underground survival of religion is even the phenomenon of socially enforced political correctness, even if it appears under a liberal banner. Indeed, the best explanation for the tabooing of certain topics and for the aggressive intolerance towards the public display of religion (such as headscarves) is that we are dealing here with pseudo-secular ersatz-religions (such as former communism).

Muslims, like members of the activist Catholic "*Opus Dei*" organization and Evangelical Christians, do not check their faith in at the front desk when going to the office. As with any political animal, it is in the very nature of Muslims to be politically active. That may well be in contradiction to the current Western ideal of an internalized, fully subjective relationship to the divine: each individual with his own eclectic, private faith, online and alone. The advocates of such a privatization of religion must let experience tell them that, in the long run, no state can survive without some transcendental moorings.

Despite being rationalists, Kant and Novalis understood that worldly powers cannot reach an equilibrium among themselves. Instead, there will always be a jungle of conflicting interests unless societies are held together by a religion. Why else would the European Commission make an effort to breathe some spirituality into the old continent by launching a program called "Giving a Soul to Europe "?

Already a quarter of a century ago, the Harvard sociologist Daniel Bell recognized in "The Cultural Contradictions of Capitalism" that capitalism – according to Max Weber the product of Calvinist values – becomes self-destructive once it loses itself in frantic obsession with scientific and economic progress. In this case, what used to be fundamental virtues like hard work, loyalty, thrift, discipline, and the drive to succeed are perverted and begin to poison the system from within in the form of consumerism, sexual promiscuity, egalitarianism, "slacker"-syndrome, and the like. This is not surprising. The post-industrial world produces virtually everything except answers to the most essential questions about life and existence: Where did we come from? Why are we here? Where are we going? Against this background, Prince Charles remarked at an Investcorp dinner in London on July 10, 1996: "Science has tried to assume a monopoly – or rather a tyranny – over our understanding .... I believe that the survival of civilized values .... depends on the corresponding survival in our hearts of the profound sense of the sacred .... I believe strongly that a world in which science and religion form an integrated part of a common understanding of our world will be better balanced, wiser and more civilized .... The Islamic world has preserved this spiritual view of the world around us to a degree we have not managed in the West."

As we see, Islam neither lacks political understanding, nor the will to shape state and economy. Quite the contrary: Muslims feel the historical obligation to create, if at all possible, only one single[9] politically organized society encompassing the entire community of believers, a framework to structurally ensure equality, justice, welfare, freedom, and dignity for all. The Qur'an gave an advance blessing to such an ideal community – a community of brothers and sisters (49:10), "*You are the best community ever evolved for mankind*" (3:110).

This is the reason why abolishing the caliphate in 1924 came as a profound shock for the entire Islamic world, even though this office had for some time been reduced to symbolic significance. Nostalgia for the caliphate is an undeniable fact to this very day. This is why it took some time before the majority of Muslim legal scholars came to terms with the emergence of national states in the Muslim world (and that within borders dictated by colonialism.) Up until recently, it went against their grain that Islam should import this utterly European 16th century creature, the nation state, including its more recent secular structure.

But the ideal of Muslim unity was saved by an insight going back six hundred years to Ibn Taymiyyah. He had discovered that the future of Islam depended less on the unity of state and caliphate than on the unity of the *ummah* (religious unity) and the *Shari'ah* (legal unity). In 1964, Sayyid Qutb, the leading theorist of the Egyptian Muslim Brotherhood, reflected this insight in his saying that the *ummah's* nationalism is its faith, its home the Islamic world (*dar al-Islam*), its ruler Allah, and its constitution the Qur'an. As a consequence, the "mythos of the *Shari'ah*" virtually replaced the caliph as symbol of Islamic identity and unity.[10]

For its ideal state, Islamic Law does not require a specific form of state. Each Muslim generation is called upon to find precisely the one state organization to serve best its developmental level and tradition. This can be a monarchy. The Qur'an mentions monarchies, deals with King Saul and, in *Surah al-Naml* (27: 28-44), extensively reports concerning a reasonable and just monarch, the Queen of Sheba (evidently Belquis). But a Muslim state can also be a republic, like the first Islamic state founded in *al-Madinah* in 622. Islamic constitutional law in no way requires a Muslim state to be a theocracy in the narrow sense of the word even though in *Sh'ite* Iran, political power is vested in clerics.

In the final analysis, any specific form of State is compatible with Islam as long as the state rests on a broad consensus, at least on the consent of a large majority. In this case one can assume that there exists an unwritten contract between the people and their state, regulating their mutual rights and responsibilities much in the manner envisaged by Rousseau (social contract). Islam calls this contract *baya'*. In Morocco, one can witness ceremonies, year after year, for the symbolic renewal of the *baya'*, with delegations convening from all over the country. The Jordanian monarchy seeks reconfirmation whenever the genealogy of the monarch is publicized, as happened again on the occasion of the crowning of Abdallah II, the present king. (His genealogy through forty-three generations does reach back to Muhammad and to an additional eleven generations preceding him.)

WE have now reached the question to which every discussion of "political Islam" invariably leads: what is democracy to Islam?[11] That this subject is still the source of discordant tunes will surprise nobody. But critical Muslim voices are becoming weaker – the voices of those who used to treat democracy as a rival religion, and therefore associated it with infidelity (*nizam al-kufr*) or polytheism (*shirk*), because democracy meant worshipping, as supposedly, the sovereign, both the individual citizen and his state.[12] Nevertheless, Sayyid Qutb's radical rejection of democracy, "*Milestones*", is being continuously reprinted: a book whose powerful punch and radical bite can only be compared to the Communist Manifesto (1848), and which caused Gamal Abd al-Nasser to execute him in 1966. Qutb had been afraid that a parliamentary democracy, even in an Islamic state, might eventually legalize what the *Shari'ah* prohibits (like charging interest).

One may wonder why Qutb was more suspicious of parliamentary democracy than of other forms of government when overseeing abuse of authority. The answer to this question is easy: just as in the case of human rights, when it comes to the issue of "democracy", highly emotional associations tend to play tricks on Muslims. The main reason probably is that they were introduced to democracy in a questionable form and by the powers that were "civilizing" them through colonization. Democracy was seen as a skillful method for alienating them from their own religious traditions. This has left a bad taste in their mouth for generations to come when thinking of "democracy".

For Muslims, the semantics alone are offensive. They translate the term "democracy" etymologically correctly as "people's rule" – sovereignty of the people – and by doing so, make the word immediately anathema, because the sole and only sovereign is of course God, the Creator, alone. Explaining the practical meaning of sovereignty (*hakimiyya*) is therefore absolutely of prime importance. As can be expected, for Sayyid Qutb any form of legislation had divine character, and therefore, any legislative act of parliament constituted a manifest act of blasphemous presumption and rebellion against God.[13] In short: for him a parliamentary institution did not have any conceivable Islamic use.

His opponents, chiefly among them Muhammad Asad, M.S. Ashmawi, Fathi Osman, Rashid Ghannouchi, Hassan al-Turabi and Jeffrey Lang, explain that rule of God (*hukm Allah*) obviously cannot mean that God is doing the job of everyday governing for His people on earth. Sovereignty here rather refers to the sovereignty of God's Word (Qur'an) and Law (*Shari'ah*). This being granted, the question remains how man, how the Muslims can best implement the divine Revelation received.[14]

According to Hassan al-Turabi, "gray eminence of the Sudan", the Islamic ideal is a democratic Islam, since "Islam rejects absolute authority, hereditary authority, and the authority of one single individual."[15] Also to Fathi Osman, those who readily dismiss democracy as un-Islamic only reveal their ignorance of Islam or of democracy – or of both. He goes on to maintain that playing Islam and democracy off against each other is unfair – to both.[16]

Not only unfair, but also totally false is the allegation that democracy needs to be accompanied by secularism. (If this were so, democracy would indeed be unacceptable for Islam). Democracy and secularism are anything but synonymous, on the contrary. Great Britain, Germany, Italy, Austria, Ireland, Sweden, Norway, Denmark, the Netherlands, Belgium and other non-secular states, aren't they all solidly democratic? Hence in Islam, a "theodemocracy" (Mawdudi) is a definite possibility.[17]

For Muslims, "people's rule" would be unacceptable if it really meant that the people can enact whatever they like, simply by virtue of having a majority in parliament. But this hypothesis does not even reflect the Western theory of democracy, which also distinguishes rule of the people from rule of the mob. For this reason, Western constitutions not only protect their citizens from the state, but also the state from it own citizens' license, and minorities from the majority.

Western democracies all know some constitutional norms that transcend the law by being considered immutable. For German constitutional scholars, it is therefore plausible that there could even be such a thing as unconstitutional constitutional law, resulting from forbidden attempts to change what must not be changed. The situation would not be much different in an Islamic democracy, since an Islamic parliament when engaging in legislation will always feel the breath of the Shari'ah on its neck and refrain from violating it.[18]

Instead of mindlessly stumbling over offensive vocabulary like "people's rule", Muslims should realize that the primary goal of democracy – preventing the abuse of power through a systematic control of government and a balance of power – is a key Islamic concern. How to improve and ensure better welfare of the people, equality, and justice? In an Islamic democracy, this goal would be addressed primarily by acknowledging the Qur'an as the supreme constitutional norm. (This would be the first cornerstone of an Islamic democracy).

This Islamic constitution would provide the yardstick against which Muslim judges, members of a supreme court, would have to measure all bills passed by legislative bodies. (Second cornerstone).

The Qur'anic foundation for an Islamic parliament (third cornerstone) is the twice repeated reference to the necessity of "consultation" (*ash-shura*) in *Surah Al 'Imran (3:159)*, and *Surah ash-Shura (42:38)*. The latter *surah* being eponymous prompted the Algerian party leader Sheik Mahfoudh Nahnah to suggest that the Islamic form of democracy be called *Shurakratiyya*.

According to verse 3:159, the Prophet himself was under obligation to "consult the believers in [current] affairs." With Verse 42: 38, the obligation to seek counsel covers the entire community of believers and is elevated to the importance of prayer and charity. Accordingly, those are rewarded, "... who (conduct) their affair by mutual consultation...". This innocuous phrase potentially is of paramount legal significance, even though historically, ever since the Umayad dynasty in Damascus (until 750), the consultative principle has been neglected over long centuries of despotism. (Little consolation that the Occident for long did no better.)

Contemporary Muslims do not deny their duty to consult, nor do they overlook the fact that in modern mass societies consultation is only feasible via representative bodies (*majalis ash-shura*), as even Moses realized.[19] (Cornerstone number four).

But which is the Islamic way of choosing people's representatives? If, as is the norm in most Muslim core states, the ruler appoints them into an advisory council, the authority to be controlled is controlling itself. For that reason, more and more Muslims are calling for free and general elections of their representatives.[20] (Cornerstone number five).

One obstacle practicing democracy this way is the Islamic principle not to nominate oneself for political office. To do so was regarded with such disapproval that Muhammad would never appoint as governor anyone who campaigned for the job.[21] As far as I can see, applying this *sunnah* to an election campaign does not mean that a candidate, once nominated by the *Ummah*, could not speak up for his cause (and thus invariably for himself); however, he must not put his name up for election himself.

Another question yet to be settled is whether consultations between government and representative assembly should be considered binding or not.[22] Making them binding is first and foremost supported by the fact that the Qur'an views each and every individual human being, man and woman, as God's deputies (*khulafa*) on earth. (That is why the chief executive should not be called *khalifa* but *amir*).[23] Everybody is a Caliph! (In that sense, something like "sovereignty of the people" indeed exists even in Islam).

The binding nature of consultation can of course be based directly on the *sunnah* of the Prophet because Muhammad honored the results of consultation even if he personally had disagreed: before the battle of Badr (624), he followed the advice of al-Khabab ibn al-Mundhir to post the Muslims before and not (as intended by him) behind the water wells. Before the "Battle of the Trench" (627), Muhammad heeded the then most outrageous counsel of Salman al-Farsi to dig defensive trenches all around *al-Madinah*. Once, on the eve of the battle at mount Uhud (625) at the outskirts of *al-Madinah*, the Prophet abided by the result of consultations against his better judgment. The ambitious Muslims lost, because their majority had overruled Muhammad's advice and engaged the overwhelming besiegers from Makkah in open battle without having the necessary discipline for it.[24] (The binding nature of consultation forms cornerstone number six).

While the Qur'an itself assumes that Muslims can be of different opinions (4:59), they seem to be obsessed with a desire for internal harmony, as if disputes were to be averted no matter what. This quest for unanimity in unity can be so strong that it becomes almost authoritarian.[25] It also comes through in the fear that political pluralism might provoke ugly confrontations between Muslim parties (as in Malaysia). This misgiving is partly due to the fact that most Muslims expect Qur'an and *sunnah* to give clear and definite (and therefore indisputable) answers to every conceivable question, also in politics. Does it not say: *"Nothing have We omitted from the Book"* (6:38) and *"This day have I perfected your religion for you"* (5:3)? In view of that, differences of opinion are easily seen as a sign of ill will.

This interpretation overlooks the fact that Islam has found its perfection only in religious matters, that is faith (*aqida*), worship (*'ibada*) and morality (*akhlaq*). This means that differences in opinion are permissible, legitimate, and even unavoidable, when no specific rules of the *Shari'ah* but broad Islamic principles (*maqasid*) are applied to fields like agriculture, military strategy, or economic policy. Only, debate should never degenerate into splitting hairs.[26] Did Muhammad not state: "The differences among the learned members of my community are a grace of God"?[27] There had actually been many heated arguments among the Prophet's followers on political and military issues and, in settling the question of succession, even fighting. 'Umar, 'Uthman and 'Ali, the 2nd, 3rd and 4th Caliphs, were assassinated.

Even if Muslim anxieties about keeping internal peace are

warranted, they do not constructively address the question of what to do in the event the desired political consensus among brothers simply won't materialize. Many Muslims hesitate to let majority decisions carry the day in situations of stalemate because they misjudge the legislative discretion of a Muslim parliament in two opposite ways: they overestimate it by recalling *Surah al-An'am (6:116)* which states, "*If you follow the common run of those on earth, they will mislead you away from Allah's path.*" In reality, however, in a true Islamic democracy no representative body would ever be permitted to diverge from, or modernize, issues long since settled by the Qur'an or the *sunnah* – no matter how large the majority.

On the other hand, the room for parliamentary discretion in a Muslim setting is frequently underestimated, because the role of an Islamic parliament is not limited to finding divine Muslim law in the Qur'an and *the sunnah* (and perhaps codifying it). Rather, it has long been recognized that there is room, and even a need, for additional man-made laws dealing with new issues on which the *Shari'ah* remained silent – as long as such legislation is compatible with the principles (*maqasid*) of the Qur'an and the *sunnah* and therefore does not contradict the spirit of the *Shari'ah*. [28] (Cornerstone number seven). After all, there is a practical need for technical regulations governing, for instance, road building, customs duties, hygiene, occupational safety standards, and so forth. No Muslim state has been able to function without legislation supplementing the penal code of the *Shari'ah* with additional misdemeanors and crimes (*ta'zir*). This, as an accepted practice, goes back to the Abbasid Caliphate where early on a kind of Islamic secularism emerged in the form of two parallel legal systems: on one level there was the divine Shari'ah, the domain of legal scholars. On another level, administrative law and supplementary criminal law, emancipated (to put it mildly) from the former, evolved at the "discretion" of the respective rulers. This way, for instance, non-Qur'anic methods of punishment such as incarceration and fines were eventually introduced.[29]

This juxtaposition of executive and legislative, together with the judiciary, equally anchored in Islam, constitutes a veritable separation of powers also for an Islamic democracy. (Cornerstone number eight). This would find its most striking expression in a direct or indirect election of the Head of State. Islamic tradition, in accordance with the Prophet's role in the Qur'an, mandates that one single (male) individual be at the helm of the state - no revolutionary council, no supreme soviet, no politburo. This head of government should be the most righteous among the citizens qualified for the position, since only a Muslim who believes in the divine nature of Qur'anic norms can be expected to observe and defend them. (Cornerstone number nine).

The chief executive, on the other hand, called Grand *Vizier* in the Ottoman Empire, does not necessarily have to be either a Muslim, or male. (Cornerstone number ten.)

In spite of the positive example set by the Queen of Sheba in *Surah al-Naml (27),* many Muslims still believe, though, that a state run by a woman chief executive could never prosper. This is because Prophet Muhammad, commenting on a concrete historical situation in imperial Persia, had expressed skepticism about whether the daughter who had just succeeded Emperor Chosroes II would be a successful ruler. (Her tenure did indeed turn out to be rather brief). But this rather popular tradition may be read as more informative than normative, as sort of a judicial *obiter dictum*. At the same time it is a rather weak, if not altogether apocryphal tradition. What makes it particularly suspicious is the fact that Abu Bukra, its narrator, unearthed the event only decades after it had happened [30], and that at a point in time when his recollection was politically propitious: The so-called Battle of the Camel near Basra, in 656, during which the Muslim army opposing 'Ali was under the nominal command of a woman, Muhammad's widow 'A'isha.[31] One may also wonder why the Prophet would only have informed a less prominent companion like Abu Bukra of such a far-reaching rule affecting the status of women instead of prominent and close collaborators, like Abu Bakr.

Be that as it may, with Benazir Bhutto (1988), Begum Khaleda Zia (1991) and Tansu Ciller (1993) the Muslim world has by now produced more female heads of government than Germany, France, Great Britain and the United States combined.

The history of the Prophet's early successors demonstrates that the Head of state of an Islamic state is to be elected without a procedure fixed once and for all. (Cornerstone number 11). Abu Bakr, his   first successor, was elected after a heated argument between the Muslims from Makkah and those of al-Madinah. 'Umar, the second successor, was appointed by acclamation. The third successor, 'Uthman, emerged from an electoral council of six. It follows that Islam understands monarchy, too, only as an elected monarchy. Any new king must be confirmed, at least by acclamation, and preferably through the described *baya'* – process, by which the successor to the throne and the people's representatives enter into not merely a symbolic, but a substantial contract spelling out their mutual rights and obligations.

THE foregoing discussion offers compelling proof that Islam cannot be considered, in itself, hostile to democracy. Rather it contains 11 cornerstones, or basic building blocks, by which the foundation of an Islamic democracy can be put into place. The counter argument, which assumes a singular, genetic flaw in Muslims with regard to democracy, qualifies as postmodern racism. One might just as well dismiss the French as essentially unfit for democracy, considering their motley collection of five republics, two empires, two monarchies and a Communist commune over as little as 200 years. A sounder argument to make is not based on myth: alas, as a religion, Islam has not had any significant impact on the political history of the Muslim world since 661, nor does it have any on the contemporary political landscape from *Maghrib* to *Mashriq*.

An Islamic democracy would not be a copy of the Westminster one, since the Arab-Islamic world knows its own unique forms of pluralism, confederation, civil society, and distribution of power which are indigenous to it alone. After all, even in the West, Westminster only exists in Westminster. At any rate, it is utterly unacceptable that democracy be defined in such a way that it excludes religious societies, i.e., societies intent on drawing political consequences from their faith. If this were the case, most North Americans would be poor democrats because de-Christianization is not an American, but only a European, phenomenon. One wonders, by the way, about the democratic spirit of those who welcome Christian parties in Germany and Italy, while questioning the democratic credentials of Islamic parties in the Muslim world, such as in Tunisia (*Mouvement de Tendence Islamique*), or Algeria (*Front Islamique du Salut*).

Concluding – not from Islam itself but from political history – that Muslims are afflicted by some congenital democratic disability would be a fallacy as well. After all, there is no region in this world, whether Christian, Confucian, Buddhist, Hindu, Jewish, or Islamic, that has not had its share of problems with democracy, most of them to this very day. Sub-Saharan Africa, China, most other parts of Asia and some Latin American countries have yet fully to arrive in the democratic camp. The Europeans, too, experienced many setbacks in their centuries – long journey towards democracy. Therefore, Mark Heller's recent attempt to label the Islamic world as "out of step with history" depicts more prejudice than insight.

Currently, it is primarily Muslim opposition groups headquartered abroad who stake their hopes for Islam back home on democratic control mechanisms. And yet, expecting the ruling powers in the Muslim world to show a genuine interest in democracy means misjudging human nature. True, nowadays hardly any governments can safely do without projecting a democratic façade (*ad-dimuqratiyya shikliyya*), but that is as far as it usually goes. Surprisingly, in a recent book with the pessimistic title *Democracy without Democrats?*, edited by Ghassan Salamé, most of the mostly Western authors nevertheless arrive at the optimistic conclusion that democracy is very gradually gaining ground inside the Muslim world as well.

If so, Islam owes this development to a number of distinguished personalities who have contributed bit by bit, each in his own way, to creating the foundations for a democratic blueprint. First and foremost among them are the Persian Jamal ad-Din al-Afghani (1838-1897), the Egyptian Muhammad Abdu (1849-1905), the Syrians Abdurrahman al-Kawakibi (1849-1903) and Rashid Rida (1865-1935), the Algerian Malik Bennabi (1905-1973), the Austrian Muhammad Asad (1900 -1992)[32], the Egyptian Fathi Osman, who now lives in California, the Sudanese politician Hassan al-Turabi, the Tunisian Rashid Ghannoushi[33], currently living in exile in London, as well as Jeffrey Lang, an American Muslim mathematician (and Arabist) in Kansas.

The forces that had been most strenuously resisting the Muslims' warming to democratic mechanisms are gradually losing their influence over the contemporary intra-Islamic debate on democracy. I am referring to the Journalist Abul 'Ala Mawdudi (1903-1979), founder of the Indo-Pakistani cadre-party Jama'at-e-Islami; Hassan al-Banna (1904-1949), founder of the Muslim Brotherhood (ikhwan al-muslimun), as well as Sayyid Qutb (1906-1966), their "chief ideologue." Curiously enough, since his execution, certain governments have feared him more for his ideological impact than during his lifetime. All three can be considered the legitimate heirs of Shah Waliyullah (1703-1762) and Muhammad 'Abd al-Wahhab (1703-1787), the two great inspirational figures and renewers of Islam in the early modern age.

In his breathless work *Milestones*, Sayyid Qutb wrote, "We ought not .... start looking for similarities with Islam and the current systems or in current religions or current ideas. We reject these systems in the East as well as in the West. We reject them all .... " [34] This was thoroughly consistent with his premise that all existing States, the so-called Muslim States included, were still – or again - tarrying in the pre-Islamic world of unbelief (*jahiliyya*).[35] That this train of thought has not yet lost its impact became evident in a heated debate, as late as 1994, in the German magazine *Al-Islam* on the pros and cons of voting in parliamentary elections.[36]

Believe it or not, only 30 years after *Milestones*, the contemporary Muslim Brotherhood leadership committed itself in writing to the following elements of an Islamic state: written state constitution; general elections to determine the head of state, for a limited term; multi-party system, i.e. political pluralism; parliamentarianism; independent judiciary; and also the Muslim women's right to vote and to be elected.[37] With that in mind, Fathi Osman's wish that the Muslims will soon abandon their fruitless "*Shura*-Democracy polemics"[38], may well be fulfilled Those doing an incredulous double take over this would be better off accepting the fact that the Islamic world is – and historically always has been – far from static.[39]

These observations should be reason enough for Western critics to reevaluate their often negative attitude towards Muslim opposition groups in Europe which are trying to change the political status quo in their home countries by adopting a democratic discourse. These "Islamist" movements have much in common with Western grass roots movements supporting civil rights, women's liberation, environmental protection, and ethnic concerns.[40]

These Islamic movements in the West are united with many a thoughtful Occidental observer in their assessment that today's societies have but three options: (i) To pursue the "Project Modernity" in the spirit of rationalist enlightenment as if nothing had happened – a prescription for disaster. (ii) To surrender to a postmodern cultural relativism and lead a life without meaning. Or (iii) to revive the transcendental links of their religions. Many young Islamic academics consider the "Project Modernity" a bankrupt paradigm and view post modernism as an intellectual dead end. For this reason, they opt for the religion of their fathers. What is dangerous about that?

That they politicize Islam into an ideology of liberation and progress is their reasoned reaction to previous colonial domination. To them, Islam is an instrument of motivation, legitimization, and justification, which is true for religion everywhere. With their involvement in social work, they counter "me-societies" with the solidarity of a "we-society" that has always been characteristic of Islam, a community defined by common conduct (group prayer, public fasting, communal pilgrimage, tax for the poor). Where dire circumstances cause such movements to slide into formal illegality, one should not rush into denying them their right to resistance against state oppression which is, after all, guaranteed by Christian and Islamic teaching (42: 40) alike.[41]

And yet it is understandable when the West suspects that groups committing acts of violence, although defensively, and those prone to it, would not deliver on democracy if they were to seize power themselves. Would the escalation of violence and counter-violence leading up to a successful democratic revolution not spiral into a renewed suppression of opposition, now by the former underdogs?

Indeed, groups prepared to use violence will typically follow the 8th century example of the Abbasid rebellion against Umayad tyranny and "excommunicate" their adversaries, so to speak, by disputing their Muslim credentials. Such groups are also likely to idealize a Golden Islamic Period of their choice, claim a Messianic mission, monopolize the correct interpretation of the Qur'an and the *sunnah*, and operate with deceivingly simple slogans of little practical use, like *"lâ hukma illa' llah"* (all sovereignty is with God).

Until the contrary is proven, it will therefore be difficult to dispel the suspicion that among politically active Muslims there are Islamists, rightly called that way, who are using Islam for their own varied purposes. Why should the Muslim world be capable today of making vanish the very phenomenon of religious hypocrisy (*nifaq*) which figured so prominently even in *al-Madinah* during the Prophet's lifetime and plays such a great role in the Qur'an?

Not to be overlooked: there are specific Muslim political opposition movements, active world-wide, like al -Hizb at-Tahrir (Party of Liberation), which renounce violence out of principle, even where it would be justified in legal theory or advantageous in practical terms. These groups follow the example of the Prophet in pre-Islamic Makkah. Even though the persecution of the small initial Muslim community was severe there, Muhammad did not call to arms. He preferred his companions to emigrate, some first to Ethiopia and then all to *al-Madinah*, rather than mounting armed resistance. It is perhaps to be expected that these groups face especially hard prosecution, because certain governments perceive their attractive tactical pacifism as even more dangerous than terrorist attacks.

"Islamic movements" based and operating in the Occident itself, for the most part are dominated by Western-educated academics – mostly scientists and medical doctors – who appreciate the rule of law as practiced in the United States and Europe and follow Western methods in dealing with academia, the political scene, and the media. There is no justification whatsoever to paint even such well-integrated Muslim groups with the suspicion of lacking sincere conviction as far as democracy and the rule of law is concerned. At present, among Muslims worldwide, there is no greater democratic potential to be found than in these youthful, Western-based Islamic groups. As even Edward Luttwak concedes: "Islamists are the only viable opposition against anti-democratic governments."[42] Their "fundamentalism" is not a "fad", but the choice of an entire generation.

In 1992, during a discussion in Washington, D.C., Hassan al-Turabi put it squarely: "If you want to keep Islam at a distance, you have to stay away from the ballot boxes!"[43] There can indeed be no doubt that in every Muslim country throughout the world, democratic Islamic parties would now win free and fair elections, if there were such a thing.

Notes

1. Ashmawi, p. 11.
2. According to Sayyid Qutb, Sufism worked like a drug on Islam, robbing this otherwise virile and dynamic religion of its formative will to shape the world, at times intoxicating the entire Muslim society (Qutb, p. 87). Already back in the 14th century Ibn Taymiyyah had blamed Islamic mysticism for corrupting Islam. It is true that most Sufi brotherhoods have become apolitical, and as a consequence the Moroccan Sufis from Wazzan stand accused of unpatriotic pacifism and collaboration with the French colonial authorities to this very day. However, their predecessors – the Murabitun – had still been belligerent defenders of the faith against the Spanish and Portuguese aggressors. For more on criticism of Sufis, see Osman (1997), p. 440.
3. The Qur'an repeatedly asks the faithful to enforce what is right and to forbid what is wrong. See 3: 110; 9: 71 and 31: 17.
4. An-Nawawi, *Forty Hadith*, no. 34.
5. Qutb, pp. 37.
6. Hamidullah (1975).
7. Qutb, S. 87.
8. Lang (1995), p. 191
9. See Tamimi (1997, 1998) for an excellent rendition of the debate.
10. According to Krämer, p. 50; for Qutb, see p. 110.
11. On the history of the argument over sovereignty see Khir (1995).
12. Qutb, p. 61.
13. Qutb, p. 61.
14. Osman (1994), p. 70; Lang (1995), p. 191; Tamimi (1998), p 35.
15. al-Turabi (1992)., p. 19.

16. Osman (1996), S. 58.
17. al-Turabi (1992), p. 24.
18. al-Turabi (1992), p. 19.
19. 7: 155.
20. Osman (1996), pp. 43.
21. al-Bukhari, vol. 8, no. 715, vol. 9, no. 58 and 261.
22. Osman (1996), p. 83, supports the binding nature, see also "Shura in Islamic Life", in: *Muslim Democrat*, vol. 1, no. 2, Washington, September 1999, p. 6, based on Qur'an 2: 30, 6: 165, 24: 55, 27: 62, and 35: 39.
23. Every man is seen as God's deputy according to 2: 30; 6: 165; 24: 55; 27: 62; 35: 39.
24. Cf. Haikal, p. 219, 221, 232, 242, 252, 254.
25. Osman (1996), S. 55.
26. So Osman (*Human Rights*, 1996), p. 11. The harmfulness of differing opinions is derived from the following *ahadith*: *al-Bukhari* no. 4.468, 5.434, 5.717, 6.510, 9.67, 9.39; and *Sahih Muslim* no. 6447. This may be partly due to fear of religious innovation (cf. *Muslim, Sahih*, no. 6450).
27. The Prophet warns of destructive hairsplitting in *hadith* no. 6450. in *Sahih Muslim.*
28. Muhammad, after all, did not want Muslims to emulate him in each and every respect. Cf. Muslim, *Sahih*, no. 5830 and 5831.
29. For more on the *ta'zir* (plural: *ta'zair*)-penal code and its potential for displacing the Qur'anic *hadd* (plural: *hudud*)-penal law, see Doi, p. 222-228, and al-Turabi(1992), p. 14, 38.
30. Not to be confused with the first Caliph, Abu Bakr.
31. The *Hadith* reads *Lan yufliha qaumun wa lau amrahum imra'a* (Never will those succeed who make a woman their ruler): al-Bukhari, vol. 9, Book 88, no. 219, p. 171; Rassoul, p. 743, *Hadith* 7.099. For its evaluation and interpretation, see Osman (1996), S. 51; Lang (1995), p. 169, finds it difficult to decide whether the *Hadith* constitutes a principle, or only a political comment. Engineer believes it is counterfeit.
32. Nobody has spurred on Muslim organization more vigorously than Muhammad Asad (a.k.a Leopold Weiss) in his *The Principles of State and Government in Islam,* first published 1961 in California and only 107 pages long. In it, he arrived at the well documented conclusion that an Islamic state could be conceived along the lines of the American form of presidential government.

33. The most important book by Ghannouchi relevant to our topic is *Al-hurriya al-'amma fi-l-daula al-islamiyya* (*Public Liberties in the Islamic State*). For a splendid summary of his thoughts, see Tamimi (1998).
34. Qutb, pp. 117 f.
35. Qutb, p. 67.
36. Burhan Kesici, "Wählen oder nicht? (To Vote or Not to Vote?)", in: *Al-Islam*, 1994, no. 2, p. 12, argued in favor of participating. In the next edition, (p. 23) two letters to the editors voiced strong disagreements: voting constituted an endorsement of the rule of the people, hence a rejection of Qur'an and *Shari'ah*.
37. "The Muslim Brotherhood's Statement on *Shura* in Islam and the Multi-Party System in an Islamic Society ; Statement of the Muslim Brotherhood on the role of Muslim Women in Islamic Society and its Stand on the Women's Right to Vote, be Elected and Occupy Public and Governmental Posts and Work in General." in: *Documentation*, *Encounters*, vol. 1, no. 2, Markfield, LE (UK) 1995, p. 100 and p. 85.
38. Osman (*Human Rights*), 1996), p.24.
39. Schulze has shown this even for the 18th century.
40. According to Pinn, p. 70. Kepel is still relevant for a comprehensive view of the topic.
41. The *sunnah* recommends much, but not unlimited patience with tyrants: al-Bukhari, vol . 9, no. 257 and following; Rassoul, *Hadith* no. 7053 and following; *Muslim* no. 4551 and following.
42. Quoted by Osman (*Human Rights*, 1996), p. 25.
43. al-Turabi (1992), p. 21.

CHAPTER SEVEN

Similar or Identical?

*Certain legal scholars condemn all women to
life emprisonment!*
(Sheik Yusuf Qaradawi in the London newspaper
ash-Sharq al-Awsat , February 5, 1990)

According to *Surah Al 'Imran* (3: 36), Mary's mother, after she had delivered Mary, exclaimed: *"O my Lord! Behold! I have delivered a female child!"* The rejoinder was priceless: *"Allah knew best what she had delivered – a male is not like a female."*

Before making this observation, surely Allah did not check whether it was politically incorrect or even unconstitutional. In any case, with this passage the Qur'an focuses all discussions of gender relations on their essence. Men and women, women and men: they are not only favored by the attribution of equal rights, but are also ontologically at par and equal in the eyes of the law

I am fully aware that putting the questions that way – let alone answering it – is already politically incorrect, both in Europe as well as North America. The mere intention of exploring any possible differences between the sexes, beyond the fundamental biological ones, is ideologically scorned. Doing research on the I.Q. of boys and girls in general, or their mathematical talents in particular, until recently could ruin an academic career in the United States, a country where censorship supposedly does not exist. For this reason, Daniel Goleman showed uncommon civil courage when, in his bestseller *Emotional Intelligence*, he objectively traced remarkable emotional differences between the genders and, on that basis, later calculated different "success quotients" for each sex. Other medical researchers have also begun to stick their necks out by publishing on gender specifics, for instance on differing hearing capabilities. According to such research, women generally discern better than men faint sounds above 2000 Hz from an otherwise silent background. Men, on the other hand, are doing better than women when it comes to locating sound directions.[1] *Honi soi qui mal y pense*: a pox on him who thinks of baby care and bear hunting!

Since Islam, not entirely without its own fault,[2] suffers from the reputation of being a misogynist religion, the debate of "women and Islam" keeps overshadowing any efforts towards a better mutual understanding between Orient and Occident. As a Muslim you can lecture on any other subject under the moon, yet the first question from the audience invariably will be: "How do you see the role of women in Islam?"

The emotional charge of this debate can become explosive whenever questions focus on something as trifling as a piece of cloth, a headscarf. If worn by Muslim women – and in that case only – headscarves apparently have the potential, as in Turkey, to shake the foundations of an entire nation. In that case, Islamic clothing has become a potent metaphor of Islam itself, an icon defining its very essence.[3] Quite clearly, Westerners are puzzled by the phenomenon as well, trying to reconcile their fanciful stereotypes of dark-eyed seductive Oriental odalisques and the sexual pleasure of the harem with real life "fundamentalist" women who insist on privatizing their charms in a fashion considered puritanical, and hence outdated.

Not only is this topic charged with emotions. It also reveals both a devastating lack of information and a high degree of misinformation about Islam. Muslims are left dumbfounded when audiences in all seriousness ask whether Islam teaches that women have no soul – whether they are allowed to go to Makkah on pilgrimage – and whether they are accepted into paradise, as envisaged by Muslims! Such loaded questions show that the future for Islam in the West depends not only on the hot topics of "human rights" and "democracy" but first and foremost on how to handle the burning issue of "women".

FOR a change, statistics do not lie: all over the world, both mothers and fathers prefer sons to daughters – whether one likes it or not. The Qur'an describes this phenomenon drastically: "*When the news is brought to any of them of (the birth of) a female (child), his face becomes dark, and he is filled with grief! With shame does he hide himself from his people, because of the bad news that had reached him! Shall he keep her with dishonor or bury her [alive]?*" (16: 58-59) A different Qur'anic passage tells of another father whose face had become dark with grief, too, and who grumbles: *"What? One to be raised in luxury [or: like a piece of luxury] and who is unable to hold her own in a dispute?"* (43:17-18) Against this background, the Qur'an prohibits the killing of newborn girls in strong terms (81: 8-9), like any murder; nothing less can apply to the unborn.

It is established that in pre-Islamic Arabia many a baby girl was done away with, out of dire need. Today, however, female fetuses are being killed in huge numbers, facilitated by prenatal analysis. Normally, ultrasound suffices to determine the sex of the unborn. This selective killing is now common place primarily in China, Taiwan, South Korea, Pakistan and India. There abortion clinics advertise with the slogan: "Pay 500 Rupees to save 50,000" (by escaping paying the dowry of a grown up daughter). This has already created a shortfall of approximately 100 million women in Asia. In India and China for every 100 boys only 85 girls are now born.[4]

But even if they are lucky enough to be born in spite of their sex, women even today are subjected to discrimination, the world over. Those who fail to see this happening in the West are looking the other way. Many different psychological, sociological, cultural, but also economic reasons account for this. Muhammad Qutb (brother of Sayyid Qutb) therefore felt entitled to conclude: "If poverty were to disappear from Islamic countries, the problems facing women for the most part would be solved."[5]

It would, however, be wrong for Muslims and damaging to Islam as a whole to hide behind economic facts. For there is a type of female discrimination that is culturally specific to the Muslim world. The Egyptian Qasim Amin (1863-1908), perhaps the first Muslim to fight for the liberation of women since the Prophet Muhammad himself, attributed this discrimination to "a hotch-potch of traditions which people call religion and identify as Islam." He rightly saw a definite connection between the backwardness of women and the backwardness of their entire nation.[6]

Already a quarter of a century ago, the Sudanese intellectual politician Hassan al-Turabi, in our time arguably the most significant trailblazer for the Islamic rights of women, saw "a revolution against the situation of women in traditional Muslim societies" as unavoidable. According to him, a biased, male-dominated jurisprudence, pursued at the expense of women, had sacrificed fundamental rights of Muslim women. In the process, "pseudo-religious arguments" had been used in order to justify "a complete metamorphosis of the model society as founded by the Prophet." For al-Turabi, the oppression of women was typical for times when the faith of their men had become weak.[7] Hassan al-Turabi probably had in mind what Louis Gardet considered to be a cult of jealousy and masculinity among Arabs, for which he subtly chose the more innocent terms *climat de jalousie* and *valorisation de la virilité*.[8] Others, less polite, would speak of the notorious tradition of semitic patriarchy.

American Muslims, too, whether of Oriental heritage or not, consider it necessary for Muslim men to reevaluate their attitude toward women. They want to differentiate the essential Islam as religion from what is merely part of Muslim civilization and therefore incidental. Otherwise, Muslims there risk repelling people from Islam who otherwise would find their way to it.[9] Fathi Osman makes it quite clear that "we have gotten used to the notion that women were destined for family and children only .... But there is nothing in the Qur'an or the *sunnah* that would unambiguously support such an idea. Such a division of labor is based on sociological experience. The fact that such an experience may have a very long memory does not necessarily mean that we are debating here with a law of nature, or God's divine commandment for Islam."[10]

All this certainly demonstrates that there is an urgent need for change in favor of Muslim women. But it does not state what precisely is it that should change (from a Western point of view) and what (from an Islamic perspective) could be changed, in accordance with the Qur'an and the *sunnah*. After all, true Muslims are not intent on modernizing Islam, but on Islamizing modernity (François Burgat)[11], not interested in Reformation (à la Luther and Calvin), but in a veritable Renaissance[12], without aping the West, and without recreating mere shadows of the past.[13]

WHY not go back all the way and begin with Adam and Eve? The image of woman in Islam – and its impact in depth on the subconscious – was influenced positively by the fact that the Qur'an does not portray Eve as a seductress. Rather, the Qur'an portrays the events leading up to the fall from grace as a "joint venture". Consequently, the burden of childbearing is not described as a specific punishment for the female gender, nor does the Qur'an indicate that Adam was created before Eve (and she from his rib).

This is a clear and very significant departure from the Judeo-Christian heritage, whose depiction of the events surrounding Adam and Eve doubtlessly contributed to the Christian vilification of women, beginning with Paul and, with the burning of witches, continuing all the way through the late Middle Ages and into the early Modern Age. Without such a negative tradition, Islam was able to maintain a much more relaxed and positive attitude towards sexual matters and to avoid the drastic swings of the pendulum from Puritanism to hypersexuality, so typical of the Christian world.

Accordingly, the Qur'an portrays female personalities almost without exception in a favorable light: the Queen of Sheba, Moses' mother and the Pharoh's wife, Mary and her mother prove this beyond doubt.

Even by modern standards, the relationship of husband and wife in marriage is described very positively in the Qur'an, even though marriage in Islam is neither considered a sacrament nor a religious covenant. *Surah ar-Rum* (30: 21), speaking of the married couple, states: "*He (God) has put love and mercy between you.*" *Surah al-Baqara* (2:187) paints this inspiring image: "*They [your wives] are your garments, and you are their garments.*" Surely, that does not sound like female submission or male domination, not like a call for male autocracy but on the contrary, it implies supportive mutual partnership. *Surah at-Tauba* (9:71) describes believing men and believing women as "protective friends" of one another.

Therefore, it should not be surprising but rather self-evident that in Islam women are equal to men in their religious and spiritual status, hence subject to the same obligations as any other Muslim, from prayer and fasting to paying the welfare tax (*zakat*) and performing the pilgrimage. In a rhetorically impressive manner the Qur'an enumerates these and other duties by expressly mentioning both men and women in ten different respects: "*For Muslim men and Muslim women, for believing men and believing women, ... for fasting men and fasting women, for men who guard their chastity and women who guard their chastity ....*" (33: 35). *Surah an-Nahl* (16: 97) succinctly states: "*Whoever works righteousness, man or woman, and has faith, verily, to him will We give a new life, and life that is good and pure.*"

In view of this, it is rather unfortunate that women have been discouraged from attending the community prayers in the mosque, which bars them as well from some of the mosque's social, political, and educational functions. This practice does not square with early Islamic tradition: how else could a woman have interrupted Caliph 'Umar during his Friday sermon in order to correct his interpretation of the Qur'anic rules governing the amount of bridal gifts (*mahr*)?

What is true of women's equal religious status is also valid for their intellectual status: biological differences between men and women do not make one naturally more pious or more intelligent than the other, even though there are proven differences between the sexes as far as certain talents and responses are concerned. If ever a female intelligence test, proving equality, had been necessary, Muhammad's young wife 'A'isha would have passed it with flying colors, e.g., by recording for posterity over 1000 meticulously memorized reports (*ahadith*) about her husband; by committing to memory the entire Qur'an; by interpreting Qur'an and *sunnah* in the manner of a legal scholar; and by turning into a major political player after the death of the Prophet.

Fatima Mernissi, an Islamic feminist without theological or historical academic competence, without much success strains to prove that women have left their mark in Muslim political history. Well, Khayzuran, mother of the legendary Abbaside Caliph Harun ar-Rashid, spinning her plots in the harem, was more of an intriguing courtesan than a stateswoman. True, in 1250, the Mameluk Sultanness Shadjara ad-Dur did rule – for a few months. So, Razia Sultan, occupying the throne in Delhi from 1236 to 1240, remains the lone exception proving the rule of male domination in Muslim politics.[14]

Most Oriental men, I am afraid to say, continue to consider women to be more irrational and more subject to emotions than themselves. Whether or not this is factual is beside the point - believing so makes it a fact of life in behavioral terms.

WESTERN criticism of the status of Muslim women is, however, not concerned with generalities. Instead it homes in on concrete elements of the *Shari'ah*, namely (a) polygyny; (b) women's status in marriage; (c) women's dress code; (d) segregation of the sexes, including total veiling; (e) unilateral divorce by the husband; (f) women's position in the law of inheritance and testimony.

Accusations involving polygyny quickly dissipate, because even Western Islamologists admit that, for all intents and purposes, monogamy is prevailing in the contemporary Muslim world, and quite in keeping with the ultimate aims of the Qur'an as expressed in *Surah an- Nisa* (4: 3,129).[15] In verse 3, Allah made the privilege of multiple marriage – with up to four wives – strictly dependent on the fulfillment of the condition of equal treatment: "But if you fear that you shall not be able to deal justly with them, then only one ...." Verse 129 assures husbands, toying with polygamy, that Allah`s condition for it cannot possibly be met: "*You will never be able to do perfect justice between wives, even if it is your ardent desire ....*" Can there be a clearer and more straightforward divine statement of no confidence in the widespread practice of polygyny?

At the same time, even most "liberal" Muslims believe that *Surah* (4: 3) is not without practical significance and thus not superfluous. On the contrary: in times of severe shortage of men, such as after the two World Wars, *Surah an-Nisa* leaves the option of husband-sharing open. And that can be a blessing, above all for war widows and their children, and for all the many single post-war women who, otherwise, in all likelihood would be condemned either to remain spinsters or to break up existing marriages.

In this debate, the least one can expect of Muslim authors like Qasim Amin is that they quote Verse 4: 3 from the very beginning instead of conveniently dropping its introductory sub-clause. Not doing so, obscures that polygyny in the Qur'an is dealt with in context of orphanage, i.e., rules designed to safeguard fatherless children.[16] The introductory sub-clause of 4: 3 as a matter of law contains a second explicit condition effectively limiting polygamy. It reads: "*If you fear that you shall not be able to deal justly with the orphans, marry women of your choice, two, or three, or four....*" From this rationale, a number of Muslims like Hamza Kaidi conclude that polygyny is only permissible with widows taking care of children.[17] Even though in the past many Muslims thought differently (and some still do), Verse 4: 3 definitely never meant to offer *carte blanche* for lewd excesses in harems, big or small, nor for continuously changing their occupants, to make things worse.

The second of the aforementioned Western complaints concerns those Qur'anic verses which used to be interpreted as establishing between men and women a relationship of (male) domination and (female) submission, i.e., 2: 228 and 4: 34. As a matter of fact, *Surah al-Baqarah* in Verse 228 states: "*But men have a degree over them.*" However, what is intended here is not a general, negative definition of the status of women in marriage. It only means that the husband under specific and thus limited circumstances may have the last word. Verse 2: 28, in fact, only deals with cases in which the husband unilaterally pronounced a divorce, the validity of which is still suspended since the three months' period for the discovery of a possible pregnancy has not yet passed. Within this period, according to the Qur'an, the husband may change his mind and take his wife back. Even if she chooses to go through with the divorce, under these peculiar circumstances, then in that case, her husband is to have the last word. The reason being that he, and he alone, would suffer financial loss, since divorced wives, as a matter of principle, keep their bridal gifts (*mahr*). One has to read the Qur'an through distinctly male glasses in order to find that 2: 28 places men "one cut above women."

The same can be said of the key phrase in *Surah an-Nisa* (4: 34) which in Arabic reads "*ar-rijal qawwamuna 'ala-n-nisa*". Up until very recently, this passage was translated in a way that would suggest dominant status of men and subordinate status of women – "Men rank above women" or "Men have authority over women." In keeping with prevailing tradition, Qur'an translators like Mirza Nasir Ahmad, Muhammad Ali, Hamza Boubakeur, Lazarus Goldschmidt, Max Henning[18], Rashid Said Kassab, Denise Masson, Sadok Mazigh, Rudolf Paret and Pesle/Tidjani derived from this one sentence the general rule that husbands, being essentially superior, were their wives' guardians.

Verse 4: 34 can, but need not be, understood that way. Linguistically, an equally correct translation is: "Men shall take full care of women" or "Men are to provide for women." In that case, men are not seen to stand above but to stand up for women. This interpretation has the advantage of being compatible with the aforementioned Qur'anic characterization of marriage as a partnership based on love and mutual support. In their translations, Muhammad Asad, Yusuf Ali, Jaques Berque, Ahmad von Denffer, T. B. Irving and Adel Khoury already followed this line of charging men with responsibility for the women. Fathi Osman, too, translates 4: 34 in much the same manner: "The men have to support the women, provide for them, and take full care of them."[19] He denies that any claim to male superiority could be gleaned from this passage.[20]

As the rest of the verse makes it clear, the Qur'an goes by

the assumption that in marriage men usually are the physically and financially stronger partners, and also that for the average women the ideal partner is bound to be someone as strong, stable and reliable as the proverbial (and now retired) *Marlboro Man*.[21]

To many it comes as a shock that 4: 34 also permits a husband to (lightly) "beat" his wife, if this promises to bring home to her that her ill conduct is about to wreck their marriage. In a family built on true partnership, this passage is bound to remain without much significance. Muhammad himself never beat any of his wives, and in this he is a binding model for all Muslims. Fortunately, Muslims never took 4: 34 as a license for physical abuse of any kind or as a justification, or even encouragement, to batter their wives.[22] How could anyone raise his hand against a being under whose feet lies Paradise, as Muhammad said about mothers?

The so-called "Pharaonic Circumcision", nowadays known as Female Genital Mutilation, is likewise forbidden by the Qur'an like all other grievous bodily injuries. In parts of Africa including the Sudan and Egypt female circumcision was, and continues to be, an objectionable practice among animists, Christians, and unfortunately, Muslims as well. This inhuman custom, alas carried out and perpetuated by women themselves, does not have any basis in Islam, in either the Qur'an or the authentic *sunnah,* and is now outlawed in Egypt.[23] Egypt's Supreme Court by applying Islamic criteria upheld this ban early in 1998.

Amazingly, Western criticism is less centered upon the points already dealt with, but rather on the dress code binding for (sexually still responsive[24]) Muslim women. The simple fact that they cover themselves decently, including their hair, leads Western people to groom on to the classical stereotype of the Orient and take the Islamic dress as evidence of widespread sexism in Islam. A young girl cannot possibly want to wear a headscarf, goes the argument, so girls covering themselves must be browbeaten into it by their fathers or brothers. Worse still, each individual headscarf is seen as an assault on the very foundations of one's secular worldview and society. The achievements of women's liberation, only recently won with great effort, seem to be put into jeopardy by these misguided Muslim sisters. Some Western women even accuse Muslim women for targeting them with a powerful, while silent, moral reproach, carrying their headscarves like a flag.

Given that approach, one rarely considers the obvious, i.e., the possibility that Muslim women wear their headscarves in voluntary compliance to God's will, submitting not to fathers or brothers but to Allah. This is quite obviously the case for Western women who have embraced Islam, particularly young American students, yet this fact does not seem to sink in. Many forget that wearing a headscarf can be an act of emancipation in itself, as it serves efficiently to uphold and defend the dignity of women in a sexist environment. One of the 10,000 British women who have converted to Islam over the last decade said, "Everything the feminist movement is aiming for, except lesbianism and abortion, we've got".[25] In this sense, the "veil" really does represent a modern counter-cultural identity, and not a mere throwback to tradition.[26] What one person considers an act of oppression, is a manifestation of personal dignity in the eyes of the other.

The Islamic approach in this context may also be misunderstood because of the conviction that sexual mores, like any kind of ethical behavior, exclusively depend on intentions, i.e., inner consent. In other words: just as morality cannot be assured by locking up a virgin girl in her chamber, so a headscarf does not necessarily do any good. What is needed here, goes the argument, is educating her to be true to herself as well as opening her eyes to the consequences of sexual license.

Of course, Islam, too, evaluates actions not in themselves but according to the intentions (*niya*) linked with them;[27] hence Muslims also know that morality cannot be force-fed. And yet, Islam is also realistic enough to know that opportunity makes a thief, and that inappropriate behavior can be easily provoked by outside circumstances (alcohol, provocative nudity, being alone with the other sex) – or, conversely, more readily precluded. Statistics prove that the Muslims are right in this respect: currently one in 10 American girls between 15 and 19 years goes through childbirth or abortion. Over 15 percent of all American women under 19 have been pregnant at least once.[28] It seems a safe bet that these statistics would look quite different if Islamic dress were the norm in the USA. In this respect, Islam is not only wise to the realities of life, but it also presents itself with "bold pragmatism" (Jeffrey Lang).

This is not ultimate pragmatism, but revolves around the question: what are the invariable, minimum standards for decent Islamic dress as established by divine revelation? Is the headscarf a must – or a recommendation? Is it based on the *sunnah* or the Qur'an, or both? As we discuss this, it is worthwhile keeping in mind that Islam, when dealing with something as mundane as clothing, is not concerned with external trappings, but rather with the problem of harnessing within marriage the elemental power of sexuality and the protection of this essential institution against assault. This is why the Qur'an's call for modesty is addressed equally to both sexes. Everybody knows that men can virtually undress women by looking at them alone, especially when inspired by shapely "curves". This is precisely why both Muslim men (24: 30) and Muslim women (24: 31) are to refrain from staring and ogling. Men must cover their body's sexual "aura" [29] (from navel to knee), much as women have to cover theirs, which is, of course, quite a bit longer.

With this purpose in mind Surah al-Ahzab (33:59) states: "*O Prophet! Tell your wives and your daughters as well as all believing women that they should draw over themselves some of their outer garments (min jalabibihinna); this will help to assure that they will be recognized (as decent women) and not be molested.*" Surah an-Nur (24: 31), gets more specific: "*And tell the believing women to lower their gaze and guard their private parts and not to display their charms (zina-tahunna) beyond what may (decently) appear thereof (illa ma zahara minha); so let them draw their shawls (khumur, sing. khimar) over their bosoms and not display their beauty except to their husbands (. . .) and that they should not adopt a gait which draws attention to their hidden charms ...*"

There are no other Qur'anic rules for dress.

Reflections on female head coverings (turban, headscarf, shawls, and the like) depend on what is to be understood as "outer garment" or "shawl". The general consensus is that at least "shawl" (*khimar*) denotes a broad cloth which Middle Eastern women for practical reasons used to wear over their heads (as women in Greece, Sicily, and parts of Spain do to this very day), as protection not from men but from sun, wind, and dust.

For that reason, Muhammad Asad, in his famous annotated English translation of the Qur'an, expressed the opinion that Verse 24: 31 was not concerned with covering women's hair (which in those days they did anyway) but with concealing their breasts (easily exposed at the time). For him that made sense because hair, contrary to a woman's breasts, constituted neither a primary nor a secondary sexual characteristic and thus was rather asexual.[30]

Based on this observation, Asad concluded that the Islamic guidelines for women's dress were to derive from the flexible formula in Verse 33: 59, according to which a woman can show everything that ordinarily can "decently appear." What must be covered beyond a woman's primary and secondary sexual characteristics, therefore, depends on the prevailing conditions of any given civilization. Propriety and decency, within those limits, are not necessarily constant values.[31] In practical terms, that means a woman must cover her hair if circumstances demand, rather than such covering being an absolute norm.

As far as I can see, Asad's position in that regard has met few endorsements, so far. Among Muslim legal scholars, he has been fully supported primarily by Prof. Fathi Osman (Los Angeles), but also by Dr. Tedjini Haddam, Algerian director of the Great Mosque in Paris; by Hamza Kaidi,[32] and in India by Asghar Engineer. Osman, too, does not find in Verse 24: 31 any strict female dress code, but rather a model which is to be enforced according to prevailing local customs and conditions. After all, "these charms have not been indicated in detail, and such details may not be possible or suitable for a general permanent law because of differences and changes in social custom from time to time and from place to place."[33]

In an interview with *Le Monde* printed October 24, 1989, Haddam said, "Islam recommends that a woman dress modestly, especially that she cover her most attractive features .... The implementation of these recommendations depends on the respective social environment." In turn, Engineer underlines that chastity is the absolute norm, while the journey to it, including the form of veiling (*purdah*), remains contextual. While chastity is an indispensable value, veiling may well assume different forms.

To Asad's initiatives, Jeffrey Lang reacted more cautiously and with more circumspection. For him, Asad runs the risk of adapting Islam to social circumstances, rather than having Islam change society. He criticizes Asad's logic for failing to draw a clear line indicating the ultimate limit of contextual flexibility.[34] In other words: once a woman's hair is allowed to show, what about her arms and legs, and how far up?

If one follows Asad's and Osman's lines of argument, what the sunnah has to say regarding Verse 24: 31 is perforce immaterial, of mere historical interest, relevant only for Arab society of the 7th century. If, on the other hand, one remains unconvinced, one must take into account that the Prophet made Verse 24: 31 considerably more   concrete. This is recorded in a *hadith* probably known to all Muslims, as told by 'A'isha and transmitted by Abu Dawud[35]: once when Asma bint Abu Bakr was improperly dressed, through mere gesturing, without uttering a single word, Muhammad indicated to her what a Muslima is allowed to show in public: her face, hands, and feet. It goes without saying that those parts of the female body that are to be covered must not be emphasized either by tight, figure-hugging clothing like mini-sweaters, or wet jeans worn to dry.

That discussions, nevertheless, continue has to do with the fact that the Prophet delivered his message non-verbally. Could it be then that he did not indicate the minimum, but rather the maximum to be concealed? Is this a normative, binding *hadith* or only a recommendation? Hassan al-Turabi seems to opt for the latter; for him, the *sunnah* gives "moral exhortations of how men and women are supposed to dress, not articles of law."[36]

At any rate, the ancient custom of veiling, concealing the face altogether, did not originate in the Islamic world, but among refined ladies of Byzantium and Persia, as a way of emphasizing superior social status. While veiling has infiltrated the Muslim world as well, it is by no means Islamically justified. As a universally binding norm, it can definitely not be deduced from the so-called Verse of the veil (*Ayat al-Hijab*, 33: 53),[37] In fact, hiding one's face was an unusual thing to do in the beginnings of Islam[38] and, while on pilgrimage, in accordance with tradition, Muslim women are definitely not allowed to cover their faces.

The instructions contained in Surah al-Ahzab (33: 53) exclusively concerned the Prophet's residence and his wives (*umm al-mu' minin*), with whom no other woman should seek to compete, even in piety. The verse mandated a strict separation between the private quarters of the Prophet and the official ones where public business was conducted. The purpose was to protect the private sphere of the Prophet's family from an avalanche of petitioners and other visitors.[39] For that purpose, a curtain (*hijab*) was employed from behind which the Prophet's wives could listen to petitions whenever any were brought before them. Verse 33 of the same Surah thus admonished them: "*And stay in your houses, and do not display yourselves as during the former times of ignorance (jahiliyyah).*"

With all this in mind, it is nothing less than an arbitrary violation of the Qur'anic rights of Muslim women to use such passages as justification and excuse for the domestic seclusion of contemporary Muslim women, unduly restricting their legitimate outdoor activities and wrapping them up from head to toe, like mummies. Thank God, at least the facial veil is gradually disappearing, also in Saudi Arabia. One can only hope that it will soon be gone for good.

The veil may yet disappear faster than its cultural corollary, the excessive public separation of the sexes which certain Islamic movements have been practicing again of late. Hassan al-Turabi is campaigning against this practice by pointing to the activism and initiative displayed by the Prophet's wives. Examples abound: Khadidja, first wife of the Prophet, with whom he lived in monogamy for 23 years, was a successful business woman, involved in international import-and-export trading. It was she, not he, who proposed marriage. The public activities of his wife 'A'isha, from today's perspective, were truly astonishing. Fatima bint al-Khattab, sister of the 2nd Caliph 'Umar, converted to Islam before he did, and without asking his permission. Even the first martyr in Islamic history was a woman: Sumayyah bint Khubbat. Umm Kulthum fled from Makkah to Madinah, by herself, covering singly this dangerous stretch of 250 miles

At the beginning of the Islamic era, women evidently participated in public gatherings and in all prayers conducted in the Prophet's Mosque in al-Madinah, just as they have always fulfilled all the rites of *hajj* – pilgrimage, then and now. The Prophet himself visited Muslim women frequently and even took his midday nap at their houses.[40]

Based on all this, Hassan al-Turabi concludes that Islam does not demand a complete segregation of the sexes. Housewives in particular, he suggests, could receive, serve, and socially entertain their husband's guests together with him, rather than merely cooking for them behind closed doors. Nor does he see anything wrong with men and women innocently shaking hands on such occasions where this is the prevailing custom and refusal might seem an unfriendly act.[41]

On the whole al-Turabi finds that "women suffer the gravest injustice at the hands of society in general through segregation and isolation."[42] He considers the liberation of Islamic women not as an inevitable side effect of Islamic renewal and revival, but as their precondition. After extensive research into the Prophetic traditions (*ahadith*) normally quoted on this matter, Jeffrey Lang also arrived at the conclusion that the widely practiced segregation of the sexes was in clear contradiction of the guidelines and principles of the Qur'an. The way this segregation is currently handled in the U.S. would make many a teenage Muslim girl feel not under protection, but under house arrest. The issue was not to exchange sex segregation for promiscuity, but to find a reasonable middle road.[43]

Fathi Osman and al-Turabi agree that Muslim women are permitted to work outside the home and hold public office. If they so wish, they could get actively involved in politics, vote in elections, run for office, enlist as soldiers, serve as members of parliament, judges and cabinet secretaries. Muslim husbands are expected to respect their wives' right to work. As domestic partner (*zawj*) they should also share household chores.[44]

This leads us to the last remaining particularities of Islamic law in as much as it affects women: divorce, inheritance, and civil procedure. What comes across as most offensive here is the legal fact that a Muslim husband can unilaterally divorce his wife, by simply pronouncing the divorce formula (*talaq*) thrice, without involving any court of law (2: 229). A married woman, however, normally has to go to court if she is the one seeking divorce (*khul*), unless in their marriage contract her husband had delegated to her the right to unilateral divorce. However, any divorce – by him or by her – ought to be preceded by family arbitration (4: 35). It is good to know that the simplified Islamic process of divorces does not seem to affect their frequency. In fact, Muslim marriages are more stable than Western marriages in our time.

Although Western-style divorce causes exorbitant legal fees and ruinous alimony obligations, its rate is steadily increasing. In Germany, the number of divorces reached a new high in 1997, with a 7% increase over the previous year. Accordingly, over the past 25 years, on an average, every third German marriage ends after barely six years.

The differences between the Western and the Islamic law of divorce are partially due to the different economic consequences of divorce here and there. Under Islamic law, divorce does not lead to a division of the couple's common property. Rather, in all cases, guilty or not, a divorced wife is allowed to hold on, not only to all assets brought into the family, but also to the bridal gift (*mahr*) negotiated before the wedding, no matter how high, and no matter how long the marriage lasted (2: 229, 2nd sentence.) It would, therefore, be highly unequitable if women could resort to unilateral divorce, perhaps semi-professionally collecting one bridal gift after the other. In this light it is not an undue burden that wives, when suing for divorce, must justify their plea in court. Wives can favorably influence the Islamic divorce law by stipulating, in the obligatory wedding contract, the specific reasons for divorce, in which event she can terminate her marriage. In women's favor as well, proposals are under way (already enacted in some Muslim countries) to curb divorces unilaterally pronounced by husbands (*talaq*), by linking this privilege as well to court proceedings – if not for judicial decision, at least for some form of registration or confirmation to reduce abuse.[45]

Under Western scrutiny is also the alleged discrimination of Muslim women under the Islamic law of inheritance, because according to *Surah an-Nisa* (4: 11), a daughter is entitled to only half of her brother's share. Nevertheless, she may yet have the better end of the bargain here since – in contrast to her brother(s) – she is under no financial obligation whatsoever for the upkeep of the family. Here, again, unequal rights correspond to unequal obligations.[46]

Finally, it causes Western people some headache that in court where one male witness would suffice, two female witnesses are required. This is indeed the rule laid down in the 9th sentence of *Surah al-Baqara* (2: 282) for civil law suits dealing with contractual arrangements on credit. Throughout history, *macho* Muslim lawyers have tried their hand at rationalizing of this rule, alas, mostly in an exceedingly unflattering manner for women.[47] A particularly embarrassing attempt was the insinuation that women's competence as witnesses – overly emotional creatures as they are, aren't they? – could be severely impaired during menstruation, after birth, or during menopause. As if men were always in top form, clear headed, and devoid of passions ....

To resolve the question, one has to notice that the Qur'an does not limit women's testimony in criminal cases, i.e., in suits where life or death may be at stake, but only in specific disputes over loan transactions – and not in any other case, even though there are altogether eight Qur'anic passages dealing with testimony and statements under oath.[48] If women's testimony was inherently unreliable, shouldn't the Qur'an rather demand two female witnesses (for one male one) in criminal cases? Evidently, the Qur'an correctly assumed that women at the time of revelation usually were ignorant in matters of finance. For that reason then, Verse 2: 282 ensured the best legal protection available, while not ruling out that improved education of women and their integration into the economic process would enable them to acquire expertise (and full testimonial competence) in this field as well.

Add to this that the great men who assiduously recorded the Prophet's works and words – al-Bukhari, Muslim, Abu Dawud, at Tirmidhi, Ibn Madja, an-Nisai – never objected to stories related by one Muslim lady alone, like hundreds of *ahadith* singly reported by 'A'isha.[49]

One can therefore confidently conclude with Fathi Osman and Jeffrey Lang that a woman's testimony is equal to a man's, except in lawsuits involving commerce and finance, unless she has relevant expertise or professional knowledge.[50] A judge may of course call up several male witnesses, too, until he is satisfied with the quality of their testimony, or reject it all.

THE common denominator of this chapter on Women in Islam can be summed up in the basic Muslim notion that women and men – surprise, surprise! – belong to two different genders marked by deep-rooted differences as well as by essential similarities. Islam views the non-identity of the sexes as a basic principle of the entire creation.[52] For Muslims, equality of rights and duties is a must where men and women are truly alike. But where the sexes are different from each other, it is not unjust to set up rules and regulations reflecting that difference. In doing so, Muslims see themselves in harmony with nature and, like Tango dancers, cherish the blissful polarity of the sexes.[52] As suggested by Hassan al-Turabi, as a rule of thumb, equal treatment of women should be assumed in all respects unless unequivocally determined otherwise in Qur'an or *sunnah*, or compelled by biological differences. Only this, then, would justify rules differentiating between the two sexes.[53]

In such an approach one cannot see any major difference to Western legal practice since Western laws, too, do accommodate gender-related differences, for instance when it comes to the military draft or pregnancy leave.

The few remaining differences – polygyny (as a kind of legal safeguard for all eventualities), divorce procedures, and rules of inheritance – do not, at any rate, play much of a role in the everyday life of Muslims in the West, subject as they are not to Islamic but to local law.

In order to enlist an uncontroversial witness, I would finally like to quote Father Michel Lelong, from his book *Si Dieu l'avait volu* (*If God had so wished*), whose title alludes to Verse 5: 48. As first-hand observer, he compares the quality of life of French and Tunisian women, arriving at the following conclusion: "Here, one frequently runs into so-called liberated women. But sometimes they are bent down by a new slavery which is more subtle, but no less pernicious." He believes those women to be prisoners of a new set of constraints: "Conformism, fashion, publicity, job, or even their cigarette." Lelong compares this to his experience of the "amazing freedom realized by the Muslim woman,"[54] and Michel Houellebecq seconds him with this succinct assessment: "What commonly has been referred to as women's liberation was more of a convenience for men, giving them a chance to multiply their opportunities for sexual encounters."[55]

What remains is the bottomline question: how will the West eventually deal with Muslim women who, out of their own free will, decide to follow the majority opinion which believes that covering hair and body is a religious obligation? The only legal principle that should pertain here is the constitutionally and internationally established fundamental right called "freedom of religion." Nobody, no court of law and least of all government bureaucrats should be so presumptuous as to decide in her place for a Muslima whether or not she is really required to cover her hair or not. Preempting her own decision would be a serious infringement of her freedom of religion. The religion of an individual is to be respected even if it is just his or her own personal, entirely private philosophy and view.

One of the next chapters, *Islam in the USA*, shows that America turned this freedom into reality, once again setting an example for Europe as to the true meaning of democratic freedoms. In the final analysis, the headscarf is not even a legal issue but, in the form of headscarf phobia and hysteria, a political one. The basic question is, therefore, whether old Europe and young America are willing to tolerate a new religion, and the "otherness" of its followers, or whether they seek to exclude Islam from their commitment to religious tolerance. The Bill of Rights, is it meant even for Muslims . . .?

Notes

1.   Rolf Degen, "Der kleine Unterschied beim Hören" (The small difference in hearing), in: *Frankfurter Allgemeine Zeitung*, 10 December 1998, p. N 2.

2. Consider for instance the uncritical reception of the *hadith* which supposedly claimed that most of the inhabitants of hell were women (an-Nawawi, no. 488).

3. When the newly elected representative of the Islamic Refah Party, Merve Kavakci, had the temerity to enter the Turkish National Assembly with her hair covered, she provoked such a ringing outcry among the laicist Turkish media that one was led to believe that this small gesture might destabilize a secular State which, after all, is supported by 80 percent of the voters. German TV documented, in the fall of 1998, how Turkish medical students in Istanbul were physically prevented from taking their final exams for wearing head-

4. Kausar, p. 150 f.

5. Muhammad Qutb, p. 115.

6. Qasim Amin, p. 34, 88.

7. al-Turabi (1991), p. 35, 38, 43.

8. Gardet, p. 373.

9. Lang (1997), p. 116.

10. Osman (*Human Rights*, 1996), p. 15.

11. Quoted in Krämer, p. 49.

12. al-Turabi (1992), p.15.

13. Garaudy, *Chartre de Séville*, p. 24.

14. Mernissi, p. 86, 145-59.

15. Lang (1995) calls monogamy "preferable"; cf. Lemu, p. 27; for Muhammad Qutb, p. 106, monogamy is a "bedrock principle"; for Gadet, p. 371, monogamy is "the rule"; according to Pinn, p. 72, the Qur'an essentially rejects polygyny.

16. Qasim Amin, p. 113, has indeed the temerity to pretend: "And God speaks (Qur'an 4: 3): '*Marry women of your choice, two, or three, or four!*' " - as simple as that.

17. Kaldi, "Le Coran à l'Usage des Femmes", in: *Afrique Magazine*, no. 113, Paris 1994, S. 63.

18. In my edition of Max Henning's German translation I have changed his version of 4: 34 from "the men are superior to the women" to "The men assume responsibility for the women."

19 Osman (1997), p. 815.

20 Osman (*Human Rights*, 1996), p. 16.

21. Lang (1995), p. 147f.; about 4:34, see p. 153.

22. Cf. an-Nawawi, no. 276-279. This is not to say that wife battering is absent among Muslims but it certainly is not more prominent than in Western society.

23. The Sheik al-Azhar, Muhammad al-Tantawi, took the position that female circumcision was not a religious matter, but a matter for doctors and the law (*Frankfurter Allgemeine Zeitung*, Nov. 12, 1998). In a conversation I had with him in July, 1997, I questioned this attitude for leaving the impression that the *Shar'iah* could be silent on such a crucial moral question. 24: 60.

24. 24: 60

25. Cf. *Islamic Future*, vol. 13, no. 69, Riyadh 1997, p. 2.

26. Pinn, pp. 67, 69; according to Holt, p. 65, Islamic dress plays a particularly significant role among Palestinian women: hope for a liberation from Israel, but also from family constraints. The Islamic garment invests them with both meaning and dignity.

27. *al-Bukhari*, vol. 8, no. 680, and vol. 9, no. 73 and 85.

28. Kausar, p. 155.

29. *Aura* (derived from the verb *wara/yari* = trying to keep secret) has the approximate meaning of "that which had better be concealed." Cf. Hans Wehr, p. 1329.

30. Asad (*The Message*, 1980), p. 53, footnote 38 regarding 24: 31.

31. Ibid., p. 538, footnote 37 regarding 24:31.

32. Kaidi, op.cit. (see above, footnote 17), p. 63.

33. Osman (1997), p. 855, 857.

34. Lang (1995), p. 172 ff., especially p. 175.

35 Abu Dawud, Sunan, *Hadith* no. 4092.

36. al-Turabi (1991), p. 23; also (1992), p. 36.

37. al-Turabi (1991), p. 26; also (1992), p. 36; Lang (1997), p. 115; Osman (1997), p. 728; only the ultra-conservative World Association of Muslim Youth (WAMY) continues to demand covering women head-to-toe. Cf. "The Significance of the Hijab", In: *Islamic Future*, vol. 13, no. 69, Riyadh 1997, p. 2.

38. Lang (1995), p. 179.

39. See al-Bukhari's *Hadith* no. 6315 for a report on the historical events surrounding the revelation of the Ayat al-Hijab. Lang (1995), p. 180, reminds us that 'A'isha rejected any accusation of having violated 33:33 during the Battle of the Camel.

40. al-Turabi (1991), pp. 24 f., with many examples.

41. Ibid., pp. 23, 27.

42. Ibid., p. 40.
43. Lang (1995), p.181.
44. Osman (*Human Rights*, 1996), p. 16 f.; Osman (1997) p. 728 f.; al-Turabi (1992), p. 47 f.
45. Osman (1997), p. 823.
46. By way of testament, Muslims can dispose of one-third of their possessions, however not in favor of legal heirs. (Muslim, *Sahih*, no. 3991-4000.)
47. Shamshad M Khan, *Why Two Women Witnesses?*, Ta-Ha-Publishers: London 1993, p.6.
48. Lang (1995), pp.165 f.
49. Kabbani only contains historical records handed down by women.
50. Osman (*Human Rights*, 1996), p. 17; Osman (1997), pp. 737, 883, Lang (1995), p. 166 f.
51. Pinn, p. 74.
52. In their book on Tango, Ralf Satori and Petra Steidl celebrate the creative tension between the two sexes more than just about anybody else. This may be anachronistic, and is yet so necessary in our time.
53. al-Turabi (1991), p. 11.
54. Lelong, p. 124.
55. Houellebecq, p. 68.

CHAPTER EIGHT

Why Muhammad?

This religion will remain until the Hour comes...
(Muslim, Sahih, *Hadith* No. 4.717)

W e have discussed three demands the West is addressing to Islam – human rights, democracy and the status of women. Now it is time to bring up three demands the Islamic world is addressing to the West. Islam being foremost a religion, and religion being the other, transcendental dimension of this world, it seems only fitting to begin with two theological wishes entertained by Muslims: acknowledgement of Muhammad and de-divinization of Jesus. This is to be followed up with a more mundane demand: to fight racism more effectively.

GOD'S designs are inscrutable. Nevertheless, it seems quite appropriate not only for Christians, but also for Muslims – especially in the homeland of George Wilhelm Friedrich Hegel – to ponder over the question as to why Allah let history take the course it did. Christians might ponder the significance of the fact that Jesus was an Aramaic-speaking Jew born in the Middle East, on the fringes of the Roman Empire. Muslims are asking similar questions – Why is it that the unlettered Muhammad, of all people, born in 7th century Arabia, of all places, was picked from obscurity by God to receive and deliver one more divine revelation – the final and universal one – and that in Arabic, of all languages?

God's ways are mysterious indeed. Therefore, replies to questions such as these will remain purely speculative. But it is not a sacrilege at least to try one's mind at possible answers. Quite to the contrary, Allah in the Qur'an constantly challenges the faithful to use their intellects. (It is, by the way, the only Holy Script to do so.)

In my opinion there are several good reasons why Allah picked none other than an Arabic prophet for His purposes. Just think of geography. In the 7th century CE, Arabia found itself far beyond the immediate sphere of influence of the two dominant regional powers, the Byzantine and Persian Empires, although the latter had reached out into the Yemen. The Christian (East-) Roman Empire of Heraclius I was at war with the Sassanide Empire of Shah Khosrau II Parwiz, where the dualistic Farsi religion – Zoroastrianism and Mazdaism respectively – was experiencing, a new prime. If Islam had appeared in a region under direct Byzantine or Persian control – as a new, nation-building religion with an anti-monarchist bend – it would have been recognized as a threat to the dominant state religions and crushed right away in both empires. Only in the power vacuum of the Arabian peninsula, in the remote Hijaz area, was it possible for Islam to consolidate into a new ideological state before either of the two regional powers could even think of intervening. When, in 628, Muhammad attracted attention by inviting all surrounding rulers to accept Islam, it was already too late.

However, powerless or not, Arabia at that time was the geostrategic center of the entire known world, almost equidistant to Morocco and England, India and China. This fact would prove enormously auspicious for the following expansion of Islam.

There is also a plausible explanation for revealing the Qur'an in Arabic. The predominant *linguae francae* of that period – Latin, Farsi, Greek, and Hebrew – had served as media of previous revelations. Consequently, they had been so closely associated with the doctrinal concepts of Judaism, Christianity, and Zoroastrianism that the paradigm shift triggered by the Qur'an required a language which was still pure, theologically and philosophically. This is still of utmost importance: whenever Orientalists translate the Qur'an, even with the best of intentions, they cannot help projecting into it Christian notions, simply by using terminology of Christian origin (like logos, Holy Spirit, redemption, or Holy War). Their languages alone make them prisoners of their Christian heritage.

It is also noteworthy that the Arabic spoken in Makkah by the local tribe of Quraysh had developed by the 7th century into a very sophisti-cated language, capable of conveying anything that words can convey and mean. Moreover, the language communicates even the most abstract of messages very clearly. To fully appreciate this, one has to study this intellectual language in more depth. Here, a few examples should suffice:

Arabic can make temporally indeterminate statements (corresponding to our clumsy saying "it was, is, and will be"). Furthermore, future events whose coming appears certain can be expressed in the past tense (being as good as having happened). Finally, every Arabic verb can be put into eight different modalities, whether or not the resulting meaning is possible in the real world. This quality makes the Arabic language particularly apt to serve speculative philosophy and hypothetical scientific thinking.

Another significant aspect was the propitious timing of the Qur'anic revelation: Since the 6th century, it had become increasingly clear that neither Christianity nor the Jewish diaspora, scattered as it was all over the world, could muster the insight and determination necessary to correct the distortions of their religions. The Jewish tribes had developed the highly problematic notion of being singled out and uniquely privileged as God's "chosen people." It was equally problematic that, for their part, large segments of Christianity, in 325 in Nicaea, had embraced the dogma of Jesus' divine nature. Thus, before Muhammad entered the world scene, both originally monotheistic world religions had completely remodeled the divine revelations they once had received, without any prospect for reform. Deeply anchored in this (now) "orthodox" Christianity was, in particular, the Byzantine superpower which dominated the Mediterranean, with Emperor Justinian I success-fully implementing "*Caesaropapism*", the Byzantine version of absolute theo-monarchism. Typical for the overall consolidation of State power and State religion was the *Codex Juris Civilis*, a codification of Roman law, in 534, which cemented Western jurisprudence for a millennium.

CODIFIED and cemented, too, was a new Christology.[1] The Jewish Christians had viewed Jesus as a great prophet, out to reform Judaism – this in accordance with the Qur'anic assertion that "*Christ, the son of Mary, was no more than a messenger*" (5: 75). Jesus, after all, had never identified himself with God, never saying "I" when referring to Him.

Nor did early Christians hint at what would later become the dogma of the Trinity, not even Paul, Christianity's real founding father. That is no surprise. The supposedly relevant passage in the First Epistle of John (5, 7), "for there are three that bear record in heaven, the Father, the Word, and the Holy Ghost, and these three are one," only surfaced in Spain, as late as 380 CE, in a new copy of the New Testament. By now, this verse (along with the chapter about the adulterous woman in the Gospel according to John) has been discovered a forgery.[2] In my Catholic edition of the New Testament (authorized by the Bishop of Rottenburg on March 27, 1940), the passage in question is bracketed off and annotated with a scientifically amusing footnote, maintaining that this verse "while substantially correct, is a late addition". Added for being correct, or correct for being added? That is the question.

It is undeniably true that the majority of bishops of the early 4th century, in both the Christian East and West, still more or less shared the belief of Arius (ca.260-336), the Alexandrian priest who taught that Jesus ranked above mankind for having been created directly by God – but was neither identical with God, nor possessing eternal life. Indeed, to believe otherwise would have been considered heresy before the Nicene Creed was adopted in 325.

In 4th century Constantinople, it had become increasingly popular to debate the four possible conceptions of the nature of Jesus. It was argued that Jesus might be:
- only God: the one-nature-doctrine of the Monophysites, embraced by Copts and Armenians to this very day;
- only human: the prevailing opposite one-nature doctrine held by Jewish Christians and Arians;
- both God and human, separately: the view of Nestorians, followers of Nestorius (d. 451)
- both God and human, consubstantially: dogma beginning to emerge as new orthodoxy in the 4th/5th century

For the history of ideas, the second of these views turned out to have the most lasting impact. It coalesced into Islam and became virulent in the contemporary intra-Christian debate on the role and status of Jesus.

In any case, Christian orthodoxy grew primarily out of rejecting the teachings of Arius who had asserted that "Son of God" could be understood only as a metaphor. For him, while Jesus was not true God, God had created him from nothing (*ex nihilo*). This, and this alone, was Jesus' privileged status. (The next chapter will show that this sounds much like definitions by the contemporary Catholic theologian Hans Küng.)

A fateful trigger for the tragic development of official Christology was the First Ecumenical Council which convened in Nicaea from June 19 to August 25, 325. In opposition to Arianism, the Council established the divine nature of Jesus with the formula that Christ was "of the essence of the Father", i.e., "consubstantial" with God, not created but begotten by Him. It should ring a bell that the vocabulary used for attributing divine nature to Jesus – the Greek *homousios* corresponding to the Latin *consubstantialis* – was a term taken from Gnostic philosophy.

The Nicene Creed did not prevent Arianism from temporarily – from 337-361 – becoming the official Byzantine State religion and from having a strong impact on the Christian beliefs of the Germanic tribes. But then, beginning in the year 451 with the Fourth Ecumenical Council in Chalcedon (Üsküdar), the Nicene Creed gradually took hold after all. This time, the Church condemned the monophysitic notion that Jesus was only God (in human form), replacing it with the hypothesis of a personal union (hypostatic union) of God and Jesus. Both are present in Jesus, "neither mixed nor separated." This paradox, paradoxical as it may sound, became, and remained, a constituent part of the Catholic and Protestant articles of faith.

In the meantime, an even newer dogma developed, inspired by the triadic ideas of Alexandrian Neoplatonism and Egyptian mythology. This time, the duality of God and Jesus was extended into a trinity by adding the "Holy Spirit" as a third divine person within the Christian deity. Under the sway of a then fashionable theology of the spirit, the Second Ecumenical Council of Constantinople in 381 proceeded to a personification and deification of the term logos (nominally: "word"). In the process, Hellenism massively entered Christianity and through Trinity acquired a dogmatic foothold. Pinpointing in the New Testament the third divine person, after the fact, was a cinch: the word "spirit", formerly understood as the spirit of God (spiritus) or divine inspiration simply had to be capitalized and personified as "Holy Spirit."

Today we know that the first ecumenical council in Nicaea (Nicaea I) was also the most crucial one in the entire Church history, up to and including the 22nd Ecumenical Council (Vatican II) in the last century. Astonishingly, this first and single most important council was convened not by the Pope, the Bishop of Rome, but by Emperor Constantine the Great, at the time an unbaptized heathen (and theological nobody). The council was not convened in the Cathedral of Nicaea, but in his nearby imperial summer residence. The emperor also refused to let a man of the Church, like Athanasius, preside over the proceedings. Instead, he assumed these delicate duties himself, and the Pope was nowhere to be seen. Even the fateful formula asserting the consubstantiality of Jesus and God was proposed by the emperor, not because of any deep interest in religion, but because he needed domestic peace after years of querulous religious nitpicking. Constantine's formula, asserting Jesus' dual nature as both man and God, for the emperor was more plausible than absurd. History records that time and again the Roman emperors promoted themselves to divine ranks.

It is only a short way from Istanbul to Iznik, the former Nicaea. Whenever I travel to this city I shudder to think of the dire consequences that were to come out of the events in 325. If only there had been a serious debate! But the Nicene Creed had been muscled through, facilitated by the incredible fact that among the 225 prelates and bishops present only five came from Western (mainly Arian) Christianity - among them one single Visigothic bishop, from Cordoba. As a consequence, the most momentous dogma of Christendom mainly emerged from a rather secular power struggle, and not out of a close reading – or exegesis – of the New Testament.

In the wake of Nicaea, each and every writing contradicting the Council was destroyed. Thus the preceding Christology of both the Jewish Christians and the Aryans got purged from Christian memory. Jesus' ties to Judaism were cut off. What had begun with Paul's exemption of Heathen Christians from circumcision under Mosaic law now turned into a clean theological break with Semitic monotheism. The Christians had been promised redemption, but what really came was the Church – *Sancta Ecclesia*. From this point onwards, Christians considered Judaism as a mere stepping stone towards Christianity, while the Jews viewed the Christian creed as a heresy.

A correction of these fateful decisions, based alone on Christian introspection and self-criticism, was inconceivable for centuries to come. On the contrary: extreme as it was, over the following centuries the Nicene Creed had to be defended against even more exaggerated Christological speculations. The impulse for the restoration of Abraham's uncompromising monotheism could, therefore, only come from without: from Arabia, from an Arab prophet who would not be an innovator but a restorer of the religion of Abraham, the religion of Moses, and the religion of Jesus – faith in the one and only God.

This convincingly explains the time, place, and message of Muhammad, whom the Qur'an charged to clarify: "I am no innovator among the prophets .... " (46: 9). Muhammad came as the last one of all prophets because at issue was no more, and no less, than the restoration of Abraham's monotheism, the natural religion (*religio naturalis*) in harmony with human nature *(fitra)*. In detail, Muhammad therefore taught but the following essentials:

- there is but one God, and He is both transcendent and immanent.
- God is concerned with all of is His creation, alike.
- He revealed Himself both in His book and in nature.
- it is man's privilege and duty to dedicate his life to God and submit it to His commands.
- there will be a Last Judgement and life after death.

In its unconditional rejection of incarnation and trinity, 900 years before Martin Luther, Islam represents the first significant attempt to reform Christianity. For 1400 lunar years now, there has not been a similar attempt at challenging the cornerstone of orthodox Christianity by confronting its Christology with the Qur'anic one, for example:

- Jesus was created , like Adam, and not begotten (3 :47, 59; 23: 91; 112: 3), but born of a virgin (3: 47);
- sent to confirm and revive previous revelations (3: 50) as a miracle-working (5: 110) prophet following other prophets before him (2: 136; 3: 84; 6: 85);
- but no divine person within a Trinity (4:171; 5: 72 f.; 9: 30; 19:35);
- nor did he die on the cross (4: 157 f.).

With the exception of the last two points, it is readily apparent that Muslims are defending the most orthodox of all Christologies, i.e., that of the original Jewish Christians.

Regarding the two controversial points, the second-most recited surah after *al-Fatiha* is *Surah al Ikhlas* (112) which, according to the Prophet Muhammad, despite its brevity comprises one third of the entire Qur'an.[3] *Al-Ikhlas* (Sincerity) is no less than a laconic and unequivocal rejection of the Nicene Creed:

Say: "He is Allah, the One and Only;
Allah, the Eternal, Absolute;
He does not beget, nor is He begotten;
And there is none like Him."

To say that God has taken a son is "a thing most monstrous", as the Qur'an puts it (18: 4 f.; 19: 88 f.), and a fact which over the past 250 years has dawned upon many people in the Christian World. Søren Kierkegaard arguably cut to the quick more sharply than others – "Essentially the fundamental misfortune of Christendom is Christianity itself, the preaching of God as man." This necessarily dissolves "the qualitative difference between God and man in pantheism." The Dane had the temerity to state: "The dogma of God-as-man has made Christianity saucy ....; they now address God informally, as a family member."[4]

The Qur'an's rejection of the Trinity is no less severe. *Surah an-Nisa* (4: 171) pleads: "*O People of the Book! Commit no excesses in your religion and say of Allah nothing but the truth. Jesus Christ, the son of Mary, was [no more than] a Messenger of Allah and His word, which He bestowed on Mary, and a spirit from Him. So believe in Allah and His Messenger. Do not say "Three". Desist, that will be better for you. For Allah is One God. Far exalted is He above having a son (...).*"

Muslims cannot help being amazed at how much, and in which detail, Christians profess to know about God, His nature and His designs. Yet, at the same time, they seem to shield Trinity from rational inquiry by presenting it as an inscrutable mystery. How is this compatible, for instance, with theorizing nevertheless that the three divine persons – Father, Son, and Holy Spirit – have distinguishing properties in their relationship to each other (*opera ad intra*), while acting externally in divine unity (*opera ad extra*).[5]

The same goes for conjecturing the opposite: denying an "ontological Trinity", but accepting the existence of a "revealed Trinity". From this perspective, the inter-personal relationship of Father, Son, and Holy Spirit remains an impenetrable enigma. However, when God acts within His creation, the three personalities of Trinity can be discerned, even though they proceed from one and the same principle.[6]

The crowning achievement in Trinity acrobatics without net may well belongs to Cardinal Nikolaus von Kues (d.1464), the German mystic who went so far as to postulate that intellectually God cannot even be conceived except in Trinitarian terms, "as the intelligent way of being God" (Kurt Flasch). The cardinal flatly stated: "God must be of trinity, if He is the intelligent principle of the world, if He is self-aware, and if He is Love."[7]

Regarding the second controversial point – crucifixion – one should first of all realize that it became dogmatically pivotal for Christianity only with and through Paul. His theory of original sin called for divine redemption; his theory of divine redemption called for sacrificial death; and his theory of sacrificial death called for an interpretation of Jesus' crucifixion as divine deliverance – ideas all of which are utterly incompatible with the Islamic image of Allah. About crucifixion the Qur'an informs us:

"As to their (boastful) saying, 'We killed Jesus Christ, the son of Mary, the Messenger of Allah'. But they neither killed nor crucified him. So it was only made to appear to them. And those whose views differ therein are full of doubts. They have no certain knowledge They follow nothing but conjecture. For surely they did not kill him, but Allah raised him up unto Himself (...)." (4: 157 f.)

Reading these two verses, one should emphasize the "they" (killed him not), meaning that he was not killed by Jews or Romans. The verses also imply that Jesus did not die on the cross for "crucifixion" means "killing" on the cross.

The Qur'an's information finds support in the fact that the reports on crucifixion in all four Gospels differ so widely as to destroy confidence in any of them. That Jesus was not tied to the cross, as usual, but nailed instead was first alleged by Tertullian (ca.160-220) not based on any of the Gospels, but on Psalm 22, Verse 16, in the Old Testament: "They pierced my hands and feet!" At that time, the apocryphal story of the unbelieving Thomas evidently had not yet been inserted into the New Testament. Tertullian quite obviously could not have known about the shroud of Turin, whose marks allegedly illustrate the crucifixion. So much the better, because this piece of "evidence" also turned out to be a 13th or 14th century forgery, as admitted by the Catholic Church since 1988.[8]

Even the crucifixes that shape our imagination are figments of imagination themselves. Crosses from Jesus' time are misrepresented, if only for esthetic reasons, because instead of a protrusion at the seat, they feature an imagined pedestal. The Romans had developed two methods of crucifixion: one quickly led to death, following a breaking of legs which in turn brought about asphyxiation. Without that, crucifixion led to death much more slowly. There is some indication that Jesus had only been tied to the cross, and that, due to the impending Sabbath, for only three hours. That is why he could have still been alive when taken down.

From an even larger perspective, Prof. Paul Schwarzenau in his *Guide to the Qur'an for Christians* characterizes the Qur'an as a veritable protest against the Christian mystique of the cross.[9] Paul, with his mystical reinterpretation of crucifixion, managed to turn the fiasco that had befallen the first Christians into a grandiose piece of luck: God's own Son, sacrificed on the cross for the sins of all mankind, had redeemed all sinners once and for all. With that stroke Paul placed the cross into the center of the Gospel, not as written but as preached by him, until the Cross (capitalized) finally mutated into the Christian badge of victory. This salvation theology, regarded by Jews and Muslims as sheer blasphemy, has been extremely divisive between the three Abrahamic religions. What kind of God is this, goes the question, who cannot correct something going wrong in His creation except by conceiving a son of His and sacrificing him in the cruelest of fashions? Is this sacrificial salvation theology not borrowed from ancient mystery-cults, like the heathen cult of Midas?

Throughout 14 centuries, the Islamic side remained steadfast in defending its Qur'anic Christology. If there is one thing taboo even for modernist or mere "cultural Muslims", it is the Qur'anic concept of Jesus. This is true from 'Ali Abderraziq, Muammar al-Qadhafi and Muhammad Said al-Ashmawi to Farag Foda, Mohamed Arkoun and Bassam Tibi. Both Christians and Muslims today jointly complain that the Occident for over 200 years has been marred by agnosticism, atheism, alienation from the Church, and flight into freewheeling, private or esoteric religions, ranging from anthroposophy and feminist-matriarchal goddess-cults to Buddhism. Indeed, Christians and Muslims currently are sitting side by side in the same boat as they are riding the rough seas of contemporary hostility against religion.

But are the Christians aware of the terrible fact that the negative turn taken by modernity has a lot to do with *Nicaea*? That it could be a long delayed reaction to the loss of theological credibility caused by the *Nicene Christology*? As early as 1934, Muhammad Asad in his book, *Islam at the Crossroads*, wrote the following: "Perhaps the most important intellectual factor which prevented Europe's religious regeneration was the current concept of Jesus Christ as the Son of God .... European thinkers instinctively shrunk back from the concept of God as presented in the teachings of the Church: and as this was the only concept to which they had been accustomed, they began to reject the very idea of God, and with it of religion."[10] *Nicaea* as root cause of atheism?

In view of the bitterness of Islamic-Christian history and the incompatibility of their respective Christologies, it was quite a theological earthquake when the Catholic Church in the course of the 2nd Vatican Council (1965-66) managed to repudiate her century-long practice of targeting Islam as the enemy. In 1964, the Papal Office for the Relationship with non-Christian Religions (pro non-Christians) was founded and staffed with priests very knowledgeable about Islam (and not without some sympathy for it). On October 28, 1985, the Pope issued an encyclical with a world ecumenical flair called, *Nostra Aetate*. It says, among other things, that "the Church has the greatest respect for Muslims, who worship the living and eternal, gracious and almighty God, creator of heaven and earth."

The document elaborated by the 2nd Vatican Council called upon both Muslims and Christians to leave their hostilities and acrimony behind. Muslims and Christians should instead make "sincere efforts toward mutual understanding" and in the interest of mankind "join hands in defending peace and working towards social justice, and by doing so promote precious moral values, especially peace and freedom for all people."[11] This was the spirit that moved Pope John Paul II on August 19, 1985, when he spoke to the Moroccan youth in Casablanca. Without indicating so, he almost verbatim quoted the very Qur'anic verse considered to be a manifest of religious pluralism (5:48), and he declared: "We all believe in the same God, the one and only God!"[12]

With this initiative, the Catholic Church had taken the helm on the long road towards normalization, ahead of the Protestant world, the World Council of Churches, and far ahead of all Christian-Orthodox Churches. At the same time, Vatican II was but one, albeit important, milestone on this path, since the above-quoted encyclical and the Pope, too, conveniently avoided any mentioning of the Prophet of Islam. For precisely that reason Hans Küng and Father Michel Lelong believe that their Church is still miles away from drawing the full theological and pastoral consequences predicated in the 1985 encyclical.[13] Ulrich Schoen thus poses the question: "Why does no one dare to say a word about Muhammad?"[14]

This is merely a rhetorical question. It is obvious enough that the Church is withholding the long overdue rehabilitation of Muhammad because it is still trapped in the mesh of its own, home grown defamation against him. Even those Christians who have long since abandoned the notion of Islam as a heresy and of Muhammad as a fraud still find it hard to accept the Qur'an as a divine revelation of (at least) the same rank as the Bible. Exactly this is of course implied if Muhammad is accorded recognition as a genuine prophet. Therefore, moving ahead will require a deeper and more emphatic study of the Qur'an on the Christian side. It seems that the Catholic Church in this endeavor has already been overtaken by some Protestants circles, who no longer deny the revelatory nature of the Qur'an.

There was a time when Karl Marx claimed that with his historical materialism he had returned Hegel from standing on his head back on his feet. Be that as it may. The West should realize at any rate that Islam has indeed the potential of turning Christianity around that way and that this would be a boon for Western civilization. But this is not the issue. Is it not a simple matter of common courtesy to break the silence on a man whom more than a billion people revere as their prophet? Is treating him like a non-person not an insult? Is it not high time to treat Muhammad with at least as much respect as James, Jesus' younger brother, who had seen Jesus' role and nature the Qur'anic way? When will Christians realize that the "Qur'an brings us nearer to original Christianity than the New Testament "?[15]

Notes

1. Cf. Lüdemann (1995) and Deschner. More detailed commentary regarding Christology is in the next chapter.
2. Since then some Protestant editions of the New Testament only begin with verse 12.
3. *al-Bukhari*, vol. 6, no. 533 f. ; vol. 8, no. 638; vol. 9, no. 638; Muslim, no. 1769-1773.
4. *Die Krankheit zum Tode*, Köln: Jakob Hegener, 1956, p. 159.
5. Ulrich Schoen in: Kirste, p. 27.
6. Borrmans, p. 111.
7. Kurt Flasch, *Nikolas von Kues*, Frankfurt 1998. Quoted in Martina Bretz, *Frankfurter Allgemeine Zeitung*, Nov. 3, 1998, p. L 24.
8. The radio-carbon dating method pegs the origin of the shroud any where between 1260 and 1390 (*Frankfurter Allgemeine Zeitung*, Oct. 10, 1988).
9. Schwarzenau, *Korankunde für Christen* , 1982, p. 110.
10. Asad, *Islam at the Crossroads* , p. 51 f.
11. Excerpt quoted from Lelong, p. 13f.
12. Excerpt quoted from Lelong, p. 18-20.
13. Lelong, p. 24.
14. Schoen in: Kirste, p. 36.
15. Schwarzenau (1991), p. 504.

CHAPTER NINE

Jesus dividing — Jesus uniting

Not everybody feels intellectually satisfied
by the phrase "the path is the goal."
(Alois Brandstetter,
Frankfurter Allgemeine Zeitung, March 24, 1999)

R eaders of recent "biographies" of God – Karen Armstrong's *A History of God* [1] and Jack Miles' *God: A Biography* [2] – are led to assume that there are about as many different individual images of God as there are Jews, Christians, and Muslims. If this analysis is correct, it is safe to assume that the variety of views on Jesus must be enormous as well. One can therefore argue that the Jesus who unites people cannot possibly be the very Jesus who separates them from each other.

The historical concepts of Jesus essentially boil down to three major categories. Jesus was said to be:

- a Jewish apostate who wrongly considered himself the Messiah (Jewish interpretation);
- simultaneously God and man (orthodox Christian interpretation);
- a Jewish reform-prophet (Islamic view).

Until about 200 years ago, there was no openly anti-dogmatic, systematic rebellion against Christian teachings – apart from a handful of skeptics, such as Johann Wolfgang von Goethe and other deists who took nature for their divinity. In the 19th century, however, a real rebellion began as Christianity's main textual sources were critically examined from an historical perspective. This work, conducted by professional theologians, had devastating consequences. Leading the new trend of demythologizing Christ were both Protestant and Catholic authorities like Rudolf Bultmann, Hans Camphausen, Adolf Harnack, John Hick, Emanuel Hirsch, Hans Küng, Gerd Lüdemann, Paul Tillich, Karl Rahner, Adolf Schlatter, Hans Joachim Schoeps, Wilfred Cantwell Smith and Wolfhart Pannenberg. Yet, as usual, the Christian rank and file would hardly notice this revisionist process as their local parish priests did their best to keep the results of modern theological research in the dark.

The first casualty of this critical inquest was the New Testament (NT) as a pseudo-historical text. Rudolf Bultmann (1884-1976) applied the historical-critical method of literary exegesis to the Holy Scripture, thus clarifying the relationship between the original Christian message of Jesus and the "historical Jesus". He proceeded to "de-mythologize" the NT, revealing the circumstances of the Gospels' origins in such unyielding fashion that it became painfully obvious that Jesus' true biography could never be reconstructed. All efforts at unearthing "Q" (short for "*Quelle*", the German word for "source") had to fail since a "Gospel according to Jesus" simply never existed.[3]

The consensus emerged that none of the 27 scripts of the NT can be called authentic in the sense that (a) the author is known, (b) was contemporary to Jesus and (c) an acquaintance of him. In fact, there are only third-party reports about Jesus, and they are neither in Aramaic, his mother tongue, nor supplied by eyewitnesses. How are we then to know what he really said? Undisputed authorship can indeed only be attributed to seven epistles of Paul; yet he never met or spoke with Jesus. The story of the Apostles was even found essentially to be a product of the 4th century.

Consequently, there was no getting around the verdict that the texts of the NT are the result not of historical events, but of sectarian interests. Specifically this means that while we know the lasting impact of the "Jesus Phenomenon", the causes of the Jesus-event are in the dark. Jesus, the "mystery man,"[4] is not so much the originator of the Christian faith as he is its object. Gerd Lüdemann of Göttingen University puts it point blank: "So I do not believe in the Bible as God's message to us, but in Jesus, the one who, crushed under the rubble of ecclesiastical traditions, is behind the scriptures of the New Testament ...."[5]

Given the circumstances of canonization and later revision of the NT, many researchers came to realize that, aside from being unauthentic, there is nothing left of the integrity, infallibility, and overall consistency that used to be imputed to it. According to Lüdemann, it even represents a rather arbitrary partisan compilation, i.e., a collection of documents pleasing the one party whose theology historically prevailed over all the others. This collection became standard long after Christianity had outgrown its beginnings, which makes the NT not the word of God but the work of man. Lüdemann concludes that "analyzing the genesis of the New Testament's canon from an historical perspective collapses the edifices of Church and theology like a house of cards."[6]

Critical theologians seemed particularly outraged at the forgery of entire documents, such as the Second Epistle of Paul to the Thessalonians and the Second Epistle of Peter. The same can be said of all of the passages implying trinity, among them 1 John 5, 7 and the baptismal formula "in the name of the Father, and of the Son, and of the Holy Ghost" (Matthew 28, 19).

Given these circumstances, it was the logical next step that incarnation and trinity, the dogmas emerging in the 4th and 5th century from Nicaea, Constantinople, and Chalcedon, became subjected to heightened scrutiny. What is more, the entire critique of the New Testament grew into a gigantic theological effort to go back before 325 to rediscover the original, if not genuine, Jewish-Christian Christology. John Hick, foremost critic of these dogmas, believes with some justification that simply opening both incarnation and trinity to discussion has already robbed them of their dogmatic status, relegating them to mere theories.[7]

That may be accurate as far as Christianity in the Western Occident is concerned. In contrast, the Orthodox Churches in the eastern Occident proved markedly more successful in sustaining their dogma of trinity even through modern times. This may be due to the fact that Oriental theologians have always treated the paradigm of trinity as a mystery eluding comprehension. The Western Churches, on the other hand, eventually fell victim to their intellectual attempts to come up with rational but contrived explanations of the trinity.

In the most extreme cases, Christian theologians would embrace Paul Tillich's conviction of Jesus as a "symbol" of such beauty that one would have to invent him if he had not existed, concluding that Jesus' historical authenticity was effectively immaterial. Bultmann as well maintained that Christian faith as "an existential encounter with Christ" was not in need of historical justification. This view is similar to Umberto Eco's opinion that even if Jesus was merely a beautiful literary figure, such poetic inspiration would be as magnificent and mysterious as any true progeny of God.

All of these are steps back towards a new aestheticization of religion in the tradition of Friedrich Schleiermacher (1768-1834). Such "religion" of course turns into a mere sentimental philosophy of life (Lebensanschauung) and finally into a "religion without God", abandoning any transcendental links. A religion reduced to individual feelings fades from the real world and, to quote Goethe, becomes "Christendom for personal convenience."[8] However, religion can either be justified as a religion, or not at all!

If it were otherwise, why not go all the way and join Carlos Castaneda and Henri Michaux in plumbing the darkest recesses of experience with the help of psilocybin and mescaline, i.e., enhance our religious sensations, as some Indians do, with natural drugs? God by intoxication as antithesis to the rationalist God of the enlightened deist?

Against this backdrop Matthew Fox, a former Dominican monk, performed a "paradigm shift" from the historical to the "cosmic" Jesus.[9] His joyous rapture carried him off into a universal, anti-dualist, postmodern philosophy of wisdom, full of gnostic-mystic certitudes. And yet, with all due respect, there is room for skepticism as to whether such cosmic Jesus-mysticism can really dispense with a historical Jesus. A fictitious, ahistorical Jesus: What could he offer beyond being just another cipher for Reality, unfathomable as it is?

Somewhat less extreme is a theological variety in which a so-called "Jesus-event" is postulated as the historical core of Christianity; everything more concrete is, however, considered mere speculation. Here Jesus is seen as a vehicle for divine manifestation, and not just as a beautiful idea.[10] According to Klaus Berger, for instance, the hidden God became visible through Jesus by his becoming transparent for God. God's "salvatory presence" became apparent in Jesus because he was "completely permeable to divine presence."[11] Michel Lelong puts it this way: "In Jesus Christ God has revealed Himself in all His abundance."[12]

In all of these three cases Jesus loses his own divinity, but in exchange is being glorified into the epitome of divine manifestation. From a Muslim point of view, these efforts are even more than mere language games: they are post-Nicene poetry! Even "event-theologians" have to face up to the fact that without some concrete historical proof as a starting point, one will forever persist in mere speculation.

In contrast, the Christology of John Hick (Birmingham) has a more realistic chance of prevailing church-wide one of these days. This Anglican professor emeritus realized long ago that Jesus could either be only human - or not human at all. Eventually, he took the radical step to opt for Jesus' unadulterated humanity. According to Hick, Jesus was ("just") a man, chosen by God for a divine mission, but neither free from error, nor free from sin. His major mission was to compliment the stern Biblical image of Yahwe with the image of a kind and loving God. In other words, Jesus was to spiritualize the Mosaic ritual and to humanize the Talmudic obsession with legal trivialities.

Hick explains the subsequent elevation of Jesus to divine status (incarnation of God) and to being the second person of a divine trinity as a mythical or poetic way of expressing his significance for us. According to Hick, the Jewish monotheistic image of Jesus as a created "Son of God" had been transformed from a mere metaphor into a Greco-polytheistic theological construct.[13]

Hick's "Theology of de-Incarnation" proceeds from the fact that Jesus never spoke of himself as God and never mentioned God as trinitarian. True, in a global ecumenical context Hick's overall view focuses more on Jesus than God. But he leaves open the question whether Jesus was, and will remain, a singular "event". Instead he writes, "We are no longer speaking of an intersection of the divine and the human which occurred only once, in the case of Jesus."[14]

The famous Catholic theologians Rahner and Küng are both open to objections against the Hellenistic concept of a trinitarian God and against Jesus as a divine person. They nevertheless try to reserve a privileged status for Jesus lest he become just one among numerous prophets. But that is the logical consequence once the incarnation doctrine is dropped. In trying to side-step this logic, both Rahner and Küng show themselves averse to real religious pluralism.

After reexamining the doctrine of incarnation even Rahner, the Catholic, found himself defining Jesus' essential humanity: "Someone saying, for instance, that 'Jesus is the human being who lives the unique and ultimate self-sacrifice to God' may have seized the true essence of Christ in all its depth ...." For Rahner, divine "incarnation" in human form remains a general possibility, Jesus being the outstandingly perfect example of its realization. But at the same time Rahner also wrote, "It is thinkable of God alone that He could constitute a difference to Himself."[15] (From a Muslim point of view, a potentially polytheistic theory!) As a consequence, Rahner's attempt to turn back the Christological clock to before Nicaea while at the same time holding fast to his childhood faith comes across as contradictory, even tortured.

Hans Küng's language is certainly less labored and pretentious. Yet he, too, does not live up to Lüdemann's demand that truth must prevail whenever truth and the Church collide. On the one hand, Küng acknowledges that Abraham's God also was the God of Jesus. Küng maintains that God had chosen Jesus in a unique way; that he had "heralded" the one and only God and had acted in His name. Thus, Jesus was a unique human being, "chosen and empowered by God." Following this way, trinity is being reduced to "God's manifestation in Jesus Christ, through the Spirit."[16]

On the other hand Küng writes that this genuinely human man, Jesus of Nazareth, in Biblical language (!) was the authentic and definite revelation of God, His Messiah, Christ, His image, and His Son. In Jesus were present God's Spirit, His might and His power. Christ as God "coincided" with the historical man called Jesus of Nazareth.[17] In this fashion, Hans Küng, too, still presents himself as a rather well behaved son of the Church – even though the Vatican deprived him of the *missio canonica,* the right to teach Catholic theology.

New light was also shed on the issues of "crucifixion" and "resurrection". The Qur'an says that Jesus did not die on the cross. This statement belatedly found support from critical theology as it discovered that the trial of Jesus and the execution of the verdict took place during a few hours on one and the same (Fri)day, on the very eve of Passover; that he was bound (and not nailed) onto the cross; that the words supposedly spoken by Jesus on the cross are a fabrication; that unknown people took him down from the cross; and that the site of his grave can no longer be identified. The belief in his resurrection – according to 2. Cor. 15, 6 a mass phenomenon based on the vision of a mere handful of people - is attributed by Lüdemann to a social "chain reaction beyond compare."[8]

Defensive maneuvers like these go to show that Christology has slipped into a serious crisis in the Christian world. Psychologizing Biblical events *à la* Eugen Drewermann is, alas, just another crisis symptom. The Qur'an describes the current situation with precision: *"Truly, those who have inherited the Book (...) are in deep doubt about it."*

(42:14). Nevertheless, this crisis cannot be expected – yet! – to drive many disenchanted Christians to "*enter Allah's religion in crowds*" (110:2). What can be expected instead is a dramatically accelerated decline of institutionalized Christianity, a development likely to increase the religious alienation of the masses. This in turn may promote the existing tendency of religiously "emancipated" individuals to help themselves to exotic offers in what functions as a multi-religious supermarket. The Qur'an also comments on this development. In *Surah al-Djathiyah* (45: 23), Allah pointedly asks: "*Do you not see the one who takes as his God his own vain desire?*"

The above mentioned developments in Christian Christology hardly, if ever, register with the faithful congregating in Sunday church, since Christianity has experienced a "schism between piety and science that is tantamount to schizophrenia."[19] In spite of the earthquakes frequently shaking Christian theology, it still seems safe to assume that the Catholic grassroots will continue to honor, e.g., the *Mother of God* with processions not only in Poland, but also in Croatia, Ireland and Spain.

This process affecting theology is paralleled by the enormous paradigm shift in physics and related sciences. There, too, one hundred years ago, a revolution took place when Newtonian physics was (partially) replaced by "new physics", sparked by people like Max Planck, Albert Einstein, Werner Heisenberg, and Niels Bohr. All of a sudden there was quantum mechanics, two theories of relativity, and the indeterminacy principle deduced from the observation of subatomic matter. All of this effectively discredited materialist metaphysics. But, as in the field of theology, too, these implications of contemporary micro- and macrophysics failed to dawn upon the general public; new physics only started to trickle down half a century after the event. Similarly, the fate of Christian churches now depends on whether or not they will allow critical theology to reach their rank and file.

In the final analysis, the demythologizing of Jesus is opening the door to a reconciliation of Christianity with all other religions, and especially with Islam. This corrective process might open breathtaking vistas: if the interpretation of Jesus as "just" a prophet of God should take hold – attributing him the highest possible status available for man – some 1700 years after the Council of Nicaea, the split between Christians and Muslims could finally be mended. It is with satisfaction, but without a sense of triumph, that Muslims take note of an increasing number of contemporary Christians who are discovering the validity of the Qur'anic Christology as described in the previous chapter. If this continues, Islam may finally fulfill its mission as (first and most radical) reformation of Christianity. In that case, there would be a real chance – indeed the first one ever – for a global ecumenical dialogue, not only on humanitarian issues but also on questions of dogma. The divinity of Jesus would have ceased being a non-negotiable taboo for discussion; it would then pay off that the Muslim *ummah* for over 1400 lunar years had held fast to their own Christology.

A noticeable change has already taken place with the Papal Encyclical mentioned above. There is no mention any more of the Catholic Church being the exclusive haven for salvation (*extra ecclesiam nulla salus*). That the Vatican should have abandoned its century-old claim to exclusivity would be good news, indeed. But it is too good to be true. As a Muslim, one now gets the impression that the doctrine of *extra ecclesiam nulla salus* was merely replaced by one holding that there is "no salvation outside Christianity." This is the case, whenever the singularity of Jesus as God is substituted by the singularity of him being uniquely privileged by God. (In secular guise, in the context of globalization, this very attitude shows when people pretend that there is no civilization outside the Occident!).

An extreme form of such Christian inclusiveness became apparent in the Papal Encyclical *Redemptor Hominis* (1979): "Mankind – that is every human being, without exception – was saved by Jesus. And Jesus has a special bond with each and every person, even if the individual does not realize it." As a consequence of such an (evidently retroactive) theological takeover – or embrace – Muslims are classified by Karl Rahner as "anonymous Christians."

With thanks (tongue in cheek) Muslims are returning the compliment. In accordance with the Qur'an, they view Jesus (and all other prophets) not only as "anonymous", virtual Muslims, but as genuine ones: People who submitted their entire selves to God. As Surah al-'Imran (3: 67) says: "*Abraham was neither a Jew nor a Christian, but one true in faith, and he surrendered himself to Allah; and he was not of those who ascribe divinity to things besides Allah.*" Surah al-Baqara (2: 136) is even more explicit: "*Say: We believe in Allah and the revelation given to us and Abraham, Ismail, Isaac, Jacob, and their descendents, and that given to Moses and Jesus, and that given to all the (other) prophets by their Lord:*

We make no distinction between any of them. And to Him we surrender." (3: 84 is almost identical).

In a way, Muslims looked upon as anonymous Christians is meaningful, when one observes Muslims watching with resentment the progressive public demolition of the reputations of both Jesus (now seen as a sort of social worker) and his (virgin) mother, all of which is perpetrated by Christian theologians like Ute Ranke-Heinemann and Dorothee Sölle in Germany. Nowadays, one may indeed conclude that Muslims, more than anybody else, are among the last people who continue to affirm, defend and cherish the glory of Jesus and his mother.

The overall demythologization of Christianity is of course bound to have far-reaching consequences worldwide. Luckily there are theologians ready to face that situation in all sincerity, including courageous academic theologians like Paul Schwarzenau, William Montgomery Watt, and – once again – John Hick. Given the decomposition of Christian dogma, they clearly see the futility of any further attempt to claim primacy for the particular Christian interpretation of reality. Schwarzenau even dares to forecast a "post-Christian era" in which a "planetary religion" begins to emerge. According to him, the age of the missionary is gone for good. Now is the hour for mankind to find its way back to the primary religion of the One and Only God.[20]

It is Schwarzenau's premise, shared by Hick and Watt,[21] that Judaism, Christianity, and Islam are equally foundational, equally valid, and equally true. For him the Qur'an is a revelation of ecumenical dimension which, in archetypal fashion, contains an authentic record of Jesus and preserves the historically earliest interpretation of his role and status. With that in mind, Schwarzenau looks at the Qur'an as a reliable supplement to the New Testament. He even predicts that the messages of Moses, Jesus and Muhammad, regardless of their historical succession, will melt into timeless coexistence: "At the end of time, we will all find ourselves in universal Islam."[22]

Both Schwarzenau and Hick are very well aware that all religions are culturally grounded. This fact implies that religions cannot but fall short of the universality they may claim. According to Hick, "religious ethnicity" motivates believers to prove the moral or cognitive superiority of their faith. For Hick, this is a hopeless undertaking, given that virtue and vice are fairly equally distributed.

He goes on to point out that all religions share the same purpose:

to transform human existence by centering it on God. One could not conclude from the difference of eschatological ideas that only one is right and all others are wrong. On the contrary, Hick asserts that all religions equally share divine wisdom. A metaphor for this state of affairs is one and the same light which, however, refracts into all the colors of the rainbow. Another telling image expressing religious equality is that of different paths all leading to the top of the same mountain.[23]

Against the backdrop of such a "pluralistic theology of religions", Hick calls upon the representatives of all denominations not to place their religion above others. To his fellow Christians, he formulates the appeal to finally cross the "theological Rubicon" by admitting that Jesus was not the only possible savior or recipient of revelation.[24]

THERE are obvious philosophical parallels between liberal religious pluralism and New Physics. Hick, too, accepts a kind of "uncertainty principle" in analyzing religions. He is ready to reconcile apparent contradictions just as in quantum physics one has learned to differentiate between reality as such and how it is perceived. Similarly, the experience of God as well is conditioned by the worshipping "observer". Hick therefore tends to forego evaluation. At best he tolerates limited partiality towards one's own religion, provided there is no negative bias against other religions. All this not only corresponds to the principles of New Physics, it also fits the intellectual fashion at the outset of the third millennium: postmodernism, in as much as it is not merely a recycling of modernity. The loss of clear standards; the cult of what is small, local, and relative; and the rise of chaos-theory are not just reflected in philosophy, theology, sociology and anthropology but even reprised in the art of dance ("*aleatoric choreography*" as practiced by Merce Cunningham) and musical works, as propagated by John Cage, star of the eternal avantgarde. Typically, his devotion to pluralism reached the point of indiscriminate appreciation of each and every sound that happened to reach his ear. Is such accidental aesthetics not reminiscent of the above-mentioned theological theory of "anything goes"?

The hallmark of postmodern sociology and anthropology is their distaste for systematization and Grand Narratives. Explanation gives way to description, a process which deconstructs the referential organization of meaning into mere modes of communication. According to Lyotard, knowledge in the postmodern world (externalized by the computer) circulates like money. A text is only what the reader makes of it – the reader turning into author! Texts become scriptures of divine revelation thanks to being revered as such (W. C. Smith). All that is small, exotic, "authentic" or discriminated by majorities – like women, children, drug addicts, homosexuals, natives, religious sects, and animals – is accorded societal protection, without consideration of merit.

All this jibes with the sheer limitless toleration shown by postmodernism towards all the many ways of covering up the spiritual deficit of modernity: "New-Age" phenomena like occultism; belief in reincarnation; syncretic, charismatic neo-Christian sects; "civil religion"; myths of holistic ecology; Shamanism; Zen Buddhism; and all other things up for grabs in today's life on malls of religiosity.

As things stand, people shy away from any sort of universally binding norms. Whereas modernity would hail the *quasi*-religious dogma of scientism, "*extra scientiam nulla salus*", postmodernism has rejected the very aim of "objectivity". Thus even the "hard" (natural) sciences are denied normative laws, formerly taken for granted. In the final analysis, postmodern scientists legitimately cannot give answers but only ask questions, *ad infinitum*. Also the fundamental questions traditionally posed by philosophy – What can I know? What should I do? What can I hope for? – remain legitimate only as open questions, without prospect of resolution. But when each and every statement is treated as tentative or speculative, to have no view at all and no goal at all becomes a virtue. Then any religious commitment automatically becomes "fanatic" (Hal French). As Roman Herzog, former German Federal President, put it: "Such relativity of values does not lead to tolerance but to indifference."[25] Indeed: only tolerance and moral commitment can go hand in hand (Peter Steinacker).

The postmodern skepticism towards the very rationality so proudly claimed by modernity must be seen in context of the horrors of the Holocaust. It dawned on postmodern thinkers like Zygmunt Baumann that "final solutions" follow a deadly logic inherent in all-pervasive modern states. According to Baumann, the moral existence of man is not really threatened by passions, backwardness, and superstition – but by reason, civilization, and science.[26] Consistent with this insight, the German social scientist and philosopher Jürgen U. Habermas in his major publication *Faktizität und Geltung* (Between Facts and Norms) rejects the very foundations of 18th century Enlightenment, i.e., universal morality and the universal law of nature. In the process, he separates law from morality and sees both as mere products of social discourse. There again, the dismissal of the idea of objective truth cannot but lead to a nihilistic culture of relativity, meaning randomness.[27] However, postmodernism keeps holding on to other crowning "achievements" of modernity like separation of church and state, linear interpretation of history, a philosophy of materialist monism (or atheistic pantheism), and a sentimental humanism.

FOR postmodern circles flirting with agnosticism the question of whether Jesus unites or divides is completely irrelevant. It is, however, highly relevant for Muslims to know where a John Hick wants to take them on his religious postmodern journey, and also to find out which niche non-religious postmodernism designs to reserve for Islam. From an Islamic perspective, postmodernism is the delayed consequence of atheism, secularism, and the loss of values and meaning as brought about by classical modernity. It is a hysterical reaction to a world which – at least since World War II – has become uncontrollable, being equally unresponsive to either the ideals of Enlightenment or the threat of annihilation.[28]

Muslims are often seen, or at least suspected, to be claiming absolute superiority for Islam by comparing it to other religions. In the process, Islam in the lineage of religions comes out with the optimum image of God, i.e., *tawhid*, with the maximum moral guidance, in short: it emerges as a superlative religion.[29] This being the case, the Muslim world does not want any part in a religious pluralism under the banner of "anything goes." After all, the dangers of systematic agnosticism are obvious. Pluralism in which the search for "truth" becomes politically incorrect is a nightmare for truly religious people, as it leads into a cognitive and moral dead end and to the loss of purpose, ontological security, tradition, and devotion. André Malraux in his *Anti-Memoires* put it perfectly, way back in 1968: "I believe that our mechanistic civilization is the first one ever without a supreme value .... It remains to be seen whether a civilization can remain one when satisfied with merely asking questions, or when it is a civilization merely for the *Here and Now*, indeed whether, in the long run, it can base its values on anything else, but religion."

Be that as it may – Muslims on their part do not believe that the current crisis of meaning and moral values can be overcome simply by reviving humanist traditions among Christians, Jews, Muslims, liberals, Marxists, and atheists, as long as man continues to be seen as the supreme measure of all things, bearer and source of all rights. This, then, is the crux: simply holding on to the optimistic but worn ideology of constant progress, to be propelled by the supreme rationality of autonomous, emancipated man, will merely lead to further catastrophes of more and more cosmic proportions. Indeed, the ideology of continuous progressive innovation is the oldest of old hats of modernity. In this respect, in view of human nature, Muslims are pessimists. For that reason, too, hardly any of the Muslims expect tangible results from Hans Küng's rather formalistic project to develop a "global ethics" or what he calls a "world ethos". The same can be said for the efforts of the former German Federal Chancellor, Helmut Schmidt, to find acceptance for a Universal Declaration of Human Duties. Whenever the task is overcoming human selfishness and the taming of human passions, artificially constructed universal Esperanto religions do not stand a chance.

A case in point was the convention of the Parliament of World's Religions from December 1 to 8, 1999 in Capetown, where a moral appeal to all the world's most influential institutions was on the agenda - no less than 106 ineffective years after its founding in Chicago. Among other beautiful things, the appeal stated: "Do not commit sexual immorality!" "Respect life!" and "We are working towards a world where our technologies serve our humanity."

Wonderfully self-serving: a string of pretty platitudes of a "world-ethos" which barely surpasses Immanuel Kant's famous "categorical imperative", nor the good old fashioned golden rule, "Don't do to others what you don't want done to you."[30]   One ends up with such abstracts, once ethics is seen as that which remains after religion has vanished Heinz-Joachim Fischer was absolutely right when stating: "A new morality will not be able to focus on clean oceans and nuclear-weapon-free South Sea Islands. It will lose all credibility if it poses as morality without morals, failing in its tradition of distinguishing good from evil and justice from injustice."[31]

I therefore did not expect much either from the religious parliament's idea to mount a global event in Thingvellír (Iceland) by piggybacking on the year 2000 "millennial moment." The same goes for Hans Küng's old project of writing a "systematic theology of the world religions."[32]

In contrast to the postmodern views as represented by John Hick, the Muslim community is not prepared to abandon the notion of "truth" altogether, although many Sunni Muslims would agree with the Iranian president Mohammad Khatami that there can be a difference between the perception of religion and religion itself.[33] Islam juxtaposes the metaphor of (divine) light refracted into rainbow colors with the image of a light so strong that it outshines all others (as suggested by 9: 33; 48: 28 and 88: 8) and also with the metaphor of gold, which can reach total purity, i.e. 24 carats, but is also called "gold" when less pure. The message of Islam, pure monotheism, is thus compared to the strongest of all lights and also to most pristine 24-carat gold. It is unimaginable to improve on the dogma of God's Oneness, Uniqueness and total Otherness (al-tawhid), which certainly is not conditioned by cultural context.

This self-assessment does, however, not mean that Muslims are not incapable of tolerance towards other religions in a pluralistic world, particularly since according to *Surah al-Ma'ida* (5: 48) religious diversity is indeed intended by God. In addition to this veritable manifesto of religious pluralism the Qur'an in *Surah al-Hajj* (22: 67) contains a directive which reads like a policy platform of ecumenism: "*To every community have We appointed [different] ways of worship which they ought to follow. Let them not draw you into dispute on this matter, but summon [them] to your Lord. Behold, you are indeed on the right way. And if they try to argue with you, say: 'God knows best what you are doing'.*" "Being on the right way" for Muslims means that there is no better way, at least for them, and that they are pleasing God by following it (3:19; 48: 28).

From a postmodern as well as an Islamic point of view, eternal values and dynamic historical progress are essentially incompatible. Based on this premise, postmodernism concludes that ahistorical, transcendentally anchored values are mere fiction. Muslims, on the other hand, draw the opposite conclusion: history is made up of transitory, passing events, fading away – as modernity and postmodernity will as well – while God's laws and revealed truth will endure through all eternity. For that reason, we should follow Daniel Brown's suggestion and reverse the image of Enlightenment (at least concerning Islam). It is not the Enlightenment which has illuminated the darkness of Islamic tradition - Qur'an and *sunnah*. Rather, their norms are releasing a light, which helps to illuminate modernity.

Another reason why Muslims view postmodernism with skepticism is that it does not afford any space for Islam. The otherwise astonishing tolerance of postmodernism for anything and everything stops cold where it touches Islam. In western Europe, too, Muslims do not enjoy any minority bonus. In fact, there is no discernible difference between modern and postmodern Islamophobia. The sociology of religion may serve as a case in point here. Whereas its founders Karl Marx, Max Weber, Emil Durckheim, and Georg Simmel were expecting Islam, like all religions, to disappear as a matter of course, their postmodern acolytes are dismayed by the general resurgence of religious "atavisms" and certainly do not harbor any sympathy for Islam. While they are far from beating the drum for "one church, one god, one king," they do advocate "one culture, one technology, one world order." Like Michel Houellebecq, many consider themselves "a-religious". Yet, at the same time, they experience a painful longing for a "new ontology" and a "religious dimension."[34]

In short: wherever they look, Muslims are facing globalism.

Notes

1. *A history of God : the 4000-year quest of Judaism, Christianity, and Islam.* New York: Knopf, 1993.
2. New York: Knopf, 1995
3. Cf. Mack. Efforts continue, though, at reconstructing as primary source a document "Q" based on parallel passages in Matthew and Luke. More promising in this respect might be the recently found Gospel according to Thomas with its sayings attributed to Jesus.
4. Deschner, p. 83.
5. Lüdemann (1995), 2, 226,
6. Ibid., p. 8f., 215.
7. Hick, in Cohn-Sherbock, Chapter 1.
8. Johann Wolfgang von Goethe, *Dichtung und Wahrheit,* Frankfurt 1993, vol. 5, p. 575.
9. Fox in: Kirste, p. 374 ff.
10. Cragg, p. 5
11. Klaus Berger, *Im Anfang war Johannes*, Stuttgart 1997. Quoted from a review by Helmut Löhr in *Frankfurter Allgemeine Zeitung*, June 3, 1989.
12. Lelong, p. 160.
13. Hick 1977, first chapter. Paul Schwarzenau shares this opinion (1982), p. 123: "In the earliest Christian community from whom the Jewish Christians emerged, Jesus was never refered to as a God in the proper

existential meaning of the term. Also, it is safe to assume that the historical Jesus would have never tolerated a deification of his person."

14. John Hick, *Islam and Christian Monotheism* in: Cohn-Sherbock, p.12.
15. Rahner, ibid. p. 137-40.
16. Küng, J. van Ess.
17. Küng (1988), p. 33, 43-45, 49 f., 54.
18. Lüdemann 1995, p. 227.
19. Lüdemann 1994, p. 209-11. Lüdemann 1995, p. 8.
20. Schwarzenau in Kirste, p. 478.
21. Watt, p. 43.
22. Schwarzenau 1982, p. 9. 22. 117. 123 f., 126.
23. Hick 1995, p. x; Hick in Kirste, 114 f., 118 f., 120 f., 123, 128-49; Hick 1988.
24. Baumann, p. 7.
25. Laudatio in honor of Prof. Dr. Annemarie Schimmel receiving the German National Booksellers' Association's Peace Prize, October 15, 1995. Manuscript p. 5.
26. Baumann, p. 7.
27. al-Attas 1996, p. 508
28. Manzoor in: *The Muslim World Book Review,* vol. 7, no. 2, 1987, p. 3, and vol. 14, no. 3, 1994, p. 377.
29. Kellerhals, *Der Islam*, 2nd ed. Basel 1956, p. 377.
30. This golden rule corresponds to a Hadith which states that you should wish for your brother what you would wish for yourself. (Muslim, no. 72 f.; an-Nawawi, no. 236).
31. Fischer, "Morality without Morals?" in *Frankfurter Allgemeine Zeitung*, Nov. 16, 1995.
32. Küng, in *Die Welt* , Berlin, March 6, 1989, p. 13.
33. Khatemi, "No Religion possesses the absolute Truth", in *Frankfurter Allgemeine Zeitung*,September 26, 1998, p. 35.
34. Houllebecq, p. 71. Jochen Kirchhoff points the way to a new ontology with his "Impulse für eine andere Naturwissenschaft" (Initiating an alternative Natural Science) in his remarkable book *Räume, Dimensionen, Weltmodelle.*

Colorblind

*I have met, talked to, and even eaten
with people who in America would have
been considered white - but the white
attitude was removed from their minds
by the religion of Islam.*
(Malcolm X alias Malik al-Shabazz in a letter from Makkah)

W e emerged from the ups and downs of theological history only in order now to descend into the pit of racism. This, too, is a topic of urgent concern to Muslims. To understand why this is so, just take a Lufthansa flight from Istanbul to Frankfurt. Before leaving the plane, the passengers are likely to be asked via intercom to be ready for an on-board passport check. They will then notice how everybody carrying a German or European Union passport or appearing sufficiently Aryan is being waved through. This leaves for closer scrutiny of passengers looking Arabic or Turkish. American security officials aptly call this procedure "passenger profiling." But then, Chicago is a place as good as any for missing one's connecting flight – as happened to me – for being trapped at the passport check behind a line of people looking dangerously Arabic or wearing either a beard or a headscarf.

There was no need to declare 1996 the "European Year against Racism" in order to be reminded of the sad fact that nationalism, easily degenerating into naked chauvinism, after a century full of Fascism is staging a successful comeback almost everywhere. Just like tuberculosis, the nationalist plague of the 19th and 20th century has also returned with aggressive virulence. From the Muslim world, those bearing the brunt are primarily Bosnians (persecuted as "Turks") and Kosovar Albanians, Kashmiris, Kurds, Palestinians, and Chechens.

All this despite the arrogant claim that nationalism was incompatible with modern rationalism and socialist brotherhood, and therefore destined to disappear. One of the many promises broken by modernity! We are in fact, facing a nationalism that is a mere variant of the very racism perpetrated on Jews and Muslims alike ever since the fall of Granada in1492. And it threatens to keep us on our toes during the 21st century, at least in the form of Eurocentric myths and the global apartheid which separates Western civilization from all the "barbaric others" (Ziauddin Sardar).

The scope and development of ethnocentric sentiments become understandable if one remembers the two main, mutually corrective factors bearing on them. Firstly, there is a natural family orientation, absolutely vital to each individual. Patriotism (nationalism in its non-aggressive form) is really nothing else than family feelings extended toward kin and tribe, a normal behavior, indigenous to humans and animals, motivated by the survival instinct. The nation is the extended family *par excellence*. And who would deny that loyalty, toward the very community which enables one's socialization and assures one's survival, is a virtue?

The reverse of the coin, which is suspicion and even fear of strangers – i.e., those as yet unfamiliar to us – is essentially a natural and even necessary reaction. Secondly, thank God! – all humans are equally prone to commit themselves to more abstract ideas and ideals and to harbor religious feelings which tend to overarch ethnic borders – thereby defusing excessive nationalism. Surah ar-Rum (30: 22) comments on this mechanism by saying: "*And among His wonders is the creation of the heavens and the earth, and the diversity of your languages and your colors; verily in that are messages for those who know.*" Here inquisitive religious minds are made curious about the world at large. Racial and cultural differences, far from being described as a possible source of danger, are displayed as something to be marveled at.

THE Qur'an recognizes special family relationships based on blood or bonds of marriage as worthy of protection (4:1; 25: 54). This is noteworthy in view of the fact that all members of the *Ummah*, the Islamic community of faith, are also considered brothers and sisters in a wider sense (8: 73,75; 33: 6). The Qur'an indeed makes allowances for closely-knit families – not only for inheritance alone. Thus, the famous Qur'an commentator Daryabadi was able to conclude that kinship was the most important of all social institutions in Islam.

But every in-group, as sociologists call them, automatically creates an out-group, and efforts to define oneself in contrast to others can easily lead to a discriminatory marking-off. There is no dearth of criteria for possible discrimination: place of residence; social class; historical experience; religious affiliation; gender; language (even a touch of dialect is enough); the color of eyes, hair and/or skin. No wonder that every one of us is a member of several in-groups and several out-groups. When favoring one of two local soccer teams or one's national team during an international match, we betray basic racial instincts. The problem is that this simple, natural mechanism can not only cause an after-match brawl but lead straight away to "ethnic cleansings", as recently in Bosnia and the Kosovo province, and Holocaust-type massacres. For instance, there can be no doubt that the lamentable expulsion of Muslims and Jews after the Reconquista of Andalusia was an early case of "ethnic cleansing" with racial overtones, well prepared by the demonization of Muslims and Jews in Christian war propaganda.

The last two thirds of the 20th century have made more people refugees for religious or ethnic reasons than any other century before. Just remember the exodus of uncounted Jews from Europe; the expulsion of 11 million Germans from Eastern Europe; the bloody population exchange between India and Pakistan; the many Palestinians who have been scattered all over the world; the flights of Bosnians and Kosovars, Hutus and Tutsis. The 20th century was, indeed, the century of displaced persons, of refugees from massacres and gas chambers. Against this bloody background of recent date, we hardly need to recall other monstrosities like the systematic extermination of American Indians in the 18th and 19th century and black slavery in the USA until the Civil War.

This discussion would nevertheless be rather pointless if it did not allow the interesting conclusion that there is one, and only one, force capable of neutralizing the combined evils of nationalism and racism, and that is religion (including pseudo-religious variants). In principle, it should be possible for all religions and ideologies to overcome ethnic conflicts internally and externally. I say, "in principle", because Christianity proved quite ineffective when facing nationalism and racism, and anti-imperialist, "internationalist" Communism did not fare much better in that respect either.

Much more important is the fact that Islam, and that religion alone, has shown an extraordinary capability to quell racism. This was already the case in the formative period of Islam, thanks to an event without precedent in history: in the years 621 and 622 CE a group of citizens from Yathrib, the oasis now called *al-Madinah,* had two meetings with Prophet Muhammad and his followers in Aqaba, near Makkah, in the valley of Mina. Although they did not belong to their tribe, the Quraysh, they not only offered them sanctuary, but also bonds of brotherhood (thereby, bestowing inheritance rights) and political leadership.[1] They did not do so on the basis of tribal kinship or economic ties, but exclusively on the basis of shared faith in Islam.[2] The two pledges of allegiance made in Aqaba launched what in retrospect presents itself as the first state ever founded on purely ideological grounds. The Muslim emigration to *al-Madinah* (*hijrah*) led to the creation of the first state in human history whose citizenship was based exclusively on religious orientation, de-emphasizing all other bonds, among them those which used to be the holiest in Arabia: blood ties to kin and clan. The Qur'an succinctly declared the emigrants (*al-muhajirun*) and their hosts (*al-ansar*) – and only them! – to be friends and protectors (*al-auliya*; 8: 72) to each other, and stated: "*The Prophet is closer to the believers than their own selves*" (33: 6), i.e., closer than their own fathers and mothers.

Ibn Majah (Sunan I) reports the Prophet as saying, "Marry women not for their beauty, for their beauty can ruin them; and likewise do not marry them for their possessions, for their possessions can make them wasteful. But marry them for their religion. An enslaved black woman with pierced nose, but who is a believer, is preferable." This illustrates better than anything else that Islam as such constitutes the closest possible kinship.

In elevating the bonds of faith above family ties the Qur'an went one step further, cautioning the believers that practicing their faith might turn even wives and children against them (64:14). But then, the Qur'an flatly notes that neither his women nor his children will be of use to a believer on Judgment Day (60: 3).

From that point on, it became Islam's ideal to choose the best and brightest of the community from the most God-fearing, without regard to social background, and not from the aristocratic elite or the most talented composers of Qasidas. Following that logic, Bilal, a former black slave, became the first muezzin of Islam; an Iranian, Salman al-Farsi, became the first minister of finance, and a woman, 'A'isha, in 656 was the nominal supreme commander during the so-called Battle of the Camel against 'Ali ibn Abi Talib.

A single *Ummah,* the egalitarian community of all believers, governed by a single *amir al-mu'minin,* a model of justice and devotion: this was the formative ideal throughout Islam's unfolding history. Until the end of the Ottoman Empire, the majority of Grand *Viziers* were not Turkish, but Albanians, Greeks, Croats, Cherkessians, etc. Whether or not Salah ad-Din al-Ayubi, the liberator of al-Quds (Jerusalem) in the 13th century, was Syrian, Kurdish, Azeri or Tartar was immaterial. All Muslims, regardless of nationality or skin color, could qualify for any service rank in government or the military. Ibn 'Arabi, the great Andalusian mystic from Murcia, worked and died as a highly revered celebrity in Damascus, as did – in exile – the great 19th-century Algerian freedom fighter and *Sufi,* 'Abd al-Qadir al-Djaza'iri.

Indeed, the Islamic world from Morocco to India was one large borderless home to Muslims of every kind. In World War I, Lawrence of Arabia was able to fan anti-Turkish, pan-Arab sentiments only because the Young Turks around Enver Pascha with their new brand of un-Islamic pan-Turkism had already begun to discriminate against other peoples of the Ottoman empire. Today's Kurdish problem, too, would not have arisen if, in the 1920s, Kemalism had not destroyed the Islamic bond that had held together the multi-racial and multi-lingual Ottoman empire for five centuries. Indeed, even today almost all the states of the Arabo-Muslim world are late colonial creations, not quite settled as "nation states", a Western construction without Islamic pattern. (Exceptions to this rule are states whose historical foundation is dynastic or of a sectarian nature, like Morocco and the Ibadite emirate of Oman.) Theoretically, such states should not even exist.

The global phenomenon of a colorblind *Ummah* finds its most beautiful expression during the annual pilgrimage to Makkah (*al-hajj*). There and then mutual feelings of equality, togetherness, and purpose are enjoyed by millions of Muslims from all continents, pilgrims from all races. In an enormous crowd, they live under severe climatic conditions. But their praying together, all identically dressed, and dealing with each other on absolutely equal footing, is an unparalleled experience. The intense feeling of universal brotherhood and peace typical of *al-hajj* even liberated a black activist like Malcolm X from his previously aggressive racism. I submit that pilgrimage to Makkah is the most potent counter-education imaginable against racism.

I experienced this reality myself not only in Makkah, but also in 1985, in San Francisco, where a congregation of black Muslims spontaneously asked me, a white foreigner fresh off the plane, to lead them in prayer. But descent, nationality and status were no issues. The decisive point here was that they considered me the most knowledgeable Muslim among them, and thus *Imam* of the day.

It is precisely this mind-set which today offers only Muslims the chance to heal troubling big town social disintegration. In several American cities, Muslim do act as credible go-betweens for white police officers and black street corner kids. The same goes for South Africa. Without Islam curbing racial tendencies, a pluralistic state like Malaysia would be unthinkable. There Malay people, Chinese, and Indians are not only coexisting but working together, despite their pronounced differences in language, dress, mores, kitchen, and religion. It is not without a sense of pride when Muslims explain that the Muslim world, while rejecting Zionism as racist and Israel's policy of expansion by settlement as downright illegal, never embraced anti-Semitism. The reason for this restraint is not that Arabs are Semites themselves. Rather they feel bound by the Qur'anic command to respect the believers of all other monotheistic "people of the Book" (*Al al-kitab*) and to compete with them, peacefully, only in piety. God forbids any compulsion in matters of faith (2: 256). Beyond that, *Surah al-Ma'ida* (5:48), frequently mentioned by me, even gives structural guarantees to other religions.

AS pointed out above, the natural roots of racism are so deep and strong that all successes notwithstanding, even Islam was never fully able to eradicate this scourge. To claim differently would be as presumptuous as to assert that Islam had managed to defeat evil itself. Righteous self-delusion will not advance the case. Already in 632 CE when the 1st Caliph, Abu Bakr, was elected, it became evident that the former asylum-seekers from Makkah (*al-muhajirun*) expected preferential treatment to their "helpers" (*al-ansar*) in al-Madinah. Eventually this approach led to a kind of Islamic aristocracy in the Damascus-based Umayyad empire. Not piety but descent, tradition, and wealth led to the absurd situation that the most recalcitrant former enemies of Islam, now "turncoats" like Abu Sufyan, began to run the *Ummah*. With this in mind, the battle of Siffin (657 CE) between Caliph 'Ali and the Umayade counter-Caliph Mu'awiyyah already had traits of a tribal conflict in an Islamic context.

Even the Abbaside revolution (750 CE), seemingly motivated by religion, ended with quasi-aristocratic pretensions. Once they had superseded the Umayyad clan and installed themselves in Baghdad, they, too, insisted that the office of the Caliph was to be reserved for members of the Makkahn tribe of Quraysh, preferably someone of their own clan. This elitist theory survived well into the late Middle Ages, with fair exceptions, until the Ottomans put an end to it when Selim I – not Arab but Turk – conquered Cairo and, in his person, united the offices of Sultan and Caliph. In passing, one should perhaps note that *Shi'ite* theology even demands the establishment of a monarchy, run by a dynasty traced back in direct line to the Prophet Muhammad via his daughter Fatima and her husband 'Ali ibn Abi Talib – a far cry from Islam's egalitarian beginnings.

The issue of equality became more pressing as Islam quickly expanded over its first two hundred years. In order to ensure a controlled assimilation of the many, many new Muslims, some Muslim commanders even rejected mass conversions. But even those non-Arabic novices who were accepted as *bona fide* believers in the Near East, Iran, India, North Africa and Andalusia, the so-called *mawali* (affiliates), had to bide their time. At any rate, they felt like second-class Muslims, especially when they witnessed an unequal distribution of booty and war pensions. Some *hadith* collections vividly illustrate this situation by including a great number of alleged statements on the excellence (or the opposite) of Persians, Turks, Berbers, and other ethnic groups.

In the 9th and 10th century, in outright defiance, the *mawali* mounted an anti-Arab movement called *shu'ubiya* (from *sha'aba*: to diverge, crumble, separate). This trend never died out fully. Even today, some Occidental, far Eastern, and African Muslims resent what they consider a privileged position of the Arab minority within Islam. But that too, although in reverse, is inadmissible ethnic partisanship.[3]

In 1377, Ibn Khaldun, the world's first scientific sociologist and historian, with his famous *Al-Muqqadima* (Introduction, i.e., to his world history) introduced a new key concept: *al-asabiyya* (group solidarity). In doing so, with a keen and sober eye, he described the strong feelings and bonds connected with ethnic identity as they prevailed among diverse communities of the Islamic world.

Who would deny that ethnicity, skin color above all, was a decisive factor when, during the early Renaissance period, the Ottoman rulers supplied Venice with galley slaves; or when some Arab traders engaged in slave trading in some African countries. To this very day, this embarrassing history continues to burden the relationship between some Muslim states like Mauritania and Senegal.

In order to be completely up-to-date, let us consider the Afghan Taliban. They trace their school of thought back to Shah Waliyullah from Delhi (1703-1762) and the conservative Indian Deobandi school that grew from his teachings. By type, they are rural, Puritan soldier-monks and as such certainly represent a religious phenomenon, at least in part. Impelled by strong and rigid moral convictions, they marched into Kabul, from their southern *madrassah* near Kandahar, just as the 12th-century Berber Morabites (*al-murabitun*), as Muslim missionaries, had descended onto Marrakech from their base high up in the Atlas Mountains. And yet, who would disagree that even the present conflict between Afghan Muslims is not only due to religious polarization (between ultra-conservative Taliban and Islamist groups around Burhanuddin Rabbani and Gulbuddin Hikmatyar), but reflects as well a tribal rift between Pathani, Tadjiki, and Usbeki forces? [4]

It would also strain credibility, if one were to maintain that on the Arab peninsula, between the Red Sea and the Gulf, ethnic and class issues did not exist between native citizens on one side, and "expatriate" Muslim guest workers from India, Pakistan, Bangladesh and Sri Lanka on the other. For such workers, a more ideal situation – the one foreseen by Islam – did not exist either in the 18th century, when Carsten Niebuhr was able to observe their pitiful situation in the Yemen and the Hijaz.[5] Receiving a cornucopia of bliss twice – first the Prophet of Islam and then an abundance of oil and gas – may well have convinced some Arabs that they belong to one more chosen people after all.

American and European Muslims, too, sometimes complain that "native" Muslims view them with a suspicious eye. But in their case the observed wariness has little to do with racism. More important are sincere Arab concerns about guarding the purity of faith, in view of the rather newly reverted brothers and sisters with limited understanding of Islamic sources and an even more limited command of Arabic. Even Muhammad Asad alias Leopold Weiss (1900-1992), a towering authority in Arabic, still has to fight posthumously for recognition in the Arab world for his monumental contribution to Islamic sciences. Why? Because of his European-Jewish roots. Indeed, many a Western Muslim feels what the *mawali* must have felt some 1200 years ago.

All this goes to show that even if pushed out, racism is likely to sneak back in through the back door. This means that Muslims cannot afford for a minute to rest on the laurels of the exemplary anti-racist dogma of Islam and its frequently exemplary implementation.

CONSIDERING the weakness of human nature, some racist stains on the Muslim world's burnoose were inevitable. And yet, all things considered, the Muslim communities all through the ages presented the following picture of an anti-racism that managed to become universal. Indeed, the overall Muslim record in checking feelings of ethnic pride and racial prejudice contains an urgent message – for Catalonia and the Basque region in Spain, for Northern Ireland and the Balkans. In fact, the Muslim example may serve as a global model for communities which seek peace by eliminating, in their interpersonal relationships all criteria save one: faith in God and submission to Him. Dealing with the same subject, the American Muslim Jeffrey Lang concluded: "I am not claiming here that Islam eradicates racial and color prejudices. That would be like claiming that Islam eradicates evil. Rather, I am asserting that Islam does not tolerate such prejudices and that when Muslims display them, they know fully well that they are violating a fundamental precept of their faith and committing a serious wrong. Of all the great world religions, I believe none has been more successful in fighting racial prejudice than Islam."[6]

Skeptics are encouraged to visit any of the Islamic centers in the United States. There they are likely to run into a motley crowd of Albanians, Bosnians, Egyptians, Emiratis, Indians, Indonesians, Iraqis, Kashmiris, Libyans, Maghrebinians, Malaysians, Mozambikis, Nigerians, Pakistanis, Palestinians, Saudi Arabians, Senegalese, Somalis, South Africans, Sudanese, Syrians, Tatars, Turks, and, of course, Afro-Americans and Americans of European stock. In Phoenix (Arizona) one could expect to come across a couple of Hopi Muslims. What is more, all these people from such different origins are on familiar, first name terms and treat each other with extraordinary warmth and cordiality; ethnic differences simply do not matter anymore. Against that background, I do not feel I am exaggerating when concluding this chapter by maintaining that Islam – well understood and well practiced – is the very antithesis to nationalism and racism.

Notes

1. The historical events surrounding the pledges of Aqaba have been well described in detail by Charles Le Gai Eaton (p. 209-11).
2. The fact that Muhammad's mother stemmed from Yathrib (later *al-Madinah*) was irrelevant.
3. Definition in Hans Wehr, p. 657.
4. About the Taliban, see "Afghanistan," the special edition of *Muslim Politics Report,* no. 11, January/February 1997. Published by the Council on Foreign Relations in New York City.
5. Niebuhr, *Reisebeschreibungen nach Arabien und anderen umliegenden Ländern* (1774) [Travels to Arabia and other surrounding Countries] Zurich, 1992, p. 318.
6. Lang 1997, p. 154.7 This does not exclude the fact that mosques are predominantly "Arabic" or "Indo-Pakistani".

What are they here for?

*We cannot possibly accept everything minorities
want, just for the sake of tolerance.*
(Peter Frisch, as President of the German Federal Office
for Protection of the Constitution, in: *Der Spiegel* 36 [1997], p. 61)

A few years ago, I was asked to speak in Bonn on the loaded question of "What is Islam's business in Germany?" It was loaded because the question already carried the (negative) response. In fact, the topic implied that Islam has no business in Germany, and never will.

It is, therefore, well worth recalling Islam's long European history, as evidenced by major Islamic architecture in Sicily, Spain, the Balkans, Edirne and Istanbul. Spain, for that matter, was much longer Islamic than so far Catholic. Thirty million Muslims now live in Europe, slightly less than half of them in western Europe, and there is a predominantly Muslim European State, Bosnia-Herzegovina. Even Moscow has half a million Muslim inhabitants now, among them many Tartars. In the United States and Canada together there may be as many as 8 million. Their religious infrastructure in the U.S. and western Europe is visible almost everywhere. One can hardly keep track of the ever-growing number of mosques, Islamic cultural centers, schools and kindergardens, associations and magazines, publishing houses and radio stations, book stores, oriental markets, *halal* butchers, *hajj* travel agencies, and cemeteries. If a minaret were standing wherever Muslims congregate for prayer, the European and North American skylines would resemble a Muslim landscape. No doubt: Islam has arrived in the Occident.

But is it going to stay? It is hard to imagine that the immigration of

Muslim guest workers to Europe, Muslim academics to North America, and the mass-conversion of African-Americans to Islam could ever be reversed. It is more likely that these immigrants – practicing Muslims or not – will take strong roots in their adopted homeland. It was symptomatic of this trend that a Turkish music group from Berlin represented Germany at the 1999 Eurovision singing contest.

Still, let us imagine for a moment that all Muslim immigrants without Western passports were to return to their countries of origin. Would Islam disappear with them? For the USA, Great Britain, and France the answer would be negative, because second and third generation immigrants there enjoy full citizenship rights and are deeply anchored in these countries.

In this respect Germany is a special case, because the majority of the 2.5 million Turks living there are still fixed upon Turkey, even into the third immigrant generation. There are several reasons for this unusual situation: contrary to the Maghribinians in France and the Indo-Pakistanis in Great Britain, most Turks did not speak the language of their host-country before arriving. Turkey is seductively close by – two hours by plane from Munich – is coming along well, and has attractive beaches in a tempting climate. Also, while many left Morocco, Algeria and Tunisia for political reasons and cannot return even if they wished, most Turks emigrated for purely economic reasons. There are, however, two other key factors in the Turkish fixation on their motherland. After World War I, the new laicistic Turkish Republic began to substitute nationalism for the cohesive power of Islam as the unifying social cement. The Kemalist slogan *Ne mutlu Türküm diyene* (How happy to [be able to] say: I am Turkish!) is not simply adorning the walls. Even practicing Turkish Muslims cannot entirely resist chauvinist temptations, with the double consequence that most Turkish emigrants first find it extra hard to sever national ties, and second, think that their being Muslim is inextricably entwined with being Turkish.

The repercussions for the German immigrant scene are two-fold as well: since Turkish Islamic centers in Germany focus entirely on Turks, they impact much less on their local German environment than Islamic centers with Arab or Bosnian orientation. Secondly, Turkish Muslims in Germany are fully embroiled in the political controversies over the role of Islam in their native country. Indeed, many actually attempt to re-Islamize Turkey from Germany. The politicization of Turkish Islam in

Germany results in its fragmentation into numerous competing movements, each one dangerously dependent on a particular, highly revered figure of absolute authority. Examples are the Nurculuk movement, still focused on Said Nursi (1877 1960), their Kurdish founder; the Süleymancılar, still focused on Süleyman Tunahan; and IMGT, the strong and socially most effective *Milli Görüş* (Islamic Worldview) organization of former Prime Minister Necmettin Erbakan.

And yet, all of these national hang-ups do not rule out the possibility that the majority of Turkish Muslims – in Germany, Austria, Belgium, the Netherlands, France, Great Britain, Denmark, and the United States – will begin to identify more strongly with their host country, rather than feeling in truth, and work toward spreading Islam where they are, rather than thousands of miles away.

WHEN asking what Islam's business is in the West, one of course questions whether it should be around at all. To give the question such a slant reveals the mistaken assumption that Islam, unlike Christianity, is merely an Arab, and Oriental religion – exclusively for Arabs and other Orientals and thus utterly misplaced in Europe and America. Such an allegation is apt to turn the stomach of historians of religion. They know, and everybody should, that not only Islam but Judaism and Christianity as well all emerged from the Near East. Their holy scriptures were all revealed in Semitic languages – Arabic and derivatives thereof like Hebrew and Aramaic. Islam, exactly like Christianity, spread over several continents. Arab Muslims are, therefore, only a small minority within the universal Muslim family, just as Near Eastern Christians are within Christianity. Believe it or not, compared to Islam, Christianity is by far more Oriental in terms of its ideological roots. This is so because, unlike Islam, Christianity absorbed important doses of Zoroastrianism, Manichaeism, Mazdaism, Neo-Platonism, Gnosis, Roman mystery-cults and – through pseudo-Dionysios Areopagita – even Iranian angelology. All this, of course, in addition to the Jewish-Mosaic legacy of Christendom. Whether you take the trinity, Christian sacraments, the priesthood, monks, mass and incense or the historically negative Christian attitude towards sex – all of these are non-European heirlooms.

On the other hand, if rationality is what qualifies for European membership and modernity, Islam easily meets this main criterion of Enlightenment. In fact, compared to Christianity, Islam is virtually devoid of mysteries. Neither are Muslims required to believe in original sin nor in incarnation; neither in trinity nor in salvation on the Cross; neither in resurrection nor in the ascension of Jesus and Mary; neither in the divine presence in wine and bread nor in the forgiveness of sin through baptism. They are only required to accept one singular miracle: the Qur'anic revelation.

For those needing further proof: it can be established that the contribution of Islam to the development of the European Renaissance was about as strong and decisive as the input of Greek classicism and Hellenistic culture. This is not the place to prove with Sigrid Hunke that "Allah's sun is shining on the Occident." And yet, all people enamored with the West ought to know that they obtained their system of numbers (including zero) via the Arab world, and that they are indebted to Arabs, Persians, Indians, Moroccans and Andalusians for much of their medicine, their pointed Gothic arches, their troubadour songs, their access to Platonic and Aristotelian philosophy – and to much, much more.

Given these facts, it is not only inappropriate but also factually wrong to speak only of the Western "Judeo-Christian heritage." To do so is an affront to Muslims and prepares the ground for their marginalization. The right way would be to acknowledge "our humanistic Judeo-Christian-Islamic heritage."

ISLAM, therefore, is not just here – it is here with justification. But what else do Muslims want beyond being tolerated as members of a religious minority? Even if this was all they wanted, that alone would amount to quite a lot. As it is, Islam is already taxing Western tolerance because it has entered a more or less mono-religious, i.e., Christian, landscape. And, as we have seen, in contrast to the Islamic world, the Christian one has not gained much practice in religious pluralism; in fact, it is downright uncomfortable with it.

This is less true of the American scene but definitely true for the European one. The terrible Thirty Years War between Catholics and Protestants (1618-1648) – it could well be considered the first World War – was so fierce that it decimated whole populations. 350 years are not much for the European collective memory. Theological subtleties, such as the disputes over whether the proper *Eucharist* formula is "this signifies my body" or "this is my body," could decide between life or death. As late as the 19th century, European Catholics still had to contend with the accusation of being poor citizens, believed to be dancing on strings pulled by the Roman Vatican. Nevertheless, Protestants and Catholics more recently learned to get along with each other. In mixed regions, their churches are still facing each other downtown, but are no longer in confrontation.

With this background, what can Muslims expect in Christian countries? They are certainly more outlandish than Catholics ever were. Aren't they oriented to Makkah? Under these circumstances, will there be a day when the churches downtown will be joined by a mosque? Will the presence of Islam in the Occident become normal? Or will it be repelled like an alien body?

Allergic reactions against Islam can be triggered by four kinds of "otherness": most Muslims can be spotted easily by their appearance: beard, headscarf, and elements of foreign dress, Mediterranean, Middle-Eastern or South Asian complexion; accent; and a language sprinkled with Arabisms (*insha'allah, al-hamdulillah, masha'allah, subhanallah*). When the number of foreigners surpasses about nine percent of the population, a single headscarf can set (majority) nerves on edge.

Muslims can get on people's nerves for other reasons as well. For instance, there are certain things they allegedly cannot do that anybody else can: in the supermarket, they linger overly long over food labels to glean from small print whether the product contains only the tiniest amount of pork. In that case, it is rejected. At the restaurant, they refuse ice cream cones if they are decorated with a cherry soaked in rum. Some restrict themselves to fish altogether, because the available meat comes from animals not slaughtered in the proper Islamic way. Whenever possible, they eat with their fingers while sitting on the floor. If you smoke in their company, you get annoyed looks and begin to feel guilty.

Worse, where ritual matters are concerned, Muslims become capricious. They insist on saying prayers when it is still pitch dark outside and continue that practice into the most productive parts of the afternoon. During the month of Ramadan, they are fasting unreasonably long. They also insist on going on pilgrimage without any regard to the company or school vacation schedule. They want to build mosques with domed ceilings and with minarets – i.e., architecture which clashes with the local standard. From those minarets they even want to call the faithful to prayer, in the middle of the night and without regard to noise pollution. In the schools, they want to run their own religion classes. In the cemetery, they create a mess by pointing their graves towards Makkah. To top it all, they then refuse to bury their dead in caskets.

Finally, with an air of superiority, they reject not only alcohol – known to be social cement – but everything a good Christian believes in. They exclusively look towards their Qur'an and their traditions for guidance in each and everything – as if there were no Bible, and as if their books were not hopelessly outdated. Just think of their attitude towards women...!

So much for irony. These four areas – appearance, dietary regulations, ritual, and worldview – do, however, really cause genuine problems for multicultural coexistence. It would, however, be wrong to make these problems disappear through total assimilation in the prevailing Western civilization. For in that case, Muslims would not only become indistinguishable, they would lose their capability of presenting their environment with a viable alternative. And this would indeed be a disadvantage for both sides. In order to make a contribution to Western society – to enrich it – Muslims need to remain themselves and visible.

This concern does, however, not relieve Muslims from the obligation of minimizing avoidable friction by clearly distinguishing that which constitutes the core of their faith from those elements that are merely idiosyncrasies of traditional Muslim civilization. Such cultural legacies may have been very valuable during other times and under other circumstances. Mere mannerisms of civilization – and only those – can be abandoned, if necessary, to pave the way towards better integration – but not for the purpose of assimilation. A mere artifact of civilization (and hence dispensable) is, for example, oriental dress, even though it facilitates praying. Women's hair can be covered far more fashionably than with a drab headscarf. Muslims are not required to eat like 7th century Arabs. They can wear a tie, eat at the table with knife and fork, and instead of cleaning their teeth with a frayed twig brush (*miswak*) they can use a toothbrush and paste.

At the same time, Western society should be strong enough to fully tolerate even the gaudy folkloristic trappings of a traditional Islamic culture that can mean so much to immigrant communities. But since obviously this is not so, it is in the interest of Muslims to meet their hosts halfway, wherever possible, in order to increase their chances of acceptance. Compromises are out of the question in the entire, non-negotiable fields of belief (*al-aqida*), morality (*al-akhlaq*), worship (*al-'ibada*) and behavioral norms of the *Shari'ah*. But concessions are possible everywhere else.

Muslims, therefore, ought not to willfully test the threshold of tolerance by acting as if Islamization went hand in hand with Arabization. They have to take into account that the fast-paced expansion of Islam – reaching all the way to Sweden and Finland, South Korea and Columbia – has caused a future shock in many people with strong cultural roots. With sociological predictability, such cultural shocks are bound to discharge themselves as a neo-conservative backlash against change. Of this danger all Muslims should become, and remain, aware.

ALAS, there are indeed indications that the European-Islamic encounter – and the American-Islamic one as well – could end on a negative note, despite the stated willingness of Muslims to compromise. Take for example the worrying fact that, in the course of the last 35 years, neither the knowledge of, nor sympathies for, Islam have noticeably increased in the Occident. Rather, due to negative media coverage and Zionist activity, the contrary seems to be unfolding. There are even fanatically anti-Islamic Christian counter-movements afoot, with an Evangelical background.

Abdul Hadi Christian Hoffmann, author of the book *Between all Chairs*, in 1999 described the situation as follows: "To the degree I integrated into the Islamic community, I found myself disengaging from German society." And: "I had to learn that the German constitution is not seen by many Germans as common basis for cultural and religious pluralism."

His impression is quite on target. According to a poll taken in 1977, only half of the Germans questioned were prepared to grant Muslims the same rights they claim for themselves. Almost 30% viewed Muslim residents in Germany – not just like Saddam Hussein – but as dangerous.

It is particularly unfortunate to notice how many people all over Europe are yielding to the temptation to turn Muslim workers into scape-goats for unemployment, even though the problem is known to be structural. This reproach – Muslims taking jobs away! – creates a truly explosive cocktail, a mixture of economic misgivings, ethnophobia and religious prejudice. Pied Pipers who are stoking such resentments are easy to come by, especially as anxieties spread due to economic globalization.

The picture grows darker in view of the fact that Muslims in the West are habitually held hostage for every outrage that shakes the Muslim world. Each poison gas shell dropped on Kurdish settlements in Northern Iraq, each Lockerbie-type assassination, each massacre in

Algeria (no matter by which side), each killing of an Iranian intellectual, each hand grenade lobbed against tourists in Egypt – all of this is summarily blamed on each and every Muslim, all over the world.

An additional hurdle for Islam's future in the West is set up by merely nominal or so-called "cultural" Muslims, i.e., fully Westernized people from the Muslim world. Some of them are more liberal than Western liberals or more Marxist than Western socialists. It is especially annoying to real Muslims that such immigrants, mainly from the Arab world, exploit their credibility with the media in order to propagate a permissive "Euro-Islam" (heavy on Euro, light on Islam) and make practicing Muslims look like raving fanatics. As a result, Sunni Muslims in the West all of a sudden have to answer questions like "Why can't you be as easy-going as those Alewites? They do not want to build mosques, go on pilgrimages, and pray at odd times. And they let their wives walk around in mini-skirts and with bare arms. Why can't you Muslims be more like them?"

It is easy to see, at any rate, how quickly the seductive Western way of life makes inroads into Muslim families as their children are exposed to the hedonism and atheism practiced in a materialistic, consumerist society. Thus, the American Way of Life may achieve within a few years what Christian Missionaries in North Africa and India had failed to achieve over decades: to alienate Muslims from their religion by making it look like an obstacle on their way ahead.

Finally, there is the never-ending admonition that the Muslims should sit on their demands until after they have successfully made up for missing out on both Reformation and Enlightenment. This viewpoint, too, impairs the chances of Islam in the Occident, as it is ranked as a pre-modern, backward culture. Against such prejudice, it is of little use to know that Islam is by no means in need of catching up, because it had never been hostile to science or controlled by clerics. It simply makes no sense to ask Muslims for those reforms which, in the West, had helped to terminate Church censorship (leading to book burnings), excommunications, the burning of thousands of "witches", and the horrible Inquisition, typified by the criminal persecution of Galileo Galilei and Giordano Bruno. It makes no sense because the Muslim world never suffered such shortcomings in the first place.

Unfortunately it is the Muslims' own behavior which helps to undermine some of their chances for acceptance in the West. One example is their fragmentation. There are ethnically oriented associations and duplicating umbrella organizations almost everywhere, all competing for funds and against each other. Single combat outweighs teamwork. And then there are the tendencies, primarily on the part of less well-educated Muslims, to move petty antics center-stage; to pelt each other with *Hadith*-quotations, Talmudic fashion, in claiming the one and only right interpretation of Islam; and to turn Islam into a rigid, life-denying sourpuss religion by over-emphasizing Puritanical elements of the Qur'an. In the process, much of Islam's spirituality gets lost, and many a potential convert to Islam is scared away.

I admit, however, that some such conversions are thwarted less for theological reasons — even the wanting to hold on to the divinity of Christ – or lack of spirituality – than for pedestrian ones: the unwillingness to renounce martinis, manhattans, beer and hot dogs. The most important obstacle is probably the idea that Muslims mistreat women. In fact, by simply refusing politely to shake hands with a woman interested in Islam, a Muslim may not only have turned her away from himself, but also from God's religion.

Here is another set of self-inflicted wounds: the aforementioned failure to develop a model Islamic State, a Human Rights code, an economic model, as well as a truly Islamic status for women. It is bad enough that Muslims feel somewhat mortified when asked to point out an existing Islamic State. Granted. But questions regarding the ideal model of such a state, its economic and legal systems, should be a lesser cause for embarrassment, and yet, it is. Here something – everything – has to change!

CHAPTER TWELVE

In for a Change

Whether we like it or not, a change there will be.
(Muhammad Asad, *State and Government in Islam,* p. 16)

*Differences of opinion among the knowledgeable
of my community are a blessing from God.*
(*Hadith,* As-Suyuti, Al-Dschami' as-saghir)

I n the last chapter we saw that both sides have to change if the West is to be able to get along with its Muslims well enough to avoid confrontation. Indeed, Muslims have to do their homework, too, for mere co-existence via cooperation eventually gives way to mutual appreciation.

This chapter sets out to discuss the two most important issues on the Muslim side: reassessment of the *sunnah* and renewal (*al-tajdid*) of Islamic jurisprudence (*al-fiqh*). Shaykh Taha Jabir al-'Alwani, Iraqi born American Director of the Graduate School of Islamic Social Sciences at Leesburg, VA., hit both nails on the head: "Without reevaluation, no reform; without reform, no revival."[1]

THE abovementioned Muslim dilemma when it comes to outlining a concrete modern Islamic polity is related to the central dilemma of all contemporary Islamic studies: the uncertainties and ambiguities of the Islamic tradition, the Prophet's *sunnah*. There exist tens of thousands of reports recording what Prophet Muhammad is believed to have said, done, or tolerated, collected in numerous *hadith*-collections considered authentic. Yet, each group - *Sunni, Shi'ite, 'Ibadite* and *Zayidite* Muslims - recognizes its respective collections, and this enormous *sunnah* is rich enough to allow the most diverse interpretations. According to Daniel

Brown, this situation is responsible for an "intellectual crisis" hitting the Muslim world. In the alternative uses of tradition, he sees a major intra-Islamic battleground.[2] This issue is indeed so important that it warrants exploration in some detail.

The *sunnah* is known as the second of the two primary sources of Islam, the first and supreme one being the Qur'an, which the *sunnah* complements and interprets but cannot abrogate. Muslims, as instructed by the Qur'an, aspire to emulate their Prophet as far as humanly possible. To be a Muslim means to incorporate the *sunnah*. In doing so, the faithful base their personal conduct on the near-exhaustive documentation of the Prophet's behavior and activities in all fields of life, the *hadith*, be they strictly binding or not. This, as Fazlur Rahman (1964) reminded us, is already a restriction: the first generations of Muslims, in addition to the Prophet's, also followed local custom and the particular "*sunnah*" (pattern of behavior) of the first four Caliphs.

In contrast to the Qur'an, the *hadith* normally do not record God's directly revealed word (except in the case of *hadith qudsi*, i.e., extra-Qur'anic, "holy" divine transmissions). *Hadith* are not based on revelation but inspiration, formulated by the Prophet himself. Since he was the Qur'an's best interpreter, his *sunnah* is considered as binding as the Holy Book itself, except in banal or morally indifferent areas like agriculture.

The problem is that, contrary to the Qur'an, all *hadith*-collections – even if called "sound" (*sahih*) – are not fully authentic, beyond doubt. One reason for this insecurity was the Prophet's concern that written *hadith* records might get mixed up with fragments of the Qur'anic text. He therefore discouraged the writing down of his *sunnah*. Therefore, it is not certain whether extensive *hadith* recordings really existed before the second post-*hijri* century.

In those days, illiterate Arabs possessed a tremendous ability to faithfully commit large texts to memory, just as hundreds of thousands of young Muslims still do with the entire text of the Qur'an, i.e., 604 pages in standard editions. Therefore, the absence of large *hadith* collections contemporary to the Prophet was no impediment to the preservation of his *sunnah*. A more serious threat to its credibility arose when legal scholars like Ibn Shafi'i later on sought to reduce the very concept of "*sunnah*" exclusively to traditions going all the way back to the Prophet Muhammad. This definition was meant to exclude subsequent, spurious material but may have been counter-productive. Because now there was additional pressure to attribute all Islamic customs and wisdom to the Prophet. In the process, with the best of intentions, some Muslims quite obviously invented traditions to further partisan political goals. The emerging *hadith*-scholarship attempted to stave this danger off with standards of proof and a scientific conscientiousness in handling sources that until then was unheard of in historiography. It was, for instance, agreed that a Prophetic *hadith* was unauthentic unless it met three criteria of provenance (*isnad*): (1) It must be traceable back to the Prophet. (2) The chain of its transmission must be unbroken. (3) All transmitters of that chain must have been reliable. In order to evaluate all of them, a biographical science (*ilm al-rijjal*) developed which critically assessed the bio-data and character traits of each individual figuring in any of the chains of *hadith* transmission. While one was less demanding in the writing of history (*sira*), extra care was taken before legal norms were based solely on *hadith* sources. For that purpose, usually several independently transmitted and verifiably sound traditional sources were demanded.

The most revered *hadith*-collector, Abu 'Abdullah Muhammad Ibn Ismail al-Bukhari (810-870), was an eminently trustworthy man. In the process of compilation he sifted no less than 600,000 reports. He purged so many of them that in the end, in the 93 books of his nine-volume collection (*As-Sahih al-Bukhari*), only 7, 500 were accepted as genuine. In addition to sifting, *hadith* scholars gave formally accepted reports different weights by distinguishing between traditions of higher and lower credibility. At the same time, piety forbade *hadith* editors to reject traditions merely on grounds of linguistic, historical, or sociological analysis.[3] Consequently, their critical work did remain somehow, formalistic. As a rule, they focused on the integrity of the transmission process (*isnad*) more than on the content (*matn*) of traditions unless they were absurd. And this is the crux of the matter.

A few Western Orientalists like Ignaz Goldziher (1896) and Joseph Schacht (1950) felt, under these circumstances, excused in dismissing the entire *sunnah*, lock, stock and barrel, as texts that can neither be verified nor falsified. Only a few Muslims were willing to join their extreme skepticism. One of them, Muhammad Tawfiq Sidqi, published a book with the revealing title, *Islam is the Qur'an only* (*Al-Islam huwa al-Qur'an wahdahu*). Raja (Roger) Garaudy, too, and also the Iranian scholar Mohammad Shahrour sympathize with this position. For the latter, only the text of the divine revelation (*tanzil*) is binding, everything else is mere judicial legacy.[4] The overwhelming majority of Muslims, while intent on keeping the canonical *hadith*-collections intact, now readily concede that, given the law of probability, they are likely to contain some unauthentic material.

This means that the most qualified contemporary Muslim scholars are called upon, for a second time, to pass the *sunnah* through a sieve, once more trying to separate sound Prophetic traditions from fabricated ones. Following in the footsteps of Numani al-Shibli, Fazlur Rahman, Muhammad al-Ghazali, and Yusuf al-Qaradawi this implies making use of the latest tools of historic and linguistic scholarship, including computer-based textual analyses: a monumental task, demanding the highest possible degree of courage, integrity, and responsibility. Without responding successfully to this historic task, Islam can hardly be ready to cope with the challenges of the Third Millennium.

The supreme importance of this work becomes abundantly clear when one lists the major questions begging for final answers:
- Are both Qur'an and *sunnah* revelations (*wahy*), or is the *sunnah* merely an inspired legal guideline (*ilham*)?
- Can the *sunnah* abrogate the Qur'an?[5] Can the Qur'an abrogate the *sunnah*?
- Are there binding traditions in addition to the Prophet's *sunnah*, such as the *sunnahs* of the Caliphs Abu Bakr and 'Umar?
- Are *sunnah* (as tradition) and *hadith* (as text) identical, or is there a "living *sunnah*" undocumented and independent of recorded *hadith*?
- Can a *hadith* be dismissed despite undoubted integrity of transmission?
- For dismissing *hadiths* on grounds of content, which are the acceptable criteria: Reason? Lack of consistency? Historical evidence to the contrary? Contextual reasons?
- Is the entire *sunnah* binding? Are normative traditions necessarily as timeless as the Qur'anic *Shari'ah*?

Muslim or not, mulling over these questions one can easily become dizzy.

IT is of almost equal importance that Islamic jurisprudence arrive at a consensus on the understanding of *Shari'ah* - a concept constantly used but little understood. In fact, there is no consensus among orthodox, secular, and neo-normative Muslim scholars on that issue.

Traditionally one went by the assumption that the Qur'an had perfectly settled everything that needed settling (6:38; 5:3), with the *sunnah* filling in and providing comprehensive commentary. Consequently, Islamic jurisprudence confidently built its legal system (*fiqh*) on these two pillars, both considered divine and thus permanent. This large body of laws was called the "*Shari'ah*" (road to travel) in the broadest sense of the term. However, this definition has rightly been challenged for some time now for treating Islamic law in all its ramifications like a closed system. Some had indeed projected the sacredness of the prime sources of Islam even onto those parts of Islamic jurisprudence which resulted from interpretation (and the interpretation of interpretation), i.e., fallible human effort.

In short, we simply have to accept that it was most devout, but nevertheless, fallible Muslims – and not God Himself – who erected the marvelous edifice of Islamic law in taking account of the historic context and the social and political needs of their time. Their legal system, next to Roman Law (codified in 534 CE as *Corpus Iuris Civilis* [6]) and English Common Law, is one of the three summits of the world's cultural heritage in jurisprudence.[7]

This Islamic legal system (*al-fiqh*) has been developed from its two prime sources mainly through drawing analogies (*al-qiyas*). Consensus (*ijma*) among all legal scholars was also considered a (secondary) legal source. And yet, in the Middle Ages, Islamic law was anything but monolithic. The different Schools of Law (*al-madhahib*), primarily the *Hanafi, Hanbali, Jaf'ari,* and *Shafi'i* schools, differed considerably, and none of their founders ever claimed infallibility.[8]

Today, there can be no doubt that Islamic law, in order to be responsive to contemporary issues and develop further, must regain its original vitality, social relevance, and flexibility. After all, neither Qur'an or *sunnah* nor the Medieval legal expertise (*fatawa*) provide direct guidance for traffic law in space or on the ski-slopes, nor for copyright on the Internet, not to speak of surrogate motherhood, genetic engineering, in-vitro fertilization and the like. However, modern Islamic jurists (*fuqaha*) will arrive at Islamic answers to all these and other questions by proceeding like their Medieval colleagues: by deriving guidance from the general principles and goals (*al-maqasid*) of Qur'an and *sunnah,* whenever, directly applicable norms cannot be found there.[9]

This procedure is in keeping with Islamic tradition at its best: when Prophet Muhammad sent Muadh ibn Jabal as governor to the Yemen, he asked him on what bases he would administer law. Muadh replied that he would adjudicate according to the Qur'an. In case, he did not find the answer there, he would resort to the Prophet's *sunnah*. When Muhammad inquired what he would do if he did not find anything in both Qur'an and *sunnah*, Muadh answered: "In this case, I will make every effort (*jihad*) and do my very best in order to form my own opinion." The Prophet was most pleased with this answer.[10]

In a 1993 Ramadan presentation in the Royal Castle of Rabat, as part of the *durus al-Hassaniyya* lecture series, the Maldive President Mamun Abdel Qayyum concluded from the above *hadith* that Islamic law knew all the flexibility needed to meet whatever challenge. I agree, but implementation presupposes – and here is the crucial point! – that Muhammad Asad's suggestions are finally accepted, namely (i) to reduce the concept of *Shari'ah* to divine law only, approximately 200 normative verses of the Qur'an and the juridical core of the Prophet's *sunnah*. (ii) The (quantitatively much bigger) remainder of Islamic law, man-made and only to be called *al-Fiqh*, while remaining anchored in Qur'an and *sunnah*, should become open to periodic revision as a matter of good principle.[11]

Some Muslims overly eager to see reform and make Islam palatable to the West at any price, act as if Qur'an and *sunnah*, while offering some useful recommendations and rather abstract principles, were devoid of timeless, legally binding rules. At best, Qur'anic normativeness is seen tied to a specific historical context, virtually obliging only the early Muslim society of *al-Madinah*. This tends to make Islam as a whole a thing of the past. Without *Shari'ah*, Islam would lack its alternative societal vision.

Proponents of the contemporary neo-normative movement within Islamic jurisprudence are, among others, Taha Jabir al-'Alwani, founder of the ground-breaking International Institute of Islamic Thought,[12] Fathi Osman[13] and Yusuf al-Qaradawi[14]. They all share Muhammad Asad's opinion that Qur'an and *sunnah* do not regulate each and every little thing. For them, between commands on one side and prohibitions on the other there is much room for personal discretion that no lawyer or ruler come of late may limit under the pretext of following God's will.[15] After all, in *Surah al-Ma'ida* (5: 87) the Qur'an admonishes us: "*(...) Do not make unlawful the good things which Allah has made lawful for you (...)."* On this basis they resist a tendency noticeable among ultra-orthodox and Islamist Muslims to turn merely recommended actions into mandatory ones, and to treat actions that are merely discouraged as forbidden. Turning the moral screw that way may look like a positive act of devotion, while in fact it may pervert the religion of Islam.

One can only hope that Fathi Osman's provocative dictum will be properly understood and ultimately observed: "God's law is not an alternative to the human mind, nor is it supposed to put it out of action."[16]

NOTES

1. al-'Alwani, p. 20.
2. Daniel Brown, pp.3, 119.
3. Abu El-Fadl, p. 53f., points out that it was always possible in principle to dismiss records because of content, for grammatical and hostorical considerations, or because they contradict the Qur`an or the laws of nature.
4. Shahrour, p. 7.
5. Taha Jabir al-'Alwani vehemently denies that the *sunnah* could abrogate the Qur'an. Comp. "al-'Alwani" in: al-Imam, p. XIV. The late Sheikh Al-Azhar, Gadd al-Haqq 'Ali Gadd al-Haqq in a fax addressed to me took the opposite view.
6 My 1735 copy of the Corpus Juris, on 1278 pages comprising the Institutiones, Digesta, Codices, Constitutiones as well as laws later added, up to Emperor Frederick II (d. 1250). This compilation is as voluminous as comprehensive compendia of Islamic law.
7. Impressive examples of the high intellectual level of Islamic jurisprudence are to be found, e.g., in the works of Imam al-Shafi'i, Ibn Hazm, Ibn Rushd, and al-Nawawi.
8. Acording to Muhammad Asad (1987), p. 20, there was no single legal issue, large or small, on which all the different legal schools held the same opinion.
9. Imran Nyazee with his study laid the foundation for a new jurisprudence on a true Islamic basis.
10. Abu Dawud, Sunan, *Hadith* No. 3585.
11. Muhammad Asad (State, 1980), p. 13.

12. al-'Alwani, p. 18, complains that the Muslim spirit has been idle far too long. He also reminds us that nature is another revelation of God that demands attention (p.22).
13. Osman's book about the *Shari'ah* does not accidentally carry the subtitle *The Dynamics of Change in the Islamic Law*.
14. In his book on what is allowed and what is forbidden in Islam (*Al-halal wa al-haram fi- l-Islam*), Qaradawi offers answers to many topical questions of the day.
15. Osman (1994), p. 22.
16. Osman (*Human Rights*, 1996), p. 6. This is similar in tenor to Fazlur Rahman's, *Islamic Methodology in History*.

Petitioners or Partners?

The entire Qur'an is soaked in a world view
that today appears both archaic and infantile.
(Letter to the Editors,
Frankfurter Allgemeine Zeitung, May 28, 1997)

I ndications of a growing resistance to Islam in the West are fortunately somewhat balanced out by indications of increased acceptance of that religion, despite the numerous problems still existing both in the West and in the Islamic world. It is for instance auspicious that Westerners in general now grant Turks, Algerians and Indians with their *Döner Kebab*, Couscous and Curry at least the same positive folkloristic status as Italians with their pasta and pizza. For adding a little exotic color, elements of Islamic culture are not unwelcome.

The growth of Islam will certainly continue, if only due to the Muslim birthrate - even though it, too, will level off with increasing living standards. At any rate, for years now, "Muhammad" has been the name most frequently given to baby boys in France.

Perchance there is no crisis of religion *per se*, if *pseudo*-religious TV programs like *Touched by an Angel* are an indication. But the crisis of institutional religion cannot be denied. How else could there be so much rambling religiosity flocking to youth sects of any kind. There we are witnessing an instinctive response to what many youngsters experience as a spiritual-intellectual vacuum and a disturbing lack of meaning. The search for a purpose and objective values in life – a possible *Road to Makkah* (Muhammad Asad) – via esoteric and revival movements can, of course, also lead nowhere. Not everyone who turns his back on the established churches finds another religion. Many embrace atheism or at least take an agnostic position. Many others find solace in their own, highly subjective private "religion".

Among the virtues of postmodernism are respect of the other ("black is beautiful"; "small is beautiful") and sympathy for the exotic, culminating in romantic infatuation with the Third World (*tiers-mondisme*), as well as resistance to globalization inasmuch as it leads to the flattening of regional cultures. I have shown that Islam is frequently singled out in that process. Nevertheless, Muslims can, and do, profit occasionally from postmodern attitudes.

Thus, (postmodern) guilt feelings over the dismal Western failure during the recent Bosnian conflict in 2000 probably saved the Muslims in the Kosovo province of former Yugoslavia from suffering the same Occidental neglect.

Also, some Muslim countries rich with hydrocarbons now use their increased influence at the international level to support Muslim minorities worldwide. They promote Islam in many useful ways, not only by building mosques but also by publishing Islamic classics in Western languages. This applies to Kuwait, Qatar, the Emirates of Abu Dhabi and Sharja as much as to Saudi Arabia and the intergovernmental Organization of the Islamic Conference (O.I.C.) and the Muslim World League, a non-governmental organization (NGO). These and other protective powers assure that Muslims in the West cannot be treated adversely without international echo and, possibly, sanctions. Thanks to petroleum, Islam now has a seat and a voice in the concert of major powers.

Private Muslim organizations, too, have recently received remarkable governmental recognition in Europe, in Austria, Belgium, and also in Spain. The British Queen appointed two Muslims to the House of Lords, Lord Ahmed of Rotherham, originally a Kashmiri, and Baroness Uddin, originally from Bangladesh. Also, in 2000 she raised Dr. Manazir Ahsan, Director General of The Islamic Foundation near Leicester, to the rank of Member of the Order of the British Empire (MBE).

The Spanish Kingdom can even be considered a model for how to establish a constructive formal relationship between Western states and their Muslim citizens. The Spanish parliament authorized the government to negotiate a contract with Dr. Mansur Abdessalam Escudero, president of an (officially recognized) Spanish Muslim umbrella organization. This treaty became ratified as statute no. 26/1992. Subsequently, on

November 10, 1991, it was entered into the Spanish legal ledger. Accordingly, if there is sufficient demand, classes in the Islamic religion must now be offered, even in private schools; Muslims in the military, and in jails as well, are to have access to Islamic guidance and worship. Spanish Muslims, if they are willing to make up the time later, now have the right to interrupt work for prayer. Their mosques, staff, and archives now enjoy immunity. Spanish imams can validly conclude marriages like authorized government officials. In Spain, Muslims can now take off on Muslim holidays, working on Christian holidays instead.[1] On that basis, after well over 600 years, a new mosque was opened in Cordoba. On October 30, 1998, in Toledo, a Friday prayer was performed, once again, in a mosque that had been closed for over 500 years. No wonder with these regulations, Spain has made its reputation in the entire Arab and Islamic world.

In view of the consolidation of the European Union, Muslim umbrella organizations in western Europe have also come together to build a central organization at the European level, the "Islamic Council for Cooperation in Europe."[2] In Germany, the Central Council of Muslims in Germany (ZMD), founded in 1994, is gaining recognition as a Muslim institution not fixated on Turkish Muslims. Each October 3, (Germany's National Day) they proclaim "Day of the Open Mosque" during which tens of thousands of people are familiarized with the Muslim life in their midst. In 2000, during the World Exhibition in Hanover (EXPO 2000), the ZMD set up a much-visited Islamic center and mosque on the fair grounds.

The Churches in Germany have all appointed liaison officers from among their clergy charged with Muslim affairs. These mostly young pastors, in particular those from the Protestant (Lutheran) Church in Germany (EKD), actively contribute to a more levelheaded inter-faith debate and establish fruitful personal contact between people from both religions. It is almost as if the conciliatory spirit of the 2nd Vatican Council, now much vanished, had been granted asylum in these Protestant Churches. Witness the tri-denominational calendar edited each year by Thomas Dreesen, a Protestant pastor married to a Turkish Muslima. (A covenant seen as incorrect from either side.) Several German cities have even begun to set aside cemetery space for Islamic burial sites, including installations for the ritual washing of the dead. Similarly encouraging signs can be reported from North America, Great

Britain, and Scandinavia.

SO there are silver streaks on the horizon, harbingers of a more widespread toleration of Islam in Europe. But Islam does not want to be barely tolerated. In view of what Johann Wolfgang von Goethe expressed in no. 122 of his "Maxims", the Muslims wish to be respected: "tolerance should be but a passing attitude, leading to acceptance. Mere toleration amounts to insult."

This goal, moving up from petitioner to partner, is within reach for Muslims in the Occident if they manage to convince their neighbors that Islam is not only asking a lot but has a lot to offer. They should get across that Islam is even offering the very things the Occident badly needs if it is to recover from its looming existential crisis. In other words, the Muslims can win, provided they present Islam not as folklore but as panacea.

True, the Occident is no longer threatened by Communism, a blue-collar proletariat mobilized by Karl Marx. Nowadays, it is rather a spiritual proletariat (Walter Lippmann) which threatens the West. As Alasdair MacIntyre put it: "This time around the barbarians are not waiting beyond our borders; they have been governing us for quite some time now."[3] If what he means is true, the roots of the Western moral dilemma reach 250 years into the past. Consequently, any healing process must begin with a radical critique of rationalism, the subsitute-religion of the modern age. There is hope for Western man only if he can be successfully disabused of his illusions about "modernity". Only then can the rationalist self-poisoning of the West be brought to a halt. Only then can Western societies reestablish transcendental ties, admitting the divine, the holy, back into their fields of vision.

At issue here is the rehabilitation of religion as a rational reaction to the conditio humana. This must be accompanied by a dethroning of natural science, inasmuch as it has been posing as an imperial pseudo-religion. In short, what is required is nothing less than a change of paradigm to make room for a renewed religious world view, renewed through the sober transcendentalism of Islam, its undiluted monotheism, free of irrationalities.

Theoretically, Christianity could achieve the same – but only in theory, I am afraid, because its Christological excesses have irrevocably destroyed its credibility. As we have seen above, none of the leading personalities of any major church is willing to pull the theological emergency break. As far as the eye can see, there are no other religions or ideologies on the scene that might help turn the ship around. In the West, Buddhism is too elitist to achieve any sort of mass-mobilization. Humanitarian liberalism relying on "natural rights" is much too frail. No, as pointed out earlier, *pseudo-* or Esperanto-religions cannot muster the forces necessary for reining in the passions and egotism, either of the individual or the masses.

ON the other hand, I have complete confidence in the ability of Islam to bring about the necessary change of paradigm to overcome the failures of modernity, notwithstanding the many shortcomings on the Muslim side. I rest my case on the following fourteen potential contributions of Islam:

1. Human kindness. In the early seventies, America's communal drop-outs, Woodstock hippies and urbanized flower children would still dream Charles Reich's dream of *The Greening of America*. They were not after a "green" political activism to preserve parks, but a new group solidarity to share the warm milk of universal kindness, a companionship cultivated by LSD and a sprinkling of marijuana. Much according to Friedrich Schiller's lyrics in the last movement of Ludwig van Beethoven's 9th Symphony ("Be Embraced, Oh You Millions!"), this appeal, enacted in real life, remained without echo. Simon & Garfunkel's *Bridge over Troubled Waters* did not lead into warmth, but into the cold. Among the cyber-generation, the temperature of interpersonal relationships plummeted perceptibly. "Cool" became not only a mental attitude but also the climate of society in general. It may well be that to "love your neighbor as yourself" is still being preached from pulpits. But the Sermon on the Mount has become mere mythology, something to read your kids to sleep with. What actually rules reality is indifference and cut-throat competition. Social envy became a capitalist institution when J.S. Mill observed that people do not just want to be rich, but richer than everybody else. The elbow-society allows men and women to box their way into consumer heaven. Husband against wife (and *vice-versa*), kids against parents (and *vice-versa*). People are spinning a cocoon around their own precious, sacrosanct selves.

Against this background, Islamic communities with their proverbial cordiality present to the West a living example of social solidarity transcending all national and ethnic borders. Western people around them witness with surprise and mouths agape how mosques are built with years of voluntary weekend labor and how Islamic festivals – the feast of break-ing the fast after the month of Ramadan (*'id al-fitr*) and the feast of sac-rifice upon conclusion of the hajj period (*'id al-adha*) – are both conducted like huge family celebrations. Muslims socialize religion, and many teenagers like just that. Many new believers are drawn to Islam by their observation of the Muslims' strong feeling of togetherness and their readiness to help each other out.

2. The racial colorblindness of Islam has already been the topic of an entire chapter. Many "colored" people – untouchables in India, Filipinos throughout the Gulf States, African Americans in the U.S. have found their way to Islam thanks to its multi-ethnic face.

3. Of equal significance is the emancipation of the believer typical of Islam. A Muslim sees himself face to face with God, without the possibility of someone else's intercession, but also without clerical hierarchy. The Qur'an and the *hadith* collections are equally accessible to anyone who can read. Nobody may claim to be their sole authorized, or even infallible, interpreter. The Saudi King in Riyadh, 'Guardian of the two Holy Sites' (in Makkah and *al-Madina*) is no Pope. Islam knows of no ecclesiastical court like the Vatican's Rota Romana in Rome, nor of any kind of church bureaucracy. No religious opinion (*fatwa*) is ever beyond questioning. Marriage is no "sacrament". Any Muslim can perform all required acts of worship without third-party assistance, which means, he can get along without clerics.

Absence of hierarchies is particularly appealing to many young people in the West who nowadays show an almost allergic reaction to false, pretentious, and affected authority.

4. Modernity has been a bit too successful at demystifying the world. Western people often make fun of anything even remotely smacking of "miracles." We know now that the road to Christianity is paved with miracles aplenty. The road to Islam, on the other hand, leads through a single miracle, the Qur'anic revelation, an event that each reader may experience anew when sincerely exposing himself to that astonishing text. Prospective Muslims will find in the Qur'an the challenge to reflect by themselves rather than have others do the thinking for them. Above all, the Qur'an cautions against automatically and unquestionably assuming one's parents' convictions. As J. W. von Goethe would phrase it, Muslims, in order really to own their faith, should seek intellectually to acquire what they inherited from their parents. This sober

Islamic rationality, reflected as well in the bright and clear atmosphere of mosques, impresses many Occidental people mightily.

5. According to Rüdiger Safranski, the world has entered the stage of 'secularized polytheism', the one God having splintered into many little domestic divinities.[4] The Muslims see it exactly the same way: the Western dependency on all kinds of crutches – cigarettes, alcohol, assorted drugs, and incessant exposure to television and the internet – has become a structural problem. This monumental addiction reflects a frantic collective quest for unending, unlimited vacuum-filling happiness and 'wellness'. While the West is perfectly aware of these ever-increasing addictions and their devastating impact on Western civilization, it is unable to cure itself, as is commonly the case with drug addicts. On the contrary, governments – as in the Netherlands – are increasingly experimenting with the legalization of drugs (which to that end are euphemistically defined as 'soft'). Only America, which in the twenties had revolted against liquor (and in the bargain got even more whiskey and the Mafia to boot), is revolting again – this time against smoking, which is fast gaining the deadly reputation of being utterly "un-American".

Muslims oppose the drug scene unarmed, with nothing but their structural soberness. Their resistance to any kind of addiction is not just motivated by health concerns or the social costs of lung cancer and cirrhosis of the liver. It is rather more an attempt to prevent the silent emergence of polytheism (*shirk*) by allowing something other than God to become all-important in one's life. For that is the only sin God will never forgive. In addition, Muslims are anxious to be ready at any time for God's call to death, in a sober state. The identification of addiction with apostasy gives the Muslim resistance to drugs the necessary punch. The beneficiaries are, for instance, the city fathers of the Philadelphia and Los Angeles, which contracted African-American Muslims to clean up their drug-infested neighborhoods exclusively by peaceful means. It worked, and it works – through an Islamization that oftentimes starts in jails.

6. William Ophuls sees in feminism the beginning of the complete collapse of bourgeois society.[5] Cultural critics indeed show panic when assessing what is to become of Western society once a generation reaches adulthood which was raised without fathers, be it because of high divorce rates, or because of the cult of single motherhood. Will this generation finish off the breakdown of the family?

By valuing the family higher than any other social institution, Muslims are sending a counter-signal: societal decadence certainly starts in the family – but also ends with it. Young people whom AIDS has shocked back into one-partner relationships willingly receive the Muslim counter-signal. Hasn't 'going steady' made a comeback? It is, at any rate, a fact that many people have found Islam after finding how vital and tightly knit extended Muslim families are.

7. One would think that the 'right to life' should be the most uncontroversial of all human rights. Yet, this right is enjoyed only by those among us who successfully made it through the most dangerous time of our existence: the prenatal period. Even in Catholic circles, resistance to the spreading legalization of abortion is sagging. The life of the unborn ranks not only behind the life of the mother, but also behind the second car, the second fur coat and the second vacation.

This trend drives some literally 'conservative' people into a clean break with their libertine societies. In the process, some are discovering that they are actually embracing Islamic positions and that Islam promises to be more successful against abortion than throwing bombs against clinics.

8. Since St. Paul, Marcion and St. Augustine, Christianity has set a pendulum in motion which swings widely between two extremes: extreme puritan demonization of women and sexuality on the one hand, and uninhibited surrender to all biological instincts without limits or taboos on the other. If we dismiss the latter extreme as un-Christian, Christianity can justly be characterized as "2000 years of forbidden lust" (Georg Denzler).

In sharp contrast, Islam has managed to integrate human sexuality into the everyday life of Muslims without negative connotation. The Islamic rules and regulations take the natural sexual needs of men and women into full consideration. It is therefore permissible for husband and wife to have sexual relations even during Ramadan nights. In Islam, sex among married people is considered a form of worship and an act of compassion. Everything here is in balance. Women and marriage are not denigrated (as they are in the New Testament), nor is marriage touted as a sacrament (as in the Catholic and Orthodox Churches). When his followers were puzzled that sexuality in marriage should be of religious merit, the Prophet explained that it could not be otherwise since extra-marital sex was a sin; one was the exact opposite of the other.

The Islamic no-nonsense attitude in sexual matters corresponds to human nature (*fitra*) and explains the conspicuous absence both of Muslim monks and of Muslim witches. For Western societies, the extreme swings of the pendulum in this area have always come at a very high cost. (Tens of thousands of women were burnt as witches, and millions of others, in cloisters, were deprived of sexuality, motherhood and fatherhood altogether.) If the West wants to escape this predicament through a religion of the middle way, shunning all extremes, Islam offers a way out.

9. As far as women's liberation is concerned, the West is in for a rude awakening now that many career women, alas too late, are rediscovering their suppressed desire for motherhood. Many also discover that, after decades of women's emancipation, the political arena, business, academe, and the media remain male-dominated. Worse, they have to admit that the sexual exploitation of women for commercial purposes is as rampant as ever and even gaining new ground.

With all this in mind, more and more thoughtful Western women are finding out that Islam's way for the liberation of women is more efficient. Surprise! This is indeed the reason why so many single women in the West choose Islam. By covering themselves the Islamic way they regain the very dignity they had lost while participating in the competition for attraction through ever-increasing nudity.

10. Regarding homosexuality, matters are similar to abortion. It is now 'in' to 'come out'. Here, too, the Western pendulum has swung from criminal prosecution on the one end to the broad acceptance of a homoerotic 'option' on the other. The image of homosexuals has been transformed from being criminals to being a protected minority with an entitlement to same-gender marriages.

In this respect, too, Islam always walked the middle ground by neither criminalizing gays and lesbians nor putting them on a pedestal. Instead, homosexuality is considered more a matter of fate than a lifestyle. Islam strictly disapproves of homosexuality but shows compassion to the afflicted. This is an attitude that should come naturally to conservative people of any faith, whether or not one dismisses them for that as terribly straight, narrow-minded or petit bourgeois. That adopting the Islamic way of life would stop the spreading of AIDS is another significant consideration in this context.

11. With bemused smiles Muslims are watching the pharmaceutical

market replete with pills and quick fixes for weight control as well as clubs like Weight-Watchers. Obesity and cellulite have become phenomena accompanying Western affluence. The Muslim smiles bespeak the conviction that diets without spiritual and mental renewal are bound to fail. They do know that properly fasting the entire month of Ramadan – observed as religious worship – achieves not only a reduction of weight and cholesterol, but much, much more: enlivened spirituality; personal discipline; readjustment of priorities, and social compassion. Many people in the West have encountered Islam first during Ramadan, discovering a religion that does wonders with people to the point of transforming their personalities.

12. Western people feel stressed not only at work, but also as tourists on 'adventure' travels, and as sexual athletes in marital and extramarital beds. Their problem is one which in the past only a few philosophical minds paid attention to: 'How to cope with life'. Real-life events are not the problem here; just being around is the unbearable burden. Thus, it seems strangely normal for Americans to have their 'shrink', unless they find comfort and other crutches for 'coping' in transcendental meditation (TM), Yoga, Japanese *tea-ceremonies*, or occult *hocus-pocus*. Other people, unaffected by existential insecurity, are considered clueless and insensitive. In view of that, William Ophuls describes psychology as the very illness it pretends to be healing.[6]

A pitiful character trapped in the three-ring psycho-circus discovers to his surprise that Islam can work miracles of mental recovery with its "technique of contemplation" (prayer, to put it simply) and commitment to an absolute, but benevolent, authority . And that Islam, as well, is much cheaper than a psychiatric couch.

13. Franziska Augstein once wrote that liberal market economy, with Hegel's help, has lately been located near the gates of paradise, in the best of all possible worlds.[7] At any rate, it cannot be denied that the Western economic system, capitalism in whatever shape, has grown into an "overly affluent and risk-free society centered on entertainment" (Andreas Püttmann).[8] For the most part, invested American capital belongs to rich widows and not to the archetypal risk-taking entrepreneurs who chiefly assure the vitality indispensable for a functioning capitalist system. Venture capital is not growing, but low-risk investments with fixed interest rates, and that increases the risk of stagnation. On the other hand, Islam allows capital gains only from a

sharing of risks and profit, be it in form of partnership or stocks. Consequently, Islam prohibits fixed interest (2: 275-280; 3: 130; 4: 160; 30: 39). This alone helps prevent the kind of rentier mentality from rising that may destabilize a financial system. Islam's concomitant prohibition of financial speculation seeks to thwart a related threat: the use of capital as a mere gambling chip, whether by means of stock exchange speculation, derivatives or other futures, activities which may shake up entire economies when getting out of control. (Malaysians know what I am referring to.) The Islamic approach might also serve to dampen the kind of "irrational exuberance" of which Allan Greenspan, chairman of the U.S. Federal Reserve Board, had spoken when the Japanese real-estate markets became overheated in 1996. The same could have been said of the overvaluation of NASDAC new technology stocks in 1999. Early in 2001, the 'dot-com' – bubble finally burst, and with it for many small investors the dreams of early retirement. If only they had read the brilliant analyses of Umer Chapra, a Saudi economist from Pakistan trained in the United States, such disappointed people might have discovered that Islam is the middle road also in terms of economics, keeping its distance as much from socialist planning (State capitalism) as from an unbridled market economy (private capitalism).

14. After presenting what Islam has to offer to the West (and what should make it an attraction there), one might reduce all the differences between the Orient and the Occident to one common denominator – at the risk of rendering the overly coarse picture that inevitably goes with abstraction. The way I see it, the main difference between both worlds can be expressed in the categories of quantity and quality In the West, nothing seems to have value unless it can be quantified or, nowadays, digitized, that is, broken down into either 0 or 1. Of course, spiritual life, moral values and noble emotions cannot be quantified that way. Thus these qualitative riches are not even worth a red penny. For this reason, life in the Western world is more about having, while life for the Oriental people is more about being.

This observation is confirmed by the fact that the 'quality of life' is hardly ever discussed in the East, but is a permanent subject for discussion in the West. In the Orient, one discovers that the quality of life there is disconnected, to a degree unimaginable in the West, from the income level. This phenomenon is due to non-commercial and even anticommercial behavior, to wit a relaxed attitude towards the passing of time; a hospitality that takes priority over virtually everything else; erudition that does not vie for scholarly fame; the demotion of all the purported 'necessities of life' to secondary rank; contemplation as a way of life. This is the metaphoric 'light' that one has seen shining from the Orient all through history: *ex oriente lux.*

It should be clear by now what Islam gives, and that it is the answer to many questions of the West and its ideological needs. Consequently, it should be apparent that Islam is not a nagging petitioner but an essential contributor furnishing meaning, values, and modes of responsible behavior. Whether the Occident acknowledges this potential of Islam is of course a different question altogether. Everybody knows sick or addicted people who fool themselves, refusing to see a doctor in order to be spared the truth. This is the condition in which Western society finds itself. In spite of in-depth cultural analyses like those by Daniel Bell and William Ophuls, most people are only vaguely conscious of the crisis shaking their civilization. Worse, the general Western mood is still a form of triumphalism – with very little heckling. In short, it looks as if nobody will be able to turn the ship around. Instead, Western people will continue to fumble about, as usual.

Proper diagnosis and medication mean nothing if the patient fails to swallow the pills on his night stand, on time – or at all. That the Occident is unlikely to admit needing help is of course part of the very problem: the West is quite capable to analyzing, but no longer able to react accordingly. This inability is symptomatic for civilizations in decline. Roman Herzog, Germany's former Head of State, put it this way: "Our problem is not perception. Our problem is implementation."[9]

The Qur'an contains many stories about peoples of old who had ignored the writing on the wall and thrown their prophets' admonitions to the wind until, all of a sudden, their civilizations were wiped from the face of the earth. The West is running a similar risk. After the triumphal defeat of Communism it faces its own, self-inflicted destruction – unless it can overcome worshipping the individual instead of God, and once again embrace all the divine norms it now neglects. Islam points the way.

Notes

1. A French version of the Spanish regulations appeared in *Le Conseil*, no. 2, Paris 1994, an English version in *Encounters*, vol 2, no. 2, Markfield, LE (UK) 1996, p. 155-167. Cf. Murad Hofmann, *Islam in Spanien - Modell für Europa*, in: Al-Islam, Munich 1996, no. 4, p. 4f.
2. Its coordinator is Dr. Abdallah Boussouf, 2, Impasse du Mai, F-67000 Strasbourg, phone from USA: (011-33) 3-8822.1095.
3. Quoted in *Ophuls*, p. 57.
4. Safranski, "Der Wille zum Glauben", in: *Frankfurter Allgemeine Zeitung, Supplement* 12/24/1993
5. *Ophuls*, p. 51
6. *Ophuls*, p. 198
7. Augstein, "Herr, Deine Helligkeit ist zu groß", in: *Frankfurter Allgemeine Zeitung*, April 23, 1998.
8. Quoted in *Frankfurter Allgemeine Zeitung*, January 27, 1995, p. 38.
9. Herzog, "Berliner Rede," *Welt am Sonntag*, April 27, 1997, p. 11.

CHAPTER FOURTEEN

Islam in America

We're risking our future
and the future of our children.
(Lloyd Kolbe, Atlanta, *USA Today*, Oct.10, 1998)

I believe that Islam is the
most plausible religion for mankind today.
(Friedrich Dürrenmatt, *Neue Züricher Zeitung*, April 6, 1990)

Unexpected but logical nevertheless: if there is any chance for Islam to make a break-through in the foreseeable future, it will happen in the United States of America. There are several causes favoring such a development, and only a few hampering it.

First and foremost, there is the exemplary religious pluralism practiced in North America. No other country in the world – with the possible exception of the Netherlands – provides more room and freedom for religions, sects, and assorted cults to thrive. This is not caused by American indifference. On the contrary, being actively involved in a particular church is still considered good citizenship, and not at all a sign of parochialism. President George W. Bush's initiative to fund faith-based social programs fits well into this picture. Historically, the country has been a haven for any people persecuted for their religion. It is therefore only natural to assure domestic peace by allowing everyone to pursue happiness in his own fashion, just as had been the case in the Kingdom of Prussia during the reign of Frederick the Great in the 18th century. American religious pluralism does not rest on agnosticism, but on reason.

America, after all, did not start out as a pluralistic nation. Rather, tolerance within its own borders was the result of a hard-won struggle against bigotry. In 1620, the Mayflower had barely cast anchor, followed by the establishment by William Bradford (1590-1657) of Plymouth Colony, when a religious dispute already ensued in the second colony in Massachusetts Bay. This taking place among the Puritans, the very people who had fled Europe from religious persecution by the Anglican Church. In his *The Scarlet Letter* (1850), Nathaniel Hawthorne described what from our standpoint today can only be seen as New England's slipping into fascism. Curiously, because of his more tolerant religious views, Roger Williams (1603-1683) was forced to flee a second time and thus became the founding father of Rhode Island and its capital, Providence.

The early American colonies even failed to escape the witch-hunt hysteria of their day. Fanatics like Increase Mather (1629-1723) and his son Cotton Mather (1663-1728) made sure of that, as evidenced in the latter's text *"Memorable Providence, Relating to Witchcrafts and Possessions"* (1689).[1] In America, witches were not only burnt at the stake in Salem, Massachusetts; but "witch-hunts", like the one inspired by Senator Joseph McCarthy, still flare up there, now and then.

Compared to Europe, the United States of today is a perfect role model for pluralism. I discovered that on a 1996 visit to the Pentagon. There I met with the Armed Forces Chaplains Board (AFCB) to discuss the mission of future Muslim "chaplains" in the Army, the Navy, the Air Force, and the Marines. Four such Imams have been approved after 7,500 American soldiers converted to Islam in the wake of the Gulf War. Even so, the percentage of Muslims serving in the American military amounted only to 0.4% of the enlisted men and 0.1% of the officers. (Incidentally, several Rabbis in uniform are also serving, although only 0.5% – or 0.6%, respectively – of American enlisted men and officers are Jewish.) The first *imam, who* began serving in the Army on December 3, 1993, was the African-American Captain Abdul-Rashid Muhammad. He was followed on August 8, 1999, by Lieutenant Junior Grade Mnoje Malik Abd al-Muta' Ali Ibn Noel, Jr., serving in the Navy. Later Yahya Hendi, formerly active in CAIR, also joined the Navy as Imam. As insignia they wear a silver crescent. Since 1998, Muslim sailors – then 725 – have a mosque at the Naval Base in Norfolk, Virginia. They now also have a place to pray at the National Naval Medical Center in Bethesda, Maryland. Every Friday they are released for midday prayers.

Rear-Admiral Muchow, whose assistant turned out to be a Muslim, placed great value on all of his soldiers' believing in something, but was

indifferent as to what they chose to believe in. Any religion was better
than none. The admiral wanted to know what was to figure in an Imam's
combat kit? The Catholic kit, for example, contained a silver cross, a copy
of the New Testament, a stole, wine and hosts, and oil for the last rites
I maintained that the Muslims did not need a kit: they memorized the
Qur'an, and can pray anywhere. But this was not going to satisfy the
admiral's sense of routine. A rule is a rule – and a military chaplain
without combat kit is no real chaplain. So I suggested, half in joke, for
the Muslims to pack a copy of the Qur'an, a short collection of *hadiths*,
a prayer rug, and *Zamzam* water from Makkah...

The admiral had taken care that his commanders were fully apprised
of all the different religious dress codes and dietary restrictions to be
observed by soldiers of different denominations. His staff had indeed
compiled a loose-leaf binder with information on 261 (two hundred and
sixty-one) faith groups represented in the U.S. military. Since it is
officially recorded therein that a Muslima has to cover her hair, American
female Muslim soldiers are allowed to wear a headscarf while on duty.
(In the Turkish armed forces they are not!)

A second advantage favoring Islam in America is the fact that the collective memory of Americans does not register Islam as a threat. Having
disposed of the British, Americans started to worry about developments
in Central and South America, as evidenced by the Monroe Doctrine, the
Cuban missile crisis of 1962, and the U.S. invasion of Panama in1990.
Pearl Harbor made Americans aware of a "yellow menace"; and since
World War I, they are wary of being drawn into European turmoil. Islam,
on the other hand, only became visible for the average, non-Jewish
American with the Iranian hostage crisis and then the bombing of the
World Trade Center.

A third reason is at least as important, and that is the fact that
American Muslims do not constitute one compact and homogeneous
ethnic group but hail from all over the world. Yes, there are some
mosques with a predominant Indo-Pakistani flavor, like the one in
Flushing, New York, and others with Arabic or African-American pre-
ponderance. But the Islamic scene in the States as a whole is decidedly
multi-ethnic. The one exception to the rule is Dearborn near Detroit,
where *Shi'ite* Lebanese inhabit two square miles almost exclusively. An
even rarer case are mystical circles; American *Sufis* are mostly white and
prefer to keep to themselves.

African-American Muslims come closest to being definable as an ethnic group. But they are anything but immigrants who could be sent home. Many black American Muslims believe that their enslaved ancestors were Muslim. They are also convinced that they were brought to America on ships owned by Jews, only to become the "property" of Christian slave holders. Lists with names of slave ships and their Jewish owners are busily circulating in black circles. The *en masse* conversions of African Americans to Islam cannot be divorced from this background. But there is much more to it than political protest and nostalgia. The amazing vitality of "black" Islam is essentially a religious phenomenon with a social frame. Nowhere can this be better seen than in the promotion of the true message of Islam in American prisons.

In retrospect, it does not appear to have been a lasting disadvantage that many of the best black American Muslims initially joined a highly heterodox form of Islam: the "Nation of Islam" under the weirdly authoritarian Elijah Muhammad, who considered himself a prophet and preached an anti-white, anti-Jewish, racist "Islam". Some of the most important African-American Muslims, like Malcolm Little (Malcolm X) a.k.a. Malik El-Shabazz (1925-1965) and Cassius Clay, a.k.a. Muhammad Ali [2], came to Sunni Islam via Elijah Muhammad. It was an achievement of tremendous significance when Elijah's own son, Imam W. D. Mohammed[3], after the death of his father, managed to guide the larger part of the "Nation of Islam" into the fold of the Sunni Muslim *Ummah*, decentralize their leadership, and make them repudiate any kind of racism. Instrumental had been that Malcolm X on his historic pilgrimage to Makkah had realized that a white man embracing the unity of God also embraced the unity of mankind. He also understood that America needed a colorblind Islam, because only such an Islam could rid American society of its deeply ingrained racism. Ever since, Louis Farrakhan, the current leader of the "Nation of Islam",[4] is the only one left who still promotes a heterodox, still racist Islam among black Americans. But before long even his followers will probably merge with orthodoxy: on 27 February, 2000, the leaders of all major Muslim organizations in the U.S., including Imam W. D. Mohammed and Louis Farrakhan, joined hands and shifted the points in such a way that unity is bound to result.

The fourth advantage for Islam in America results from the fact that most Muslim immigrants came to the U.S. as students (and not – as in Europe – as unskilled labor). Consequently, the ratio of university graduates among Muslims is particularly high. In America, to be Muslim more often than not means to be an academic. As a result, Islam is not suspected there, as it is in Europe, of being a backward religion for illiterates and simpletons. Rather, thanks to its student element, Islam in the U.S. has acquired both social prestige and financial prowess. Whenever Muslims congregate for a fundraising dinner, just a few tables may easily yield 100,000 dollars. I have even witnessed collections totaling half a million dollars.

Take for instance the tremendously active director of the Islamic Information Service (IIS) in Los Angeles,[5] Dr. Nazir Khaja, an Indian-born, Harvard-trained urologist. The President of the American Muslim civil rights organization CAIR (Council on American Islamic Relations), Omar Ahmad[6], is of Palestinian origin and is a specialist for computer-chip testing. In Santa Clara, the heart of Silicon Valley, where Intel is literally "inside," 700 Muslim computer specialists are making a living (and an impact). It is there and in Palo Alto (the home of Apple) where Muslims are successfully running their own software firms, like AST and Focus Software International. They are profiting particularly from mathematically gifted employees from India.

The fact that almost all these Muslims are American citizens adds to the attractiveness of this business location, especially when compared to Germany (whose Muslims are mostly foreigners). But it is not only citizenship which allows Muslims to become quickly rooted in the U.S. The vast geographic distances separating them from their countries of origin render frequent family trips there, be it to India or Syria, quite unaffordable, especially for those blessed with numerous children.

Taking a cue from the Jewish minority, quite a few American Muslims have become politically active. Only small groupings, like the Hizb al-Tahir, reject this. The "American Muslim Council"[7] is the highest level of organization representing the interests of Islam to the government. Its first director, Abdurrahman Alamoudi, hails from the Yemen. He single-handedly made sure that Jewish and Christian symbols are not the only ones put on display before the White House during the Christmas season.

Another organization, the "American Muslim Alliance," is working in every election district to inform people about the candidates' attitudes on issues of concern to Muslims. So far Muslims have not given blanket endorsements to either Republicans or Democrats; instead they make independent decisions for each and every individual voting district. Thus Talat Othman and Dr. Maher Hathout each opened the last conventions of both parties with an Islamic prayer (*du'a*). Appeals for voter registration are made before every presidential election, and so far have succeeded in drawing an additional million or so Muslim voters to the ballots. The last presidential election may have been an exception inasmuch as most Muslims, for once, voted for George W. Bush, given that his opponent, Al Gore, had added a Zionist to his ticket, and that during the bloody second (*al-Quds*) Intifada. It is quite possible that the joint "Election 2000" project of the American Muslim Political Coordination Council (AMPCC) and the Council of Presidents of Arab-American Organizations (CPAO) contributed decisively to the election of President Bush. (Does he know that he owes his office to Muslim voters? Does he care?)

Jewish-Zionist organizations, among them the Jewish-American Anti-Defamation League, have been the model for CAIR (www. cair-net.org), an organization focusing its activities on public relations and media-watch as well as on efforts to protect individual Muslims from discrimination. They rely on the services of Ibrahim Cooper, a seasoned media professional. Each morning an employee monitors the Internet for reports on anti-Islamic incidents, ready to trigger a media-alert, if necessary. In the event, many Muslims are simultaneously notified and urged to lodge their protests. An employer who fired a Muslima for wearing a headscarf, at the least can expect picketing. Early in 1999, CAIR prevailed against the Dulles airport authority in Washington, D.C., which had laid off employees for wearing head scarves. They were reinstated with back pay plus 2,500 dollars in damages, a written apology and a promise to give airport personnel sensitivity training.

For CAIR, this was just a routine case. The organization has a good record of bringing even more powerful opponents to their senses, among them Master Card (because of an outrageous commercial set in a mosque), Nike (because of shoes whose sole-profile could be read as "Allah" in Arabic), and Simon & Schuster (because of a blasphemous, anti-Islamic chapter in a children's book). Each year, CAIR publishes a report on "The State of Muslim Civil Rights in the United States" with a statistical analysis of anti-Islamic incidents.

An always inspiring event is the annual convention of the Islamic Society of North America (ISNA), chaired by its Secretary, Dr.

Sayyid Muhammad Sayeed, a fiery Kashmiri.[8] When he calls – 1996 to Columbus, OH, 1998 to St. Louis, MO, 1997 and 1999 to Chicago – 12,000 to 18,000 Muslims from all over the United States come together. Most of them are young, and a majority of the young are women. Part of these conventions is a bazaar the size of a large city department store. All the merchandise near and dear to Muslims can be had there: clothing, jewelry, oriental cosmetics and Islamic computer software (MacHadith; MacQur'an), Qur'an recitations on audio tapes and CDs, books, prayer beads (tasbih), prayer rugs, and oriental delicacies. The land of unlimited possibilities makes this possible, too.

ISNA conventions are used by several other professional Muslim organizations as a platform for their own statutory meetings. There are the gatherings of associations of Muslim physicians, lawyers, psychiatrists, architects, teachers, or students. This is another reminder of the academic leaning of the American Ummah.

With their overall dynamics, organizational talent, civic virtues and efficient professionalism, American Muslims show themselves to be typical Americans, as far as that goes. This professionalism ought to increase even more as grants and stipends provided by Muslim organizations will help to produce many more activist Muslim journalists and lawyers. The "American Journal of Islamic Social Sciences" (AJISS)[9] is the most scientific Muslim journal in the social sciences. America is also home to the first university of Islamic studies accredited in the West, the "School of Islamic and Social Studies" (SISS)[10] in Leesburg, Virginia. On the faculty are Dr. Taha Jabir al-'Alwani (Iraqi born American), Dr. Mona Abul-Fadl, Dr. Iqbal Unus and the American Arabist Yusuf Talal DeLorenzo. A second Western faculty of Islamic studies at university level was launched in 2001 with the Markfield Institute of Higher Education (MIHE), located at the Islamic Foundation in Markfield, Leicester, U.K., and affiliated with Portsmouth University.

Add to this a plethora of Islamic publishing houses (Amana publications; Kazi; American Educational Trust; Threshold Books), journals,[11] research institutes - like the "Institute of Islamic and Arabic Sciences in America" (IIASA) in Fairfax, Virginia[12] – and a network of about 400 Muslim private schools coordinated by the "Council of Islamic Schools in North America" (CISNA - http://www. post tool.com/cisna). It is especially gratifying to see quite a few Muslims, many of them Palestinians, teach at university level, like professor Khalid Yahya

Blankenship at Temple University in Philadelphia.

American Muslims do not yet operate an Islamic TV channel or an all-purpose, all-Islamic radio station. But there is the I.I.S., producing quality videos for telecast. The Canadian Broadcasting Corporation, just like French State Television, routinely sets aside airtime for Muslims, as do several radio stations. An extended resource on national Muslim Organizations in North America is given on their web site at http://www.msa-natl.org/resources/Orgs.html.

On the whole, Islamic intellectual activity seems to be concentrated in and around New York, Chicago, Washington, and in Los Angeles, where Dr. Fathi Osman works.

In a lecture called "Islamic Center: Flagship Ferryboat" Dr. Shafi A. Khaled once pointed out that Muslim activity in the U.S. had originally started with the setting up of Muslim Student Associations (MSA), followed by Islamic Centers at state level. Then typically came Muslim schools in all major cities and prayer halls in smaller communities. Next, American Muslims got involved in *dawah* among prisoners and intra-faith dialogue. Only then did they start focusing on the media and the national political process.

Under these circumstances it is hardly surprising that as early as 1988, there were no less than 3596 mosques in America. It is, however, difficult to believe that now there are more than 60 of them in the metropolitan area of Los Angeles alone. And one has to blink twice upon discovering in Phoenix, deep in the desert landscape of Arizona, a replica of the Dome of the Rock in Jerusalem; it serves, among others, converted Hopi Indians as a mosque.

The oldest American of note to find his way to Islam is Professor T. B. Irving (al-Hajj Ta'lim 'Ali). He had the country's first Sunni mosque built in his hometown of Cedar Rapids, Iowa, and was the first to translate the Qur'an into American English.[13] Did he, in his wildest dreams, ever imagine in his lifetime the emergence of such a wide-ranging Islamic infrastructure, reaching as far as Harvard Law School?[14] Could he ever imagine having six to eight million brothers and sisters in his home country?

BECAUSE of the high concentration of intellectuals among North American Muslims, their dynamics, and their country's ideal research environment (including the absence of censorship), the entire Islamic world places high hopes in their brothers and sisters in the USA. Could it possibly be that the strongest and most important impulses for a world-wide renaissance and reinvigoration of Islam in the third millennium will come from the American continent? What an awesome responsibility for the American Muslim!

This is not to imply that America is all milk and honey for Muslims. They even suffer from a particular disadvantage, in that intensity typical for America alone: the stupendous manipulative power of Zionist organizations and lobbyists that shape the media and politics. Some of them seem to believe that Israel is served best by them if they denigrate the image of Islam and cast all Muslims as potential terrorists. At least in this respect Muslims in Europe are better off – even though, there as well, critique of Israel is "taboo".

Even in the USA, the climate for Muslims lately has begun to deteriorate. One cause for alarm was the nation-wide knee-jerk reaction to the terrible bombing in Oklahoma City on April 19, 1995. Despite a glaring lack of evidence, the attack was immediately attributed to Muslims. (Who else could do such a thing?) A bearded Arab, Abraham Ahmad, was locked up right away. Within but a few days there were 201 attacks on Islamic institutions and individual Muslims in America, among them rifle shots, muggings, the breaking of windows, and the worst kind of telephone threats. Muslim children suddenly found themselves snubbed in school. In the meantime, Timothy McVeigh, the ultra-conservative, white, non-Muslim perpetrator of the crime had been arrested. But the American Muslims are still waiting for an apology.

Equally alarming was the arrest of the former "Black Panther" Rap Brown (the namesake of rappers in music). While in prison, he had converted to Islam, in 1971, studied Arabic, and become the most peaceful and pious imam imaginable, known as Jamil Abdullah al-Amin. Today he runs the Community Mosque in Atlanta, Georgia, as one of the most influential Muslims in North America.[15] Still, the FBI contrived an accusation against him for nothing less than murder. However, Brown could not be found guilty since the main witness admitted in court to having been coerced into making false statements. He proceeded to cause a minor sensation when he pronounced the Islamic confession of faith (shahada) in the middle of the trial.

For the American *Ummah* it is depressing as well that Anwar N. Haddam, representative of the Algerian F.S.I., after years of unofficially tolerated activities in Washington was arrested upon trying to leave for Sweden. For years, he has been held under "secret evidence" – a procedure absolutely incompatible with the rule of law of which Americans are so proud.

Thus it was no surprise to anybody anymore when a movies like *The Siege* in1998 very deviously portrayed American Muslims as a threat to the entire nation. (You can have one guess about the affiliation of the film makers.)

Nevertheless, whenever I feel the need for a spiritual uplift and better morale, it is not only another pilgrimage to Makkah that comes to my mind, but also another uplifting visit to my Muslim sisters and brothers in the United States of America.

Notes

1. The religious controversies among the early America settlers are well documented in Joe Lee Davies, et al., *American Literature, An Anthology and Critical Survey*, vol 1 (From the Beginning to 1860), Chicago, 1948. The documents relating to witches are on p.104 ff.
2. For an interview with Ali documenting his touching activism on behalf of Islam see Barboza, p. 223 ff. Ali's daughter, May Ali is also a Muslim activist.
3. For an interview with Imam W. D. Mohammed see Barboza, p. 99.
4. For Farrakhan, see Gardell.
5. P.O.B. 6220, Altadena, CA 91003, Phone (626) 791-9818; fax: (626) 793-0710.
6. 453 New Jersey Av., S.E., Washington, D.C. 20003. phone (202) 488-8787, fax (202) 488-0833. E-mail: cair@ix.netcom.com, url: http://www.cair-net.org
7. Suite 400, 1212 New York Ave., Washingon D.C. 20005, Phone (202) 789-2550. url: http://www.amconline.org
8. 262 Old State Road, Plainfield, IN 46168, phone (317) 839-8157, fax (317) 839 1840. The competing umbrella organization is called "Islamic Circle of North America" (ICNA) Its address: 166-26 89th Ave., Jamaica, NY 11432; phone (718) 658 -1199; fax (718) 658 -1255.
9. P.O.Box 669, 555 Grove St., Herndon, VA 22070, phone (703) 471-1133; fax (703) 471-39222. http://www.iiit.org/AJISS.htm.
10. 750 750-A Miller Drive, S.E., Leesburg, VA 20176, phone (703) 779-7477; fax (703) 779-7999. http://www.siss.edu.

11. E.g., *Middle East Affairs Journal*; *The American Journal of Islamic Finance*; *Islamic Law Journal*; *Journal of the Islamic Medical Association of North America*; *The Washington Report on Middle East Affairs*; *The Minaret*; *Horizons*.

12. 8500 Hilltop Road, Fairfax, VA 22031, phone (703) 641-4890; fax (703) 641-4899. http://www.iiasa.org.

13. In my opinion, his translation of the Qur'an is less "American," but rather banal in style and thus inappropriate for any holy script. Cf. Irving, *The Qur'an, The First American Version*, Amana Books: Brattleboro, Vermont, 1985 .

14. By now even Harvard Law School has jumped on the bandwagon and established a Harvard Islamic Legal Studies Program, which is on the fast track of becoming the most comprehensive Islamic law library worldwide. (HLS already owns the most complete collection of German and French law) Address: Pound Hall 501, Harvard Law School, Cambridge, MA 02138, phone (617) 496-3941; fax (617) 496-2707. http://www.law.harvard.edu.

15. For more on Rap Brown, see Barboza, p. 48 ff.

CHAPTER FIFTEEN

What if they come?

The third possibility is that
Islam will overrun us.
(Bishop Tibha from Fulda, Germany,
in Der Spiegel, December 22, 1997)

As far as anyone can see, a real "breakthrough" for Islam is not on the horizon any time soon, not even in the USA, unless God Himself intervenes. Still, Surah al-Nasr (110) announced: "When Allah's help comes, and victory, and you see people enter Allah's religion in crowds, praise your Lord, and ask His forgiveness (...)".

Possibly al-Nasr does not presage future events at all but refers to a past event: either the Prophet's death (632 CE) or the peaceful occupation of Makkah on January 11, 630, which actually went hand-in-hand with a massive conversion to Islam which included many a turncoat. The latter interpretation is supported by two independent sources – Jabir ibn 'Abd Allah and Abu Hurayrah – who report the Prophet Muhammad as saying: "People have certainly joined God's religion in droves – and when the time comes, they will leave it again in droves."

Let the future take care of itself. What counts here and now are the following, almost tangible, fears: many people in the West are seriously asking themselves what would happen to them and their way of life if the Muslims were to become the majority. This anxiety may be vague. It is nonetheless real. How else could irresponsible authors stoke it up, as in Germany with Holy War for Allah (Wilhelm Dietl), The Islamic Challenge (Gerhard Konzelmann), Mullahs on the Rhine (Rolf Stolz) or Like Fire and Water (Bassam Tibi).[1]

Therefore, a discussion of the specter of an Islamic majority in the

Occident is not just academic, and this book will conclude with it. The issue here is how fears of the future impact the present. At the same time, the following exposition tends to show that the treatment of minorities foreseen by Islamic law is the most liberal the world has ever known. This in turn shows that Muslims in the West demand less than they are willing to give.

THE dispute on whether or not Islam is essentially tolerant with respect to other religions stems mainly from a misunderstanding of two Qur'anic passages: *al-Imran* (3: 19) and *al-Tawbah* (9: 33). The first one – *inna ad-din 'ind' allah al-Islam* – is frequently translated as "The religion before [or: of] Allah is Islam." This sounds terribly exclusivistic. Fortunately, it is a translation open to debate, because the noun *al-Islam* here should be taken in its original meaning as understood by the Prophet's earliest companions, i.e., as "submission to God," and not as a reference to the religion called "Islam" as it evolved in history.[2] Taking this into account, the sentence in question would read: "The religion before [or: of] God is submission to Him."[3]

The same goes for the statement in *Al Imran* (3: 85) which sounds awfully triumphalist when translated: "*If anyone desires a religion other than Islam, never will it be accepted from him.*" This, too, should be read: "*If anyone desires a religion other than submission to God, (...).*"

The following passage in *Surahs al-Tawbah* (9: 33) and *al-Fath* (48: 28) sounds similarly non-ecumenical and exclusionist when translated: "*It is He Who has sent His messenger with guidance and the religion of truth, to make it prevail over all religions.*" Again, the crucial Arabic verb (*zahara*) also permits the following reading: "*It is He Who has sent His Messenger with guidance and the religion of truth, to let it outshine all religions.*" In that case, Islam's light is simply brighter than other sources of light without eclipsing them.

Religious intolerance is not typical of Islam. The reverse is true, in a fundamental sense, as already shown by the grandiose manifesto of religious pluralism announced in *Surah al-Ma'ida* (5: 48). Its centrality bears repeating word for word: "*To each among you have We prescribed a law and a way. If Allah had so willed, He would have made of you one single community, but (His plan is) to test you in what He has given you. So compete with each other in good deeds. The return of you all is to Allah; then He will inform you about the matters over which you used to differ.*"

There are a large number of equally liberal Qur'anic statements:

- "*No compulsion in matters of faith*", Surah al-Baqara (2: 256). Thus coercion in matters of conscience is not only prohibited but declared useless.
  - "*To you your way, and to me mine.*" Surah al-Kafirun (109: 6).
  - "*Say, 'The truth is from your Lord: Let him who wills believe in it, and him who wills reject it.'*" Surah al-Kahf (18: 29).
  - "*To every people have We appointed [different] ways of worship for them to follow. Hence, do not let them draw you into disputes on this matter, but invite them to your Lord.... If they argue with you, say 'Allah knows best what you are doing.' Allah will judge between you on the Day of Judgment concerning all about which you used to differ.*" Surah al-Hajj (22: 67-69).
  - "*O mankind! We have created you all from a male and a female and have made you into nations and tribes, so that you might come to know one another. Verily the most noble of you in the sight of Allah is the one who is most deeply conscious of Him.*" Surah al-Hujurat (49: 13).

These verses show that, as viewed by Islam,
  - Religious and ethnic pluralism are intended by God and are thus entirely normal;
  - Faith must remain a matter of personal decision;
  - Dogmatic disputes are fruitless.

This fundamental attitude would be remarkable enough even if it only envisioned peaceful coexistence. But Islam aims higher. It considers both unity and diversity as values per se.

From an Islamic point of view, the unity of all mankind rests on two mutually reinforcing foundations. The first of these consists in the ontological sameness of the entire creation whose unified purpose is to recognize and praise God. The Qur'an describes this vividly:

  - "*Are you not aware that it is Allah Whose praises all beings in the heavens and on earth extol, and the birds as they spread out their wings? Each one knows its own prayer.*" Surah an-Nur (24: 41).
  - "*Have they considered all the things that Allah has created - how their shadows turn right and left, prostrating to Allah, and that in the humblest manner? And to Allah does obeisance all that is in the heavens and all that is on earth, every moving creature, and the angels (...)*" Surah al-Nahl (16: 48 f.)

- *"Are you not aware that to Allah prostrate all that are in the heaven and on earth – the sun, and the moon, and the stars, and the mountains, and the trees, and the animals, and many human beings?..." Surah al-Hajj* (22: 18).

Considering the scope of this cosmic unity of the entire creation, what difference is there between Sunnis and Shi'ites, Catholics and Protestants, Christians and Jews, Buddhists and Hindus? They all share the same human essence (*fitra*). This is precisely what God refers to in *Surah al-Anbiya* (21: 92) when speaking about the unity of mankind: *"Verily, this community of yours is one single community, and I am your Lord and the Sustainer; therefore, worship Me."* This describes the universal *Ummah*, the community of all the people worshiping God: the global ecumenical brotherhood of all believers.

A second foundation of unity is found in the Abrahamic link that binds all believers of monotheism together. This is unambiguously expressed in *Surah al-Shura* (42: 13): *"In matters of faith, He has ordained for you what He had enjoined upon Noah – and into which We have given you insight through revelation – as well as that which We had enjoined on Abraham, and Moses, and Jesus: be steadfast in upholding the [true] faith, and do not break up your unity therein."* Abraham's role is so pivotal that the 14th *Surah* carries his name – "Ibrahim".

It is unfortunate that many Christians continue to misunderstand not only the ontological, existential unity of mankind, but also the Abrahamic link as an inclusionist trap, meant to assimilate them. Nobody is to be appropriated! Unity is possible in spite of diversity. The Abrahamic link is the manifest basis for both a Christian-Muslim dialogue and a trialogue between Christians, Jews and Muslims in full equality. If everybody involved would approach discussions in this spirit, at long last Paul Schwarzenau, John Hick, and Hans Küng could go into retirement.

Muslims, for their part, would not want to see this global trialogue result in a relativism bordering on agnosticism. The Prophet Muhammad shows a path to God that is specific. The Islamic doctrine of the One and Only God (*tawhid*), Who neither begets nor is begotten (112: 1-4), will always remain non-negotiable. As mentioned earlier, 24-karat-gold cannot be purified further nor otherwise enhanced.

THE broad and solid theological basis for the toleration of other religions and their followers, as exemplified above, allowed Muslim jurisprudence very early to develop a detailed code for the protection of religious minorities (*al-siyar*). It continues to be relevant to this day, almost 1400 years later.[4]

Already ancient Arabic customary law, strongly anchored in the tradition of hospitality, permitted each individual member of a tribe, women included, to grant sanctuary to strangers. This to be honored by the entire community (*al-aman al-ma'ruf*).[5] This normative custom eventually evolved into a protected legal relationship between the Islamic State and its non-Muslim citizens (*dhimmi*), formalized by written stipulations for the specific protection of what the Qur'an calls *ahli-l-kitab*, i.e., "People of the Book", to wit: Jews, Christians, Zoroastrians, and Sabians.[6]

Thus in this status religious minorities enjoyed a high level of autonomy in religious matters, including inheritance, family, and criminal law. In this respect, the protected minority was not subject to the legal monopoly normally exercised on their territory by sovereign states. Rather, *dhimmi* were partially extra-territorial. This would for instance allow Christians to raise pigs and trade wine; Jews were permitted to charge interest for credit.[7] At the same time, the minorities enjoyed the state's general protection of life and limb, property, public worship of their own religion in synagogues and churches – exactly as the Prophet's envoy, Abu Ubayda, had promised a group of Christian emissaries from Najran in 631.[8] Killing of a Christian was prosecuted as severely as the murder of a Muslim.[9] Prophet Muhammad is reported as saying: "*Those hurting a protected person are hurting me; and whoever hurts me also hurts Allah.*"

The protected minorities were to be treated differently in but three ways:

- They were not subject to military draft.[10]
- In exchange for this exemption they paid a kind of conscription-tax (*jizya*) by way of a poll tax (per head) that was not necessarily higher than the basic tax (*zakat*) levied on Muslims.[11] Beginning with Caliph 'Umar, in cases where the Islamic State was militarily too weak to protect the community from outside aggression, religious minorities had their poll tax refunded. His commander in Syria, again Abu Ubayda, abided by this rule when it became clear that he would be unable to protect Damascus from the approaching Byzantine troops.
- Whereas protected minorities were allowed an active role in governing and decision-making – as in the federalist Muslim-Jewish city-state of *al-Madinah*, as of 622[12] – the highest office, i.e., head of state,

was reserved for Muslims. But non-Muslim ministers frequently served in Islamic government throughout the course of history. To this day, Christians and Jews serve as cabinet ministers in Egypt, Iraq, and Morocco.

The Islamic code for the protection of religious minorities had been so generous and liberal that it contributed to the undoing of the Ottoman Empire. The relative autonomy and self-administration permitted by Islamic law inadvertently encouraged the emergence of nationalist sentiments and organizations among the various ethnic groups in the Balkans – Croatians, Hungarians, Greeks, Serbs, and Bulgarians. All they had to do was to use the existing dhimmi – infrastructure as the basis of their own nation state.

In spite of this reassuring background, many Westerners are afraid that Muslims in Europe might not protect atheists or agnostics, since they do not fall under the traditional definition of *"People of the Book"* (*ahli-l-kitab*). To be sure, in the beginning only Christianity and Judaism were considered religions of the Book, to be joined later by the religion of the Sabians or Zoroastrians (in Bahrain). Eventually even Hindus were included as *ahli-l-kitab*.[13] This shows that the definition of *People of the Book* has become fuzzy. This fact probably encouraged Ahmed El-Borai to suggest, in 1995, that all those be considered "People of the Book" "who have religious scripture or something that could have become a book - unless they are polytheists."[14]

Surprisingly, so far, the very verse has been overlooked that, in my opinion, solves the problem. It reads: *"If one of the pagans (mushrikun) seeks your protection, grant him protection, so that he may hear the word of Allah; and then escort him to a place where he can feel secure. That is because they are people without knowledge"* Surah al-Tawbah (9: 6). Muslims today tend to accept that atheists can be considered "pagans" (mushrikun) in the sense of this verse. Is not any form of drug addiction also now regarded as a form of polytheism (*shirk*)? This suggests the conclusion that atheists – like members of religious minorities – must also not be subjected to coercive measures in a Muslim country. In fact, by signing international human rights covenants, more and more Islamic authorities are committing themselves to protecting atheists against persecution as well. After all, how could one withhold such protection without violating the commandment that forbids coercion in religious matters (2: 256)?

So much for theory. And what about practice? Fortunately, throughout Islamic history, practice usually corresponds to doctrine. There were exceptions, of course, mostly bred in the context of mutual Christian-Muslim warfare. This poisoned atmosphere explains humiliating dress codes imposed on non-Muslims, their being prohibited from riding horses (while donkeys were allowed ....). In some cases even the ringing of church bells or building of new churches was forbidden.[15] In rare cases, Christians found themselves also banned from consuming alcohol and pork.[16]

In medieval times such behavior, contradictory to the letter and the spirit of Islam, was easily justified with a phrase selectively picked from Surah al-Tawbah (9): 29, which was understood to say: *"Fight those who formerly had received revelation but do not believe in Allah, nor the Last Day (...) until they pay the poll tax (jizyah) with willing submission, and feel themselves subdued."*[17] The Arabic text allows, however, a more contextual translation, keeping in mind that the Qur'an only permits fighting in a defensive mode, i.e., against aggression. Verse 29 can then be read: *"Defend yourself against those who formerly had received revelation (...) until they surrender at last and pay the poll tax according to their ability (or: voluntarily)."*

No mentioning here of "humiliation" or personal "submission"![18]

Remember: there simply does not exist any Qur'anic justification for being disrespectful to non-Muslims.

On the whole, the Islamic minority statute enabled Christians and Jews in the past to make significant contributions to Muslim society. After all, Muawiyya, the fifth Caliph, was not the first one to have a Christian wife; Prophet Muhammad had one before him – Maria, a Copt.

LET us now return to the present situation in the West. You will recall that the issue there is not how Muslims would act if they became the majority, because that is utopian. The question is rather what kind of behavior their neighbors are expecting of Muslims in such an unlikely case. Because these expectations and suspicions nourish the anxieties and fears which shape the current Occidental attitudes towards Muslim minorities. In fact, it is entirely unlikely that Western governments and societies will reciprocate to Muslim minorities the same liberal spirit that Muslims are bound to show to Christian minorities.

Muslims of course acknowledge gratefully that the structural medieval intolerance against them has significantly abated since the eighteenth century. Pivotal was the above-mentioned development of the United States of America into a society exemplary for its religious pluralism.

The Enlightenment also turned France into a permanent haven of asylum.

The waves of immigrants pouring into Europe during the previous century from the *Maghrib,* the Indian sub-continent, and Turkey proved similarly important since they managed to diversify the Old Continent's formerly mono-religious culture.

This is the backdrop against which the United Nations and the European Council were able to weave a fabric of treaties, all designed to protect human rights in general and religious freedom in particular. Representative are the *Universal Declaration of Human Rights,* dated December 10, 1949,[19] the *European Convention for the Protection of Human Rights* and *Fundamental Freedoms* of November 4, 1950,[20] and the *International Covenant on Civil and Political Rights* dated December 16, 1966.[21] Article 27 of this Covenant decrees the following: "In those states in which ethnic, religious or linguistic minorities exist, persons belonging to such minorities shall not be denied the right, in community with the other members of their group, to enjoy their own culture, to profess and practice their own religion, or to use their own language."

These developments have left their beneficial mark on the West. Without this, the existence of a purely Muslim neighborhood in Andalusia, the *Communidad Islámica en España of Granada* (!), would not have been conceivable. (Believe it or not, their currency are self-minted gold dinars and silver dirhams.)[22] At the same time, the Western protection of religious minorities is still far behind the semi-autonomy that Islamic law had granted religious minorities already 1400 years ago. Tell me: Who is to be afraid of whom?

Muslims would of course be naive if they waited for Western national states to abandon the principle of territoriality, which insists upon equal rights for everybody within the national borders. (For that reason Germans don't like to be reminded that the German Empire had indeed permitted aristocratic families to apply their own, separate inheritance laws, until 1919.) However, people need to be enlightened that application of the Islamic minority code, partially suspending the territorial principle with its concept of religious semi-autonomy, would have the potential to resolve otherwise insoluble territorial conflicts.

Ready examples are Northern Ireland, the Basque region, Catalonia, Corsica, Bosnia-Herzegovina, Kosovo, and Macedonia.

Muslims are not naive – and no born rebels either. With few exceptions, they are ready and willing as a minority to abide by the laws and regulations of the non-Muslim states in which they live. Here they are what might be called *dhimmi* of Christianity. The idea that Muslims might voluntarily live outside the *dar al-Islam*, sort of a minority protected by Christians, if not unthinkable, has been so strange that Muslim legal scholars did not deal with the eventuality until quite late. Since the fifteenth century, however, the picture has profoundly changed, with ever greater numbers of Andalusian Muslims coming under Catholic rule.[13] Already earlier, some Muslim lawyers had been farsighted enough to consider Muslims in the Christian world as an asset for Islam provided they were allowed to fulfill at least the minimum requirements of their religion. Only where this was not possible, emigration became a must. Already in those medieval days, Muslims in the diaspora, as a matter of principle, were expected to comply with local laws. The Hanafi school of law even exempted Muslims abroad from the prohibition of interest on capital, wherever the taking of interest was customary. So, who is to be afraid of whom?

By now it should be clear what contemporary Muslims expect from a Western state: not necessarily the adoption of the liberal, model Islamic minority statute, but – as a minimum – a strict observation of the rule of law, i.e., no double standards for Muslims and non-Muslims.

Unfortunately, in this respect there is a lot left to be desired. The prototypical example here is the building of mosques. It takes years to get a permit, particularly if the mosque is to be built downtown rather than behind the railroad tracks or next to a slaughterhouse. There will be haggling over every little inch of the minaret, as if construction codes limited its height below that of church steeples. In Darmstadt, Germany, the design of a mosque was not approved because the *cupola* was considered ten inches [sic!] too high. Little did it matter that the design observed those classical dimensions that had made Sinan (1489-1578), the Turkish master architect, famous. Once a mosque is built, local authorities frequently refuse to permit the use of the minaret as a *minaret*: for the call to prayer (*adhan*).

Most of the time, administrative restrictions of that sort have no basis in the law, or are based on regulations which would not stand ground in court. Wherever there is freedom of religion, the call for prayer, modestly amplified, should enjoy constitutional protection. Yet, while being by far not as loud as city traffic and factory sirens, the *adhan* is frequently treated as a threat to public health, traffic and even the environment (the call for prayer as "noise pollution"). Sometimes each and every step in the construction of a mosque has to be fought out in court.[24] Of course, democracies do not function that way. They can only function if most bureaucrats and city councils in most cases routinely apply the law.

The second prime example of a double standard is the headscarf.

I am referring to that small piece of cloth that seems to shake the foundations of entire republics, like Tunisia and Turkey. If the headscarf is an illicit article endorsement for Islam, what about the wearing of crucifixes and the ringing of church bells? If wearing a headscarf bespeaks oppression, why not ask the woman wearing it about who forced it on her? If the scarf violates work regulations, why not change the   rules? And what about Christian sisters, and paintings of Mary? Was she oppressed?

Muslims are absolutely aghast when non-Muslims attempt to interpret the Qur'an for them – as constantly happens in and out of court. Muslims are astonished to hear from such non-Muslim "experts" that they are after all free to eat any kind of meat, wear bikinis in mixed company, and that a Muslima's hair does not need to be covered.

It may sound harsh – but Muslim society views such chutzpah as Eurocentrism or cultural imperialism. Nobody would ever have the audacity to even suggest to Jewish citizens how to read the Torah, the Mishna, and the Jerusalem Talmud.

A double standard, worse: a cynical ploy is also at work in the case of halal slaughtering of animals. The Islamic ritual of slaughter is identical to the Jewish ritual as permitted to Jewish citizens. A Muslim butcher, however, in many countries is considered to violate animal protection laws if he slaughters like his Jewish colleague. In Germany, a judge recently even tried the following cynical chain of arguments to prove that Muslims could do, after all, without halal meat: the Qur'an allowed the consumption of prohibited food in an emergency situation, didn't it? Well, by forbidding *halal* slaughtering, the government brought about exactly that emergency... The good judge merely overlooked that an emergency according, to the Qur'an, pertains only to eating or not, and is a question of life and death. Muslims are indeed permitted to consume non-*halal* meat as guests at a Christian table, but even then never pork or alcohol.

No Muslim will deny that the fate of Islam in the West depends on whether parents can transmit their faith to the next generation, and that in the midst of a consumer society. The answer is of course good Muslim schools, run by and for Muslims. Some states, like the U.S. and France, exclude religious instruction from public schools altogether. Predictably, private Islamic education is strongest there. Most other European states, however, provide for the teaching of religion, Christianity that is, in public schools. Currently, European Muslims are fighting for Islam to be taught in public schools as well. Where they win, their success is, however, often self-defeating. This is definitely the case when school authorities install their own Islamic curriculum or employ instructors to teach Islam. The newest trend in Europe is, however, to set up non-denominational, non-confessional classes in comparative religion and "ethics" to be attended by all children, regardless of their religion. This is to make a homogenous society. The children – before having learned enough of their own religion – are called upon to apprise each other of their faiths. Nobody denies that there is a need to reduce mutual suspicions and fears, also in school. In 1997, a poll conducted in Germany bore out that 48 percent considered Islam as a "threat to Western culture", as opposed to 37 percent who thought otherwise, and 15 percent who were undecided.[25]

But children can learn about each other's religions in history and geography, and perhaps in philosophy class, without sacrificing proper religious teaching to a non-denominational stew called "ethics".

Countries like the United States and France neither have a "state religion", nor do they recognize religious organizations officially, or raise taxes for them. Other countries, like Great Britain and the Scandinavian kingdoms, recognize the Anglican or Lutheran Churches as the official religion of the State. Germany is a very special case. There, religious communities can be recognized by the state as public corporations. In that case, the state raises "church taxes", a percentage of the income tax, for them. Also, representatives of recognized religions figure, for instance, in the boards of overseers of public TV. Christian holidays are protected, and Christian religion must be offered in public school.

German Muslims discuss of course whether they should also seek such recognition, but the issue currently is not a priority for them. There is, in particular, the fear that Islam, in the process of recognition, would somehow be forced into accepting a centralized church structure entirely foreign to it – institutionalized Islam. Also, would it not be a mixed blessing if the Muslims found themselves showered with large amounts of tax money?

THIS, by and large, is the state of affairs of the West and its Muslims at the dawn of the Third Millennium: a new century which promises to be exciting. One way or the other, Islam is going to play a major role in it. Why not allow this role to be a positive one?

I am closing with *Surah al 'Asr* (103) which begins with an adjuration about time. Time, this dizzying phenomenon, which inspired us with particular awe when we set the clock to 2001.

(1) By the flight of Time!
(2) Verily, man is in loss,
(3) Except those who have faith and do good works,
    and exhort one another to truth,
    and exhort one another to patience.

Notes

1. Under this title, Bassam Tibi, e.g., claimed in *Der Spiegel,* 37/1994, p. 170 that traditional Islam " does not leave any room for individual human rights"; for him even free speech is incompatible with Islam. He concluded: " The *Shari'ah* separates Muslims from the civilizations who embrace human rights." (p.172).

2. Take for instance the Qur'an translations of Muhammad Hamidullah (Brattleboro 1985), Denise Masson (Paris 1967), T. B. Irving (Brattleboro 1985), Rashid Said Kassab (Amman 1997), Marmaduke Pickthall (London 1930), and the officail Saudi translation into English (al-Madinah 1992).

3. There are passages where "Islam" actually does mean "Islam", as for instance in 5: 3.

4. *al-Siyar* is the plural of *al-sira*, here meaning "behavior" relative to international law or international private law.

5. Cf. Doi, p. 426-437; Kruse, p. 74-154.

6. Cf. Ramadan, p. 106-155.

7. Cf. Turabi (1992), p. 33-35.

8. Cf. Salem, p. 153. Regarding the agreement with the Christians from Najran, he quotes from Abu Yusuf, *Kitab al-Kharaj*, Cairo 1933, p. 72 f. See also Abu Dawud, Sunan, *hadith* no. 3035. Abu Dawud was one among the ten men whom Prophet Muhammad predicted would enter paradise.

9. *Al-Bukhari*, vol. 9, no. 49; Abu Dawud, *Sunan*, no. 2635; al-Misri, 52.1 (382).

10. This did not exempt the minorities from contributing fiancially or otherwise to support their own defensive efforts.

11. In the Middle Ages, the annual per-capita tax was between 12 Dirham and 1 Dinar. See an-Nawawi (1914), p. 467.

12. The Jewish tribes had an equal part in building the federation. Thus even the very first Islamic State was far from being purely Muslim.

13. See *al-Misri*, ch. 11.1, p. 607.

14. *La condition des minorités en Islam*, Studie für die 7. Generalversammlung des ägyptischen Hohen Islamrats in Kairo, July 1995, p. 19.

15. Accordig to al-Nawawi (1994), p. 467-469.

16. Salem, p. 155-158.

17. This is the view of al-Nawawi.

18. Cf. Muhammad Asad (*The Message*, 1980) regarding 9:29.

19. Relevant here are Article 2 (non-discrimination), 14 (asylum law) and 18 (religious freedom)

20. Relevant here are Article 9 (religious freedom) and 14 (non-discrimination).

21. Relevant here is Article 18 (religious freedom).

22. Address: P.O.Box 674, E-18080 Granada, phone (011-34) 958-207-519, or, - 220-760; fax -207.639 or -221-368.

23. Cf. El-Fadl's very detailed study.

24. The legal scholar Dior Diop wrote a very elegant article on this entitled "Construire une mosquée - est-ce si difficile?" (in: *La Medina*, Paris, no. 1, 1999, p. 56): The legal text itself is not the problem, but its application whenever Muslims are involved.

25. Cf. Reinhard Hesse, "Enemy Islam", in *Die Woche*, April 23, 1997.

NAME INDEX

BIBLIOGRAPHY

Der Koran. Translated into German by Max Henning, Edited and revised by Murad Wilfried Hofmann. Munich: Diederichs, 1999.

The Meaning of the Holy Qur'an. Revised translation and commentary by Abdullah Yusuf 'Ali, 7th edition. Beltsville, MD: amana, 1989.

The Message of the Qur'an. Translation and commentary by Muhammad Asad. Gibraltar: Dar al-Andalus, 1980.

Die Bedeutung des Korans. Translated by Fatima Grimm, et al. 2nd ed., 5 vol. Munich: SKD Bavaria, 1998.

Abd el-Wahab, Ahmad. *Dialogue Transetionnel entre le Christianisme et l'Islam*. Paris: Centre Abaad, 1987.

Abdou, Mohammed and Rissalat al-Tawhid. *Exposé de la Religion Musulmane*. Paris: Geuthner, 1984.

Affendi, Abdel Wahab El-. *Turabi's Revolution*. London: Grey Seal Books, 1991.

--- *Who Needs an Islamic State?*, London: Grey Seal Books, 1991.

Afifi, Zeinab. Die Stellung der Frau im Islam. In *Gesichter des Islam*. Berlin: Haus der Kulturen der Welt, 1992. 119- .

Afkhami, Mahnaz. *Faith & Freedom - Women's Human Rights in the Muslim World*. London: I.B. Tauris, 1995.

Ahmad, Kurshid. ed. Elimination of Riba from the Economy. Islamabad: Institute of Policy Studies, 1994.

---"Man and the Future of Civilization: An Islamic Perspective." Encounters 1, no. 1 (1995): 103.

Ahmad, Mumtaz. "Islam and Democracy: The Emerging Consensus." *Middle East Affairs Journal* 2, no. 4 (1996): 29-.

Ahmed, Akbar. *Post Modernism and Islam*. London: Routledge, 1992.

Ahmed, Akbar S. and Donna Hastings. *Islam, Globalization, and Postmodernism*. London: Routledge, 1994.

Ahsan, Manazir. and A.R. Kidwai. *The Satanic Saga - Muslim Perspectives on the Satanic Verses Affair*. Markfield, LE (UK): The Islamic Foundation, 1991.

Ahsan, Manazir. "Arrival, Expulsion and Return: Muslim Experience in Europe." *Al -Mizan* 2, no. 1 (1996): 23- .

230   Bibliography

Ali, Ausaf. "An Essay on Public Theology."
  Islamic Studies 34, no.1 (1995).
Alwani, Taha Jabir al-. *Ijtihad*. Herndon, VA: I.I.I.T., 1993.
Amin, Hussein. *Le livre du musulman désemparé*. Paris:
  La Découverte, 1992.
Amin, Qasim. *Die Befreiung der Frau (1889)*. Würzburg: Echter, 1992.
Ansari, Zafar Ishaq and John Esposito, ed., *Muslims and the West,*
  Encounter and Dialogue, Washington, D.C.: Center for Muslim-
  Christian Understanding, 2001.
Antes, Peter. *Der Islam als politischer Faktor*. 2nd ed. Hannover:
  Niedersächsische Landeszentrale für Politische Bildung, 1991.
Arkoun, Mohammed. *Pour une critique de la raison islamique*. Paris:
  Maisonneuve, 1984.
--- *Ouvertures sur l'Islam*. Paris: Jacques Grancher, 1989.
Armstrong, Karen. *Holy War - The Crusades and their Impact on*
  Today's World. New York: Papermac, 1992.
--- *A History of God*. New York: Alfred A. Knopf, 1993.
Asad, Muhammad. *Islam at the Crossroads*. Lahore: Ashraf Press, 1934.
--- Muhammad, *The Principles of State and Government in Islam*
  (1961). Gibraltar: Dar al-Andalus, 1980.
--- *This Law of Ours and other Essays*. Gibraltar: Dar al-Andalus,1997.
--- *Vom Geist des Islam* (1979). Translated by Hasan Ndayisenga.
  Cologne: Islam. Wiss. Akademie, 1984.
--- *Muhammad Asad und die Reise nach Mekka*.
  Interview with Karl Günter Simon.
  Frankfurter Allgemeine Zeitung, November 18, 1988.
Asad, Talal. *Genealogies of Religion: Discipline and Reason of Power*
  in Christianity and Islam. Baltimore : John Hopkins Univ. Press,
  1993.
Aschmawy, Muhammad Said. *L'Islamisme contre l'Islam*
  (al-Islam al- siyasi). Paris: Ed. la découverte, 1989.
Atlan, Henri. *A tort et à raison - Intercritique de la science et du mythe*.
  Paris: Seuil, 1986.
Attas, Syed Muhammad Naquib. *Islam and Secularism*.
  Kuala Lumpur: ABIM, 1978.

--- ed. *Islam and the Challenge of Modernity*. Kuala Lumpur:
I.I.I.T., 1996.

Ayoub, Mahmoud. "Islam and Pluralism." *Encounters* 3,
no. 2 (1997).103.

Azzi, Abderrahmane, "Islam in Cyberspace."
Islamic Studies 38, no. 1 (1999): 103- .

Azmeh, Aziz al-. *Islam and Modernities*.
2nd. ed. London / N.Y.: Verso, 1993.

Bachelard, Gaston. *Le Nouvel Esprit Scientifique*.
10th ed. Paris: Presses Universitaires de France, 1968.

Badri, Malik. *The Dilemma of Muslim Psychiatrists* Landon: MWH,
1979.

--- *The Aids Crisis: a natural product of modernity's sexual revolt*.
Kuala Lumpur: ISTAC, 1997.

Bahnassawi, Sali El-. *Die Stellung der Frau zwischen Islam und
weltlicher Gesetzgebung*. Munich: SKD-Bavaria Verlag, 1993.

Balic, Smail. "Die islamische Überlieferung in der Postmoderne."
In *Gottes ist der Orient, Gottes ist der Okzident*. Köln: Böhlau,
1991. 108-.

Banna, Hasan al-. *Five Tracts of Hasan al-Banna* (1906-1949).
Translated by Charles Wendell. Berkeley: Univ. of California Press,
1975.

Barboza, Steven. *American Jihad - Islam after Malcolm X* N Y:
Doubleday, 1994.

Barrett, Swaantje. *Islam, Blasphemie und freie Meinungsäußerung -
Was hat Salman Rushdie getan?* Hildesheim: Internat. Kulturwerk,
1994.

Baumann, Zygmunt. *Modernity and the Holocaust*. Oxford: Polity
Press, 1991.

--- *Modernity and Ambivalence*. Oxford : Polity Press, 1993.

Behrens, Michael and Robert von Rimscha.
"Politische Korrektheit." In *Deutschland Eine Gefahr für die
Demokratie*. Bonn: Bouvier, 1995.

Bell, Daniel. *The Cultural Contradictions of Capitalism*.
London: Heinemann, 1976.

Benchekroun, Mohamed. *L'Islam et les obligations fondamentales.*
Rabat: Arrissalat, 1988.

Benjamin, David. *Muhammad in der Bibel.* Munich: SKD Bavaria
Verlag,1987.

Berque, Jaques, e. al. *Aspects de la foi de l'Islam, Facultés
universitaires.* Brüssel: Saint Louis, 1985.

Bielefeldt, Heiner. " 'Schwächlicher Werterelativismus?' Zur
Notwendigkeit des interkulturellen Dialogs über Menschenrechte,"
In *Der Islam und der Westen,* edited by Kai Hafez. Fischer:
Frankfurt 1997, 56.

Boisard, Marcel. *Der Humanismus des Islam.* Kaltbrunn: Verlag zum
Hecht, (CH) 1982.

Borrmans, Maurice. *Wege zum christlich-islamischen Dialog.*
CIBEDO: Frankfurt, 1985.

Brown, Daniel. *Rethinking tradition in modern Islamic thought.*
Cambridge, U.K.: Cambridge University Press, 1996.

Buaben, Jabal Muhammad. *Image of the Prophet Muhammad in the
West.* Markfield, LE (UK): Islamic Foundation, 1996.

Bürgel, Johann C. *Allmacht und Mächtigkeit, Religion und Welt im
Islam.* Munich: C.H. Beck, 1991.

Bukhari, al-. *Sahih al-Bukhari.* Translated by Muh. Muhsin Khan.
9 vols. Chicago: Kazi Publications, 1976-1979.

Bukharyy, al-. *Auszüge aus Sahih al-Bukharyy.* Translated by Muh.
Ahmad Rassoul. Köln: IB Verlag, 1989.

Blumenberg, Hans. *The Legitimacy of the Modern Age.* Cambridge,
MA: MIT Press, 1984.

Bucaille, Maurice. *Bibel, Koran und Wissenschaft - Die Heiligen
Schriften im Licht moderner Erkenntnisse.* Munich: SKD Bavaria
Verlag, 1984.

Bunt, Gary. "Islam in Cyberspace." *The Muslim World Book Review* 18,
no. 1 (1997): 3- .

Buti, Muhammad Sa'id al-. *Jihad in Islam - How to Understand &
Practice It.* Translated by Munzer Adel Absi. Damaskus: Dar al-Fiqr,
1995.

Cahen, Claude. *Orient et Occident au temps des croisades*. Paris: Aubier, 1983.

Chapra, M. Umer. *Islam and the Economic Challenge*. Herndon, VA: I.I.I.T., 1992.

---*Towards a Just Monetary System*. Leicester (UK): The Islamic Foundation, 1995.

Cherfils, Christian. *Napoleon and Islam. From French and Arab Documents*. Kuala Lumpur: Utusan Publ., 1999.

Chimelli, Rudolph. *Islamismus*. Zürich: Vontobel Holding, 1993.

Choudhury, Masudul Alam. *Reforming the Muslim World*. London/ N.Y.: Kegan Paul, 1998.

Cohn-Sherbok, Dan. ed. *Islam in a World of Diverse Faiths*. London: Macmillan, 1991.

Conferences of Riyad on Moslem Doctrine and Human Rights in Islam. Beirut: Dar al-Kitab al-Lubnani, (n.d.).

Cooper, John, Ronald Nettler and Mohamed Mahmoud, eds. *Islam and Modernity*. London: Tauris, 1998.

Coury, Ralph. "Neo-Modernization Theory and its Search for Enemies: The Role of the Arabs and Islam," *Islamic Studies* 35, no. 4 (1996).

Cragg, Kenneth. *The Christ and the Faiths: Theology in Cross-Reference*. London: SPCK, 1986.

Daniel, Norman. *Islam and the West. The Making of an Image*. 2nd ed. Oxford: One World Publ., 1993.

Davutoglu, Ahmet. *Alternative Paradigms: The Impact of Islamic and Western Weltanschauungs on Political Theory*. London: Univ. of America Press, 1994.

--- *Civilizational Transformation and the Muslim World*. Kuala Lumpur: Mahir Publications, 1994.

---"The Clash of Interests: An Explanation of World [Dis]order." *International Discussion* 2, no. 2 (1994): 107- .

Daweke, Klaus, ed. "Der rechte Weg - Versuche einer Annäherung an den Islam." *Zeitschrift für Kulturaustausch* 42, no. 4 (1992).

Denffer, Ahmad von. *Der Islam und Jesus*. Munich: IZM, 1991.

Deschner, Karlheinz. *Der gefälschte Glaube*. Munich: Knesebeck & Schuler, 1988.

Diamond, Larry. "The Globalsation of Democracy." In *Global Transformation and the Third World*, edited by Robert Slater, Barry Schutz, and Stephen Dorr. Boulder, Colo.: Lynne Rienner, 1993. 31-.

Dirks, Jerald F., *The Cross & The Crescent*, Beltsville, MD., amana publications, 2001.

Doi, Abdur Rahman. *Shari'ah, The Islamic Law*. London: Ta Ha Publishers, 1984.

Dunn, Michael. "Islamic Movements at the End of the 20th Century." Middle East Affairs Journal 2, no. 4 (1996): 3-.

Dürr, Hans-Peter, ed. *Physik und Transzendenz*. Munich: Scherz, 1989.

Duran, Khalid. "Demographic Characteristics of the American Muslim Community." *Islamic Studies* 36, no. 1 (1997): 57-.

Eaton, Charles de Gai. *Islam and the Destiny of Man*. London: G. Allen & Unwin; Islamic Texts Society, 1985.

Eisenmann, Robert, und Michael Wise, *Jesus und die Urchristen*, Bertelsmann: Munich, 2. Aufl. 1992.

Elmessiri, Abdelwahab. "Feature of the New Islamic Thought." *Encounters* 3, no. 1 (1996): 45-.

--- "Towards a More Comprehensive and Explanatory Paradigm of Secularism." *Encounters* 2, no. 2 (1997): 137-.

Engineer, Asghar. *The Rights of Women in Islam*. London: Sterling Publ., 1992.

--- *Rethinking Issues in Islam*. London: Sangam Books, 1998.

Esposito, John. *Voices of Resurgent Islam*. Oxford: Oxford Univ. Press, 1983.

--- *The Islamic Threat: Myth or Reality?* Oxford: Oxford Univ. Press,1992.

Fadl, Khaled Abu el-. "Islamic Law and Muslim Minorities." *Islamic Law and Society* 1, no. 2 (1994).

--- *The Authoritative and Authoritarian in Islamic Discourses*. Los Angeles: MIV, 1997.

Falaturi, Abdoljavad. ed. *Islam: Raum-Geschichte-Religion, Der Islamische Orient, Islam*. Köln: Wiss. Akademie, 1990.

Falk, Richard. "False Universalism and the Geopolitics of Exclusion: the Case of Islam." *Third World Quarterly* 18, no. 1 (1997): 7-.

Faruqi, Ismail Raji. ed. *Trialogue of the Abrahamic Faiths*. Herndon, Virginia: I.I.I.T., 1991.

Feindt-Riggers, Nils, and Udo Steinbach. *Islamische Organisationen in Deutschland*. Hamburg: Deutsches Orient-Inst., 1997.

Findley, Paul. *Silent No More -Confronting America's false images of Islam*, Beltsville, MD., amana publications, 2001.

Fox, Matthew. *The Coming of the Cosmic Christ: The Healing of Mother Earth and The Birth of A Global Renaissance*. San Francisco: Harper & Row, 1988.

--- *Vision vom kosmischen Christus, Aufbruch ins Dritte Jahrtausend*. Kreuz: Stuttgart 1991.

French, Hal. *Adversary Identity: A Study of Religious Fanaticism and Responses to it*. Lampeter (Wales): Edwin Mellen Press, 1990.

Fricke, Wedding. "Standrechtlich gekreuzigt". *Person und Prozeß des Jesus aus Galiläa*. Mai Verlag: Buchschlag, 1986.

Fukuyama, Francis. "The End of History?" *The National Interest*, Spring (1990).

--- *The End of History and the Last Man*. New York: Penguin, 1992.

Fulton, John, and Peter Gee. *Religion in Contemporary Europe*. Lampeter, Wales: Edwin Mellen, 1994.

Garaudy, Roger. *Pour un Islam du XXe siècle* (Charte de Seville). Paris: Tougui, 1985.

--- *Verheißung Islam*. Munich: SKD Bavaria Verlag, 1988.

Gardell, Matthias. *Countdown to Armaggedon - Louis Farrakhan and the Nation of Islam*. London: C. Hurst, 1996.

Gardet, Louis. *Les Hommes de l'Islam*. Paris: Hachette, 1977.

Gellner, Ernest. *Relativism and the Social Sciences*. Cambridge : Cambridge Univ. Press. 1985.

--- *Postmodernism, Reason and Religion*. London: Routledge, 1992.

Ghannouchi, Rachid al-. "Towards Inclusive Strategies for Human Rights Enforcement in the Arabs World - a Response." *Encounters* 2, no. 2 (1996): 190- .

Ghaussy, Ghanie. *Das Wirtschaftsdenken im Islam*. Bern: Haupt, 1986.

Ghazali, Abu Hamid al-. *Ihya Ulum-id-Din*. Translated by Fazul-ul-Karim. 4 vols. Lahore: Sind Sagar Academy, n.d.

Ghazali, Muhammad al-, The Socio-Political Thought of Shah Wali Allah, Islamabad: International Institute of Islamic Thought, 2001.

Gibb, H., and J. Kramers. *Shorter Encyclopaedia of Islam*. Leiden: Brill, 1974.

Gleave, Robert. "Elements of Religious Discrimination in Europe: the Position of Muslim Minorities." *Encounters* 4, no. 2 (1998), 169. -

Goethe, Johann Wolfgang von. *Werke*. Frankfurt: Insel, 1993.

Guazzone, Laura, ed. *The Islamist Dilemma*. Reading (UK): Garnet, 995.

Habermas, Jürgen. *Between Facts and Norms* (Faktizität und Geltung): *Contributions to A DiscourseTtheory of Law and Democracy*. Translated byWilliam Rehg. Cambridge, Mass.: MIT Press, 1996.

Haddad, Yvonne, and Jane Smith. eds. *Muslim Communities in North America*. Albany: SUNY, 1994.

Hafez, Kai, ed. *Der Islam und der Westen*. Frankfurt: Fischer, 1997.

Haikal, Muhammad Hussein. *Das Leben Muhammads*. Siegen : Tackenberg Verlag, 1987.

Haleem, Muzaffar and Betty (Batul) Bowman, *The Sun is Rising in the West, New Muslims tell about their Journey to Islam*, Beltsville, MD: amana publications 1999.

Hamidullah, Muhammad. *The First Written Constitution in the World*. 3rd ed. Lahore: Sh. Muhammad Ashraf, 1975.

--- *The Emergence of Islam*. Translated by Afzal Iqbal. Islamabad : Islamic Research Institute, 1993.

Hart, Michael. *The 100. A Ranking of the Most Influential Persons in History*. New York, N.Y., 1978. 33.

Hasenfratz, Hans-Peter. *Das Christentum - Eine kleine "Problemgeschichte"*. Zürich: Theologischer Verlag, 1992.

Harrington, Michael. *The Politics at God's Funeral: The Spiritual Crisis of Western Civilization*. New York : Holt, Reinhart & Winston, 1983.

Hashemi, Nader. "How dangerous are the Islamists?" *Middle East Affairs Journal* 2, no. 4 (1996): 12- .

Hathout, Hassan. *Reading the Muslim Mind*. Plainfield, IN: American Trust, 1995.

Heine, Peter. *Halbmond über deutschen Dächern*. Munich: List, 1997.

Herman, Edward. "Free Expression in the West: Myth & Reality."

Encounters 2, no. 1 (1996): 23. -

Hesse, Reinhard. "Feindbild Islam." *Die Woche*, 23 April 1997.

Hibri, Aziza al-. "Islamic Constitutionalism and the Concept of Democracy." *24 Case Western Reserve Journal of International Law* 1 (1992).

Hick, John. *The Myth of God Incarnate*. London: SCM Press, 1977.

--- *God an the Universe of Faiths*. London: Macmillan, 1988.

--- *An Interpretation of Religion*. Basingstoke, Hampshire, U.K.: Macmillan, 1989.

--- *The Metaphor of God Incarnate*. London: SCM Press, 1993.

--- *Religiöser Pluralismus und Absoluthoitsansprüche*. In *Kirate*, Interreligiöser Dialog 128 - 149.

--- *Wahrheit und Erlösung im Christentum und in anderen Religionen*. Ibid. 113 - 127.

--- *The Rainbow of Faiths*. London: n.p., 1995.

Hick, John, and Edmund Meltzer, eds. *Three Faiths - One God; A Jewish Christian–Muslim Encounter*. London: Macmillan, 1989.

Hicks, Neil. "Islam and Human Rights." *Muslim Politics Report* 12. Council on Foreign Relations: New York, 1997.

Hilal, Iyad. *Studies in Usul ul-Fiqh*. 2nd ed. Walnut, CA, Islamic Cultural Workshop, n.d.

Hilf, Rudolf. *Weltmacht Islam*. Munich: Bayr. Landeszentrale für pol. Bildung, 1988.

Hodgson, Marshall. *The Venture of Islam*. 3 vols. Chicago : Univ. of Chicago Press, 1974.

Hofmann, Murad Wilfried. *Der Islam als Alternative*. 3rd. ed. Munich: Diederichs, 1995.

--- *Islam: The Alternative*. Translated by Christiane Banerji and Murad Hofmann. 2nd. ed. Beltsville, Maryland: amana, 1997.

--- *Islam 2000*. 2nd ed. Beltsville, Maryland: amana, 1996.

--- *Journey to Makkah*. Translated by Andreas Ryschka. Beltsville, Maryland: amana, 1998.

--- "The European Mentality and Islam." *Islamic Studies* 35, no.1 (1996): 87- .

--- *L'Islam que cherche-t-il en Europe?* Casablanca: Ministère des Habous, 1997.

--- "The Protection of Religious Minorities in Islam." *Encounters* 4, no. 2 (1998): 137- .

Holt, Maria. "Palestinian Women and the Contemporary Islamist Movement." *Encounters* 3, no.1 (1997): 64.

Hughes, Thomas Patrick. *Dictionary of Islam* (1886). Chicago : Kazi,1994.

Hunke, Sigrid. *Allah ist ganz anders - Enthüllungen von 1001 Vorurteilen über die Araber.* Bad König: Horizonte, 1990.

Huntington, Samuel. "The Clash of Civilizations." *Foreign Affairs* 72, no. 3 (1993): 17-33.

--- *The Clash of Civilizations and the Making of a New World Order.* New York : Simon & Schuster, 1996.

--- "The West: Unique, Not Universal." *Foreign Affairs* 75, no. 6 (1996): 28-46.

Imam, Ahmad 'Ali al-. *Variant Readings of the Qur'an.* Herndon, Virginia: I.I.I.T., 1998.

Ihsanoglu, Ekmeleddin. "Europe and Islam. New Challenges, New Horizons." In *The West and Islam.* Istanbul: İRCICA: 1999, p 3.

Iqbal, Muhammd. *The Reconstruction of Religious Thought in Islam.* Oxford: Oxford Univ. Press, 1934.

Izetbegovic, 'Alija 'Ali. *Islamic Declaration* (1979). N.p. (Samisdat-Druck).

--- *Islam between East and West.* 2nd ed. Indianapolis, IN: American Trust, 1989.

Jamil, Javed. *Islamic Model for Control of AIDS.* Saharanpur (Indien): Mission Publications, 1996.

Jayyusi, Salma Khadra. ed. *The Legacy of Muslim Spain.* Leiden : HdO, Brill, 1992.

Jaweed, Najma. "Human Rights in Islam." *Al-Mirzan* 2, no. 1 (1996): 65- .

Kabbai, Shaykh Muhammad, and Lalah Bakhtiar. *Encyclopedia of Muhammad's Women Companions and the TraditionsThey Related.* Chicago: ABC International / Kazi Publ., 1998.

Kant, Immanuel. *Kritik der reinen Vernunft* (1781). Vol. 1 and 2. Frankfurt: Suhrkamp, 1996.

--- *Kritik der praktischen Vernunft* (1788). Frankfurt: Suhrkamp, 1996.

Karic, Enes. "In Europe There Are No 'Indigenous' and 'Imported' Religions." *Islamic Studies* 37, no. 1 (1998).

Kathir, Ibn. *Tafsir Ibn Kathir*. London: Al-Firdous –published continuously since 1996.

--- *The Life of the Prophet Muhammad - al-Sira al-Nabawiyya-.* 4 Vols. Reading: Garnet, since 1998.

Kausar, Zeenath. "Sexuality and Reproductive Rights in 'Platform for Action' and Islam." *Encounters* 3, no.2 (1997): 149.

Kepel, Gilles, and Yann Richard , eds. *Intellectuels et militants de l'islam contemporain.* Paris: Seuil 1990.

--- *Die Rache Gottes, Radikale Moslems, Christen und Juden auf dem Vormarsch.* Munich: Piper, 1991,

Khaldun, Ibn, *The Muqaddimah. An Introduction to History.* Translated by Franz Rosenthal. Bolligen Series. Princeton: Princeton University Press, 1967.

Khaleel, Shawki Abu. *Islam on Trial.* Beirut: Dar el-Fikr el Mouaser, 1991.

Khan, Mujeeb R. "Bosnia-Hercegovina and the Politics of Religion and Genocide in the 'New World Order' ." *Islamic Studies, Special Edition, Islam in the Balkans* 36, no. 2 and 3 (1997): 287- .

Khir, Bustami Muhammad. "Concept of Sovereignty in the Contemporary Islamic Movements." *Encounters* 1, no. 1 (1995): 5 .

Kierkegaard, Sören. *Die Krankheit zum Tod.* Köln: Jakob Hegner, 1956.

--- *The Sickness unto Death.* Edited by Robert L. Perkins. Macon, Ga.: Mercer University Press, 1987.

Kirste, Reinhard. "Entwicklungslinien der Bibelauslegung - Chancen für ein sachgemäßes Koranverständnis?" In *Gottes ist der Orient, Gottes ist der Okzident.* Köln: Böhlau, 1991. 362-395.

Kirste, Reinhard, et al., eds. Interreligiöser Dialog zwischen Tradition und Moderne, *Religionen im Gespräch (RIG).* Vol. 3. Balve: Zimmermann, 1994.

Köse, Ali. *Conversion to Islam.* London: Kegan Paul, 1996.

Krämer, Gudrun. "Der 'Gottesstaat' als Republik." In *Der Islam und der Westen.* Edited by Kai Hafez. Fischer: Frankfurt 1997. 44.

Kramer, Martin. *Arab Awakening & Islamic Revival.* New Brunswick, N.J.: Transaction Publ., 1996.

Kreeft, Peter. *Ecumenical Jihad.* San Francisco: Ignatius Press, 1996.

Kremer, Alfred von. *Geschichte der herrschenden Ideen des Islams* (1868). Hildesheim: Georg Olms, 1961.

Kruse, Hans, *Islamische Völkerrechtslehre.* 2nd ed. Bochum: Brockmeyer, 1979.

Küng, Hans, and J. van Ess. "Islam". *Christentum und Weltreligionen.* Vol. 1. Gütersloh: Mohn, 1987.

Küng, Hans, and Karl-Josef Kuschel, eds. *A Global Ethic: The Declaration of the Parliament of World`s Religions.* London: SCM Press, 1993.

Küng, Hans. *Pourquoi suis-je toujours chrétien?* Paris: Centurion, 1988.

--- *Projekt Weltethos.* Munich: Piper, 1990.

--- Vorwort. *New Horizons for Faith and Thought.* Edited by Karl-Josef Kuschel and Hermann Häring. London: SCM Press, 1993.

Kuschel, Karl-Josef. *Abraham - a Symbol of Hope for Jews, Christians and Muslims.* London: SCM Press, 1995.

--- *Vom Streit zum Wettstreit der Religionen - Lessing und die Herausforderung des Islam,* Düsseldorf: Patmos, 1998.

Lang, Jeffrey. *Struggling to Surrender.* 2nd ed. Beltsville, Maryland: amana, 1995.

--- *Even Angels Ask.* Beltsville, Maryland: amana, 1997.

Laoust, Henri. *La profession de foi d'Ibn Taymiyya - La Wasitiyya.* Paris: Geuthner, 1986.

Lawrence, Bruce B. *Shattering the Myth - Islam beyond Violence.* New Jersey: Princeton University Press, 1998.

Lee, Robert. *Overcoming Tradition and Modernity: The Search for Islamic Authenticity.* Boulder, Colorado: Westview Press, 1997.

Lelong, Michel. *Si Dieu l'avait voulu... .* Paris: Tougui, 1986.

Lemu, Aisha, and Fatima Heeren. *Women in Islam.* Leicester (UK): Islamic Council of Europe, 1978.

Lincoln, C. Eric. *The Black Muslims in America.* Grand Rapids, MI: Wm. B. Eerdmans Publ., 1994.

Little, David, John Kelsay, and Abdulaziz Sachedina. *Human Rights and the Conflicts of Culture: Western and Islamic Perspectives on*

Religious Liberty. N. p.: Univ. of South Carolina Press, 1989.

Lüdemann, Gerd. *Die Auferstehung Jesu*. Göttingen: Vandenhoeck & Ruprecht, 1994.

--- Ketzer - *Die andere Seite des frühen Christentums*. Stuttgart. Radius, 1995.

Lyotard, Jean-François. *The Postmodern Condition: A Report on Knowledge*. Manchester (UK): Manchester Univ. Press, 1986.

Maalouf, Amin. *Les croisades vues par les Arabes*. Paris: Edition J'ai lu, 1991.

Mack, Burton. *The Last Gospel - The Book of Q and Christian Origins*. N.p.: Element Books, USA 1993.

Malley, Robert. *The Call from Algeria*. Berkley: University of California Press, 1996.

Malik b. Anas. *Imam, Al-Muwatta*. Translated by 'Aisha 'Abdarahman and Yaqub Johnson. Norwich (UK): Diwan Press, 1982.

Mantran, Robert. *Les grandes dates de l'Islam*. Paris: Larousse, 1990.

Manzoor, Parvez. "An Epistemology of Questions: The Crisis of Intellect and Reason in the West." *The Muslim World Book Review* 7, no. 2 (1987).

--- "Human Rights: Secular Transcendence or Cultural Imperialism." *The Muslim World Book Review* 8, no. 3 (1994): 3- .

--- "Hubris and Humility: Christian Perplexity at the Plurality of Faith." *The Muslim World Book Review* 15, no 4 (1995): 3- .

--- "Desacralizing Secularism." *The American Journal of Islamic and Social Sciences* 12, no. 4 (1995): 545- .

--- "Against the Absolutism of Science and Society." *The Muslim World Book Review* 18, no. 2, (1998): 3- .

--- "Freedom as Transcendence? Contemporary Islam and the Puzzle of Modernity." *The Muslim World Book Review* 19, no. 2 (1999) 3- .

Martinez, Florentino Garcia. *The Dead Sea Scrolls*. Leiden: Brill, 1994.

Marty, Martin, and Scott Appleby, eds. *The Fundamentalism Project* 4 vols. Chicago: University of Chicago Press, 1993, 1994.

Maqsood, Ruqaiyyah Waris, *What Every Christian Should Know About Islam*, Markfield, LE. The Islamic Foundation 2000.

Masud, Muhammad Khalid, *Shatibi's Philosophy of Islamic Law*, Islamabad: Islamic Research Institute, 1995.

Maududi, Abu 'Ala. *Islam in the Face of Contemporary Challenges.*
Kuwait: Dar al-Arqam, 1971.

Mayer, Ann Elizabeth. *Islam and Human Rights.* 2nd ed. Boulder, CO:
Westview, 1995.

Mazrui, Ali. "Islam and the End of History." *The American Journal of Islamic Social Studies* 10, no. 4 (1993): 512 -535.

--- "North American Muslims: Rising to the Challenge of Dual Identity." *Islamic Studies* 34, no. 4 (1995): 451- .

--- "Human Rights between Rwanda and Reparations: Global Power and the Racial Experience." *Encounters* 2, no. 1 (1996): 3- .

--- "Islamic and Western Values." *IQRA* 18, no. 1 (1998): 13- .(1997 in Foreign Affairs).

Meier, Andreas. *Der Politische Auftrag des Islam.*
Wuppertal: Peter Hammer, 1994.

Mernissi, Fatima. *Sultanes Oubliées, femmes chefs d'état en Islam.*
Casablanca : Le Fennec, 1992.

--- *Der politische Harem, Mohamed und die Frauen.* Frankfurt:
Dagyeli, 1989.

--- *Die Angst vor der Moderne.* Hamburg: Luchterhand, 1992.

Miles, Jack. *God : A Biography.* New York: Alfred A. Knopf, 1995.

Misri, Ahmad ibn Naqib al-. *The Reliance of the Traveller.* Translated by Noah Ha Mim Keller. Dubai: Modern Printing Press, 1991.

Monshipouri, Mahmood. Islamism, *Secularism, and Human Rights in the Middle East.* Boulder, Col: Lynne Rienner, 1998.

Moore, Kathleen. *Al-Mughtaribun: American Law and the Transformation of Muslim Life in the United States.* Albany, N.Y.:
State University Press, 1995.

Moten, Abdul Rashid. *Political Science: An Islamic Perspective.*
Basingstoke, Hampshire (UK): Macmillan, 1996.

--- "Democratic and Shura-based Systems." *Encounters* 3. 1 (1997): 3- .

Motzki, Harald. *The Origins of Islamic Jurisprudence – Meccan Fiqh before the Classical Schools*, Boston/Leiden: Brill 2002.

Mousalli, Ahmad. *Radical Islamic Fundamentalism: The Ideological and Political Discourse of Sayyid Qutb.* Beirut: American University of Beirut Press, 1992.

Munoz, Gema Martinez, ed. *Islam, Modernism and the West.* London: I.B.Tauris, 1999.

Murad, Khurram. "Islam and Terrorism." *Encounters* 4, no. 1 (1997): 103- .

Muslim. *Sahih Muslim.* 4 Vols. Translated by Abdul Hamid Siddiqi. Lahore : Sh. Muhammad Ashraf: 1976.

Muzaffar, Chandra. *Human Rights and the New World Order.* Penang (Malaysia): JUST, 1994.

Nadim, Abu'l-Faraj Muh. b. Ishaq al-, *The Fihrist,* New York: Columbia University Press (1970) 1998.

Nadvi, Syed, *Habib ul-Haque* Durban, South Africa: Academia, 1995.

Nagel, Tilman. *Staat und Glaubensgemeinschaft im Islam.* 2 Vols. Zurich / Munich: Artemis, 1981.

--- *Geschichte der islamischen Theologie.* Munich: C.H.Beck, 1994.

Nasr, Seyyed Hossein. *Ideal and Realities of Islam.* Kairo: American University in Cairo Press, 1989.

Nawawi, an-. *Minhaj-et-Talibin, A Manual of Muhammadan Law.* Lahore (1914): Law Publishing Co., 1977.

--- *Vierzig Hadite.* Translated by Ahmad von Denffer. Leicester (UK): The Islamic Foundation, 1979.

--- *Riyad us-Salihin, Gärten der Tugendhaften* Vol.1. Garching: Dar-us-Salam, 1996.

Na'im, Abdullah A an-. *Human Rights in Cross Cultural Perspectives.* Philadelphia: University of Pennsylvania Press, 1992.

Nielsen, J S. "Muslims ins Europe or European Muslims: the Western Experience." *Encounters* 4, no. 2 (1998): 205- .

Nietzsche, Friedrich. *Werke in Zwei Bänden.* Munich: Hanser, 1967.

Nu'man, Fareed. *The Muslim Population in the United States.* Washington, D.C.: American Muslim Council, 1992.

Nyazee, Imran Ahsan Khan. *Theories of Islamic Law, The Methodology of Ijtihad.* Islamabad: I.I.I.T., 1994.

O'Ballance, Edgar. *Islamic Fundamentalist Terrorism 1779-1995.* Basingstoke, Hampshire (UK): Macmillan, 1997.

Ophuls, William. *Requiem for Modern Politics - The Tragedy of the Enlightenment and the Challenge of the New Millenium.* Boulder, CO: Westview Press, 1997.

Osman, Fathi. *Jihad - a Legitimate Struggle for Human Rights.*
Los Angeles: Minaret, 1991.

--- *Shari' a in Contemporary Society -The Dynamics of Change in the Islamic Law.* Los Angeles: MVI, 1994.

--- *The Children of Adam - An Islamic Perspective on Pluralism.*
Washington, D.C.: Georgetown Univ. Press, 1996.

--- *Human Rights on the Eve of the 21st Century - Problems for Muslims and Others.* London: Islam & Modernity, 1996.

--- *Concepts of the Quran - A Topical Reading.* Los Angeles, CA:
Multimedia Vera International (MVI), 1997.

Otaibi, Moneer al-, and Hakim Rashid. "The Role of Schools in Islamic Society." *The American Journal of Islamic Social Sciences* 14, no. 4 (1997): 1- .

Ott, Claudie. "Das Feindbild in den westlichen Medien." *CIBEDO* 7, no. 3 (1993): 76.

Otto, Rudolf. *Das Heilige - Über das Irrationale in der Idee des Göttlichen und sein Verhältnis zum Rationalen.* Munich: C.H. Beck, 1997.

Packard, Vance. *Pyramid Climbers.* Harmondsworth: Pelican, 1962.

--- *The Sexual Wilderness.* New York: David McKay, 1968.

Parrinder, Geoffrey. *Mysticism in the Worlds Religions.* Oxford: One World, 1995.

Pasquier, Roger du. *Unveiling Islam.* Cambridge : The Islamic Texts Society, 1992.

Pearl, David. "Conflicts and Tensions in the Proposal for a System of Personal Law for Muslims in the UK." *Encounters*, 4, no. 1 (1998): S. 4 - .

Phipps, William. *Muhammad and Jesus.* London: SCM Press, 1996.

Piscatori, James. *Islam in a Word of Nation States.* Cambridge :
Cambridge University Press, 1986.

PLD (The All Pakistan Legal Decisions), Supreme Court Judgments on Riba, Lahore: PLD Publishers, n.d.

Popper, Karl R., and John C. Eccles. *The Self and its Brain.* Heidelberg:
Springer, 1977.

Pryce-Jones. *At War with Modernity: Islam's Challenge to the West.*
London: Institute for European Defence and Strategic Studies, 1992.

Qaradawi, Jusuf al-. *Islamic Awakening between Rejection and Extremism*. Herndon, VA: I.I.I.T., 1987.

--- *Erlaubtes und Verbotenes im Islam*. Munich. SKD Bavaria Verlag, 1989.

Qutb, Muhammad. *Einwände gegen den Islam*. München: SKD Bavaria Verlag, 1994.

Qutb, Sayyid. *Milestones (Ma'alim fi-l-Tariq)*. Indianapolis: American Trust Publ., 1990.

Rahim, Muddatili 'Abd al-, *The Development of Fiqh in the Modern MuslimWorld*. Kuala Lumpur IKIM, 1996.

Rahim, Muhammad 'Ata ur-. *Jesus - A Prophet of Islam*. London. MWH Publishers,1977.

Rahman, Fazlur. *Islam*. New York: Holt, Rinehart and Winston, 1966.

Rahman, Mohibur. *Clash of Civilizations or Clash of Ideas?* Al-Mizan, Jahrgg. 2, no. 1, London 1996, S. 38.

Ramadan, Said. *Das islamische Recht*. Wiesbaden: Harrassowitz, 1980.

Ramadan, Tariq. *To be a European Muslim*. Markfield, LE: The Islamic Foundation 1999.

Rehs, Michael. "Die Welt des Islam zwischen Tradition und Fortschritt, I / II." *Zeitschrift Fur Kulturaustausch* 35, no. 3 (1985).

Reich, Charles A. *The Greening of America*. New York: Random, 1970.

Riesmann, David, et al. *Die einsame Masse*. Reinbek: Rowohlt, 1958.

Riße, Günter. "Der Islam, eine politische Religion?" *CIBEDO* 7, no. 2 (1993): 33.

Robinson, Neal. *Discovering the Qur'an - A Contemporary Approach to a Veiled Text*. London: SCM Press, 1996.

Rodinson, Maxime. *Die Faszination des Islam* (1980). Munich: C.H. Beck, 1985.

Rusdh, Ibn, (Averroës). *The Distinguished Jurist's Primer (Bidayat al-Mujtahid)*. 2 vols. Reading (UK): Garnet, 1994, 1995.

Runnymede Trust, " 'Islamophobia' in Britain." *The Muslim Politics Report* 15. New York: Council on Foreign Relations, 1997, p. 2- .

Safi, Louay. "Islam and the Global Challenge: Dealing with Distortions of the Image of Islam by Global Media." *Islamic Studies* 35, no. 2 (1996): 191.

Salem, Isam Kamel. *Islam und Völkerrecht*. Berlin: Express, 1984.

Salvatore, Armando. *Islam and the Political Discourse of Modernity*. Reading (U K) 1997.

Said, Edward. *Orientalism*. New York: Random House, 1978.

--- *Covering Islam*. New York: Pantheon, 1981.

--- *Culture and Imperialism*. London: Chatto & Windus, 1993.

Sardar, Ziauddin, Ashish Nandy and Merryl Wyn Davies. *Postmodernism and the Other: The New Imperialism of Western Culture*. London: Pluto Press,1997.

Sardar, Ziauddin. Ashish Nandy und Merryl Wyn Davies, *Barbaric Others: A Manifesto of Western Racism*. London: Pluto Press, 1993.

Schacht, Joseph. *An Introduction to Islamic Law*. Oxford: Clarendon, 1964.

Schimmerl, Annemarie. *Mystische Dimensionen des Islam, Die Geschichte des Sufismus*. Munich: Diederichs, 1985.

Schlatter, Adolf. *Die Geschichte der ersten Christenheit* (1926). 5th ed. Darmstadt: Wiss. Buchgesellschaft, 1971.

Schönig, Hannelore. "Die rechtliche Stellung der Frau im Islam." In: *Die Welt des Islam zwischen Tradition und Fortschritt*. II. Stuttgart: Inst. für Auslandsbeziehungen, 1985. 439- .

Schulze, Reinhard. "Gibt es eine islamische Moderne?" In *Der Islam und der Westen*. Edited by Kai Hafez. Frankfurt: Fischer, 1997. 31- .

Schuon, Frithjof. *Den Islam verstehen*. Bern: O.W. Barth Verlag, 1988.

Schwarzenau, Paul. *Korankunde für Christen*. Stuttgart: Kreuz Verlag, 1982.

--- "Biblische und koranische Grundlagen für den christlich-islamischen Dialog." In *Gottes ist der Orient, Gottes ist der Okzident*. Köln: Böhlau, 1991. 499-508.

--- *Das nachchristliche Zeitalter*. Stuttgart: Kreuz Verlag, 1993.

Shafi'i, al-, Risala. *Treatise on the Foundation of Islamic Jurisprudence*. Translated by Majid Khadduri. Cambridge: Islamic Texts Society, 1991.

Shahrour, Mohammad. "The Divine Text and Pluralism in Muslim Societies." *Muslim Politics Report* 12. New York: Council of Foreign Relations, 1997, p. 3-9.

Sharif, M.M., ed. *A History of Muslim Philosophy.* 2 vols. Wiesbaden: Harrassowitz, 1963, 1966.

Siddiqi, Muhammad Nejatullah. "Towards Regeneration: Shifting Priorities in Islamic Movements." *Encounters* 1, no. 2 (1995): 3- .

--- "Christian-Muslim Dialogue: Problems and Challenges." *Encounters* 2, no. 2 (1998): 123- .

--- "Future of the Islamic Movement." *Encounters* 4, no. 1 (1998): 91- .

Siddiqui, Jawed ul-Haq. *21st Century & the Birth of United States of Islam.* Karachi: ISI Publ., 1997.

Sigler, John. "Understanding the Resurgence of Islam: the Case of Political Islam." *Middle East Affairs Journal* 2, no. 4 (1996). 79 ff.

Smith, Wilfred Cantwell. *What is Scripture?* London: SCM Press, 1993.

Spuler-Stegemann, Ursula. *Muslime in Deutschland.* Freiburg: Herder, 1998.

Stolz, Rolf. *Mullahs in Deutschland - Der Sprengstoff von morgen 2nd ed.,* Frankfurt / Munich: Ullstein, 1996.

--- *Kommt der Islam? Die Fundamentalisten vor den Toren Europas.* Munich: Herbig, 1997.

Swinburn, Richard. *The Existence of God.* Oxford: Clarendon Press, 1979.

Tahtawi, Rifa'a al-. *Ein Muslim entdeckt Europa.* Munich: C.H. Beck, 1989.

Talbi, Mohamed, and Maurice Bucaille, *Réflexions sur le Coran.* Paris: Seghers, 1989.

Talbi, Mohamed. "Is Cultural and Religious Co-Existence Possible? Harmony and the right to be different." *Encounters* 1, no. 2 (1995): 74- .

Tamimi, Azzam, "Fundamentalist Islam and the Media." *Al-Mizan* 2, no. 1 (1996).

--- "Democracy in Islamic Political Thought." *Encounters* 3, no. 1 (1997): 21- .

--- "Democracy: The Religious and the Political in Contemporary Islamic Debate." *Encounters* 4, no. 1 (1998): 35- .

Tibi, Bassam. *Die Krise des modernen Islams.* Frankfurt: Suhrkamp, 1991.

--- "Wie Feuer und Wasser." *Der Spiegel* 3 (1994): 170-172.

--- *Der wahre Imam. Der Islam von Mohammed bis zur Gegenwart.*
Munich: Piper, 1996.

Troll, Christian. "Witness meets Witness: the Church's Mission in the
Context of the Worldwide Encounter of Christian and Muslim
Believers Today." *Encounters* 4, no. 1 (1998) 15- .

Turabi, Hasan al-. *Women, Islam and Muslim Society.* London:
Milestones, 1991.

--- *Islam, Democracy, the State and the West.* Edited by Arthur
Lowrie. Tampa, FL: WISE, 1993.

Turner, Bryan S. *Orientalism, Postmodernism and Globalization.* New
York: Routledge, 1994.

Tworuschka, Udo, ed. *Gottes ist der Orient - Gottes ist der Okzident*
(Festschrift for Abdoljavad Falaturi). Köln: Böhlau, 1991.

Wagner, Peter. *Soziologie der Moderne.* Frankfurt: Campus, 1995.

Walker, Dennis. "The Revived Nation of Islam and America's Western
System in the 1990s: Ambiguous Protest of A New Black Elite."
Islamic Studies 37, no. 4 (1998): 445-

Watt, William Montgomery. *Religious Truth for Our Time.* Oxford:
Oneworld Publ., 1995.

Wehr, Hans. *Arabisch-Deutsches Wörterbuch.* 5th ed. Wiesbaden:
Harrassowitz, 1985.

Westerlund, David, and Carl Hallencreutz, eds. *Questioning the Secular
State: The worldwide Resurgence of Religion in Politics.* London:
Hurts & Co., 1996.

Woods, John. "Imagining and Stereotyping Islam," In *Muslims in
America - Opportunities and Challenges.* Chicago: Intern. Strategy
and Policy Inst., 1996, pp. 45-77.

Yassine, Abdessalam. *Winning the Modern World for Islam.* Iowa City:
Justice & Spirituality Publishing, Inc. 2000.

Zakzouk, Mahmoud, et al. *Gesichter des Islam.* Berlin: Haus der
Kulturen der Welt, 1992.

Zaman, Muhammad Qasim. *The Making of a religious Discourse – an
Essay in the History and Historiography of the Abbasid Revolution.*
Islamabad : I.I.I.T., 1995.